With

JOURNEY
IN
WONDER

A global adventure and personal discovery

KEITH CORCORAN

ORIGINAL WRITING

© 2010 Keith Corcoran

Cover painting by Morgan Ferriter
www.morganferriter.com

978-1-907179-91-4

A CIP catalogue for this book is available from the National Library.

Published by Original Writing Ltd., Dublin, 2010.

Printed by Cahill Printers Limited, Dublin.

This book is dedicated to my father Donal, my mother Maura, and my sister Donna, and all their love and support.

ACKNOWLEDGEMENTS

I would firstly like to thank my good friend Ruairí Mc Kiernan who inspired me to write this book and who has been a constant source of support and trusted counsel. I would also like to thank Michael Mc Monagle who offered his advice and experience as a published author and more recently as a friend and confidante.

I am also deeply humbled to have such a friend as Morgan Ferriter who shared his abundant talent as an artist to create a very special painting for the front cover. Thanks also to the kindness and copy reading skills of Eimear O'Tuathaigh who took it upon herself to proofread my manuscript and offered very timely advice on changes and edits the book greatly benefited from.

I would also like thank Anna Lally for her last minute proof-reading interventions and Steven and Garrett at Original Writing who gave me the opportunity to get this book out into the world and for being so generous with their time and support. Thanks also to up and coming photographer and neighbour Shaneen Gorman for conjuring up such good promotional shots for the book.

This book needed initial financial backing to get self-published and I am very grateful for the support of Liam Hyland from the Donegal Times and also Joe Murray from Afri (Action from Ireland). A big thank you also to Finbar Rock and all at Simple Simon for their creative and much appreciated support.

Last but not least I would like to thank Ann Mc Gowan, Eddie Erskine, Billy Johnston, Larry Masterson, Ken Donnelly, Harveys Point, The Central Hotel, and all my family and friends for their vital support. A final special thanks goes to my girlfriend, Jana, for her continued patience, care and love.

INTRODUCTION

I was sort of compelled to write this book. It felt like it was ready to burst unto paper and I might as well have had a hand in its writing since it's a journey that happened to me. I'm thirty-five years of age now and that doesn't seem so real somehow. I've lived in a townland called Trummon in South Donegal for most of my life and that seems very real. I have two loving parents, Donal and Maura and one younger special sister Donna. Happily, we are family all the time and friends most of the time.

This is not an autobiography but I think a few shared memories and events from my earlier years might help make more sense of this book for both reader and writer alike. My parents moved back from Dublin to live in Donegal and less than a mile from my Mother's home place, when I was four years old. Around this time I was sitting in the backseat of our car. We were driving through some part of Donegal when my eyes took in a scene my mind will never forget. Time seem suspended in that instant and out of the back window I saw a beautiful Donegal glen in the fading light of an overcast evening. It was a complete vision. I gazed upon an ancient rocky mountainside, its summit cloaked mysteriously in swirls of cloud. A torrent of water gushed out of the mists and tumbled down unto a valley floor of deepest greens and bog browns. Even at such a young age, some part of me was mystified. I felt deeply at home.

At eleven years of age I cut a hazel staff from a nearby woodland called 'The Scrug', and set off directly for the mountain called 'The Ought' to the east of my local world. Across drains, over sheep wire fences and around marshes I tramped. I might as well have been trekking to Mount Everest such was my excitement. Reaching the summit was like standing on the shoulders of the world. All of Donegal Bay stretched out below me and beyond to the Atlantic Ocean. Then in amazement I realised I could see my own house, the size of a pebble, nestled in a basket of egg shaped emerald green drumlin hills.

Aged thirteen, I put on a grey uniform and went to secondary school which began a tough, challenging time for me. Life is tough though and even difficult experiences can be a blessing. At sixteen I drank my first alcohol, a pint of lager and lime. Aged twenty, I sat at a bus stand in South London on a cold lonely Sunday night surrounded by concrete and glass skyscrapers and cried my heart out. At twenty-seven I completed my college education back in Ireland and although grateful for much of what I been facilitated and funded to learn, I was left with more questions than answers.

That same year I read out one of my poems called 'From Darkness be Light', at a peace gathering on the Diamond in my home town of Donegal. It was around the time the Bush led US administration began its War of Terror against Iraq and later Afghanistan. Through this gathering I met Ruairí Mc Kiernan and after just a few meetings I threw in my support to set up a non-profit company called Community Creations. Working alongside Ruairí taught me that you can create and achieve whatever you wish for in life if you believe in it strongly enough.

Through our work with Community Creations projects and a new national youth health website we had come to understand that while the Celtic Tiger was bringing great economic prosperity and opportunities, there were all these social problems coming to the surface. We saw an increase in suicide, self harm, racism, alcohol and drug abuse, low self esteem, depression, loneliness and family break up. When we spoke to groups on the margins of society things were even worse. I felt that trying to solve these problems within the current norms of thinking was like trying to use an empty bucket to keep the tide out.

Working with Ruairí and Anna Lally in Community Creations challenged me in many ways and in return gave me a massive injection of confidence, self-belief and a decent wage to put money aside for my travels. For me, Community Creations and SpunOut.ie has successfully engendered Mahatma Gandhi's wise words as its core ethos that "all change comes from within." With nothing but support and encouragement from family, friends and work mates I called 'time-out' in June 2006 and began planning and preparing to go on a journey.

I had carried two dreams from about the age of eleven years old. One dream was to see the Great Plains of North America and to visit a Native American tribe. The second dream was to gaze up at the mighty Himalayan mountains and experience the sights and mysteries of India. For ages, however, I could not decide which direction to take. Should I go East or should I go West? Now at the age of thirty, I was finally in the financial position to take a year out and go travelling.

One day around this time the thought occurred to me, "why choose one dream over the other. Why not visit both lands and make it into a journey of some kind." Later I came to realise a wonderful secret about this trip. Although I had gathered the will and money to go to these places of my dreams, the journey had a course of its own for me to take. The more I let go and accepted this, the more the unexpected happened and the greater the adventure that unfolded.

Keith Corcoran

CONTENTS

United States of America

Seattle· ·Great Falls, Montana

·Billings, Montana

Rapid City, South Dakota·

·Chicago

·New York

Montana

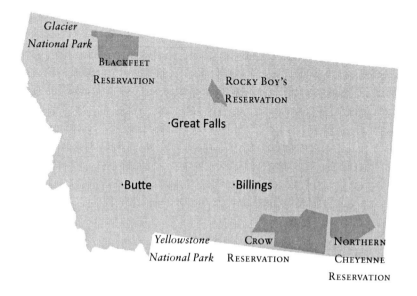

Glacier
National Park

BLACKFEET
RESERVATION

ROCKY BOY'S
RESERVATION

·Great Falls

·Butte
·Billings

Yellowstone
National Park

CROW
RESERVATION

NORTHERN
CHEYENNE
RESERVATION

Tamil Nadu and Kerala

INDIA

·Chennai
·Mamallapuram

Calicut·

Tiruchchirappalli· ·Thanjavur

Kochi· Madurai·
Kollam·
Trivandrum·

SRI LANKA

Sri Lanka

INDIA

Negombo·

·Sigiriya Rock

·Kandy
·*Nilambe Meditation Centre*

Colombo·
Aluthgama·
Ambalangoda·
Galle·

SRI LANKA

Northern India and Nepal

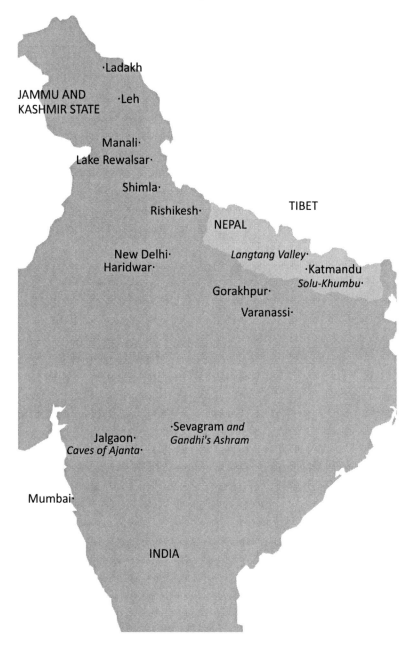

·Ladakh

JAMMU AND   ·Leh
KASHMIR STATE

Manali·
Lake Rewalsar·

Shimla·

Rishikesh·   TIBET
                NEPAL

New Delhi·   *Langtang Valley*·
Haridwar·   ·Katmandu
                        Solu-Khumbu·
                Gorakhpur·

                Varanassi·

·Sevagram *and*
Jalgaon·   *Gandhi's Ashram*
Caves of Ajanta·

Mumbai·

INDIA

Solu-Khumbu Trek

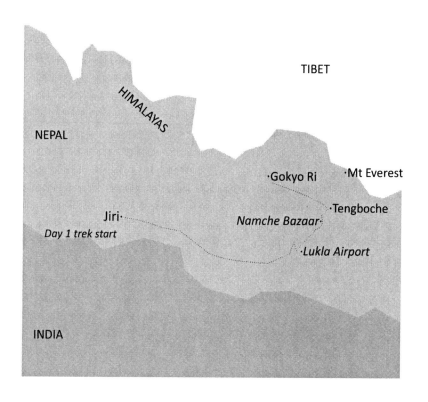

"The heart has its reasons of which reason knows nothing of"

BLAISE PASCAL

French scientist, mathematician and philosopher.

1623-1662

PART 1

WHAT THE FOX KNOWS

It all began one fine sunny June evening back in 2006 while driving home from a work meeting. An hour earlier I had left my work colleagues and good friends Ruairí McKiernan and Anna Lally. I had made a decision to take a year out from Community Creations and shared with them my travel ideas to go West and then East on some sort of journey. With full support and encouragement they granted me a year's leave and wished me good luck and a safe journey.

Driving home that evening I felt a growing sense of excitement and anticipation but also uncertainty. How was I going to make contact with a Native American community in the U.S. and go as a cultural visitor? I didn't want to stumble into some remote reservation as a wide eyed naïve tourist and I certainly had no interest in gambling at their casinos. As events turned out I would have my tribe to visit sooner that I could ever have imagined. Even inside the self contained space of my car that evening in June, I could see and sense the Donegal countryside bursting with new life and growth. These were the precious warm, sun-filled days of mid-summer. The rare jewels that made you forgive and forget the countless dull, wet and windy ones. Soon I was off the main road and driving along familiar country lanes near home. Just as I was driving down along a steep tree lined brae called Menin, a young fox suddenly burst out of the green undergrowth to my right and bolted across the road in front of me. I touched the brakes lightly more out of reflex surprise than alarm. A split second later and he was gone but not before I got a magical glimpse of his fiery red coat.

Then a short distance further along the road I passed a woman walking in the opposite direction. I had passed by before recognising her. It was Sister Nellie McLoughlin from Inishowen. But what was she doing walking along my local country roads? I stopped the car, beeped the horn to catch her attention and reversed back into a lay-by. I had first met Nellie on the day

of my thirtieth birthday at an outdoor festival called the Inishowen Summer Gathering. She had signed and gifted me a copy of
her book 'Out of Wonder'. Nellie was the kind of person who
could lighten the mood of a room by simply walking into it.
She seemed always close to a laugh or smile and was one of the
coolest religious Sisters I had ever met.

Nellie had stopped and was walking back towards the car. We
exchanged greetings and were both quite surprised to see each
other. She explained how she had recently moved into a nearby
house to be closer to her work. In excited tones I then explained
how I had decided just a few hours ago to take leave from work
and go travelling. When I shared with her my dream to visit a
Native American tribe she laughed and smiling brightly replied,
"I actually spent time out in Montana just a few summers ago
and visited the Northern Cheyenne. I still have a contact and
could make a few enquiries on your behalf if you like..."

With less than four weeks to prepare and organise flight tickets, I began to think how I could make my visit to the Northern
Cheyenne more of a cultural exchange than an ordinary visit.
Although separated by a vast ocean I felt a natural affinity to the
Native American people. There was certainly common ground
between our older Celtic and Native American cultures. A deep
rooted family rather than national civic sense of belonging was
one. A respect for ancient ancestral places and generations past
was another, while a weakness for alcohol or 'firewater' was
a less fortunate one. The fact that both our cultures had been
conquered and dominated by emerging world military powers
after a brave yet doomed struggle, was a tough reality of history
that also linked us together.

I needed a special gift to take with me and I knew just the
person to make it, my good friend Charlie Gallagher. Charlie is quite an extra-ordinary character in his late-20's. In his
early teens Charlie had decided to take up his great grandfa-
thers trade of blacksmithing. An even more ancient calling soon
became apparent, however, in his craftsmanship. Charlie began
hammering out medieval swords and other alarmingly sharp
ancient looking objects on his anvil as opposed to your average

horse-shoes and iron gates. If ever there was a case for re-in-carnation then Charlie would surely make an interesting study. Standing six feet tall with long black hair to his waist and the solid sinewy stature of a Gaelic warrior he would have possibly been turned down for a part in Mel Gibson's Braveheart movie on account of looking too realistic!

His ancestral clan were the Gallaghers, spelled Ó *Gallachóir* in Irish. They had provided captains, cavalry, swordsmen and advisors to the powerful medieval armies of the O'Donnells' who once were kings of Donegal and much of Northwest Ireland. As well as possessing an intuitive understanding of many ancient crafts and beliefs sadly lost to the great majority of Irish people, Charlie is the funniest person I've ever had the good fortune to know.

I explained my plans to him over the phone and entrusted Charlie to make a special gift for my Native American hosts. We both agreed that entering the United States brandishing a sword might not be the wisest option. "Leave it with me for a while Keith and I will think of something", was his solid reply.

Three weeks later I set off through Barnes Gap in my car to a quite rural townland in East Donegal where Charlie and his young German wife Katja live in an old two-storey farmhouse. I had attended their wedding just a few months earlier. They married each other on May Day underneath a grove of ash and oak trees, dressed in medieval clothing completed by two jewel-inset crowns, while friends and loved ones gathered around. It was one of the most enchanting spectacles I had ever witnessed.

The memorable festivities were held in a marquee on the street in front of their house. At any moment I imagined an angry mob of hotel owners and irate 'wedding fayre gurus' would come blustering through the front gates demanding that everyone come to their senses and spare a thought for the proper excesses of a real Celtic Tiger wedding. It was re-assuring to see that Charie's sword hung by his side during the festivities!

The sun was just beginning to set when I arrived at Charlie and Katja's house. I was welcomed inside and the kettle was boiled for tea. When Charlie showed me what he had made I

3

was utterly lost for words. He had metal crafted a circular disc of bronze, rimmed by silver, and about 10 inches in diameter. As he tilted the disc under the kitchen bulb, a dazzling wave of reflected light moved across its surface. It was visually stunning. The face of the disk was inset with gem stones, ancient symbols and elaborate etchings. I sat down and listened attentively as Charlie explained the disc he had created for me to take. He had etched an eagle with outstretched wings on the top half of the disc. This depicted a powerful totem bird for most Native American tribes and represented their 'Great Spirit' or God. Below the eagle's head and appearing to be born from its opened beak was a golden coloured bronze spiral symbol. When I asked Charlie with quiet reverence what this symbol meant, he described it as symbolising the birth of universal or clockwise motion. This is the directional movement of our Moon, Earth, Solar System and Galaxy. He had based this symbol on a treasure unearthed in South America which had been dated conservatively to between two to five thousand years ago.

Across the centre of the disc from left to right Charlie had inset in silver the three phases of the moon. The new moon, full moon and waning or old moon. A small bright round gem known as the moon stone was inset upon the full moon and the disc had even been created on the eve of a full moon.

The head of a red stag deer was etched on the bottom half of the disc and represented the spirit of ancient Ireland. An ogham message from a Celtic ancient form of writing was inscribed on one antler while a message in ancient American writing was inscribed to my Cheyenne hosts on its other antler. Set above and between the antlers and made of silver was an ancient Celtic symbol called a tri-spiral, representing youthfulness, maturity and old age. The ruby gem stone set inside the tri-spiral was of amethyst. "It is a stone of healing", Charlie explained, "it's meaning is that we receive healing from the earth." At this point in our conversation I felt a strange tingling sensation in the centre of my forehead which gradually faded away after a few moments. Charlie revealed that even the disc itself had great meaning as the inner disc was set in copper to symbolise the sun.

I was transfixed in awe at the disc now placed into my keeping. When I asked Charlie how long it took him to make it he replied, "the best part of a day, it sort of flowed through me." In times past Irish people considered anything the blacksmith made to be 'gentle' or enchanted and carried good luck and protection. Even today many people still hang a horse-shoe over the door of a barn or shed as a good luck charm.

Before I left, Charlie performed a short ancient protection ritual for me outside in the nearby tree grove. "This will insure that your journey is a safe one", he assure me, as the last light of evening faded to the West. We then shook hands and embraced like brothers. His final words to me were, "this disc will accompany you on a journey of forgiveness but also don't forget the ancient links that connect our ancestors. Let them know there are people here who wish to express their solidarity through these difficult times."

On the Saturday before departing I put a turf fire in the kitchen hearth of the old cottage I live in and awaited some visitors I had invited around. Ted Hall arrived and signed a copy of his enchanting book 'The Thinness of Light' to bring with me. Eamonn Monaghan then arrived with a traditional musician by the name of Donal Kelly. Eamonn had only recently published a collection of his poems and songs and I was honoured to take a signed copy along with me. A poet in the traditional rhyming style, Eamonn's poems are steeped in local folklore and history, nature, the Donegal landscape, rambling houses and characters.

I set out cups, milk and sugar and brewed up tea for us all. Removing Charlie's disc from its silk covering I passed it around while answering questions like "who made it?" and "where are you going with it?" Someone threw a few turf on the hearth fire and I asked Eamonn would he recite one of his poems for my journey. He leafed thoughtfully through the pages of his poetry collection for a few moments and then chose;

The Highway of Life;
As I journey on the highway of life,
Over many a weary mile,
I meet the folk who hurry with a frown,
And I meet the men who go in eager hope,
With those who trudge in timid throng,
But each pilgrim on the highway of life,
Will love a helping hand to get along.

I will go upon my way with lightsome thread,
By rainbow glen and plain,
For I can never retrace my footsteps there,
Nor pass that way again.
And when the rising mountains loom ahead,
And weary is the burden then to bear.
I will give a cheery smile, a friendly word,
And a helping hand to share.

Donal Kelly then brought his accordion in from the car and
played a few tunes. Donal had recently been crowned Ulster
Champion for his accordion playing at the *Fleadh Ceoil* traditional music festival. His face became animated as he began
playing. His fingers moved up and down the keys and his body
seemed to flow and move with the music he brought alive. As
night fell slowly outside, the embers at the centre of the hearth
fire grew a deep ruby red. Galaxies were born from such fires
I thought to myself. As I looked around the room it felt like I
was being honoured with some kind of special traditional send
off. Three elders, a poet, a bard and a storyteller, all gathered
together in a wee Donegal cottage in the summer of 2006, just
a few years into the 3rd Millennium AD. In times past this very
place had been a rambling house. Neighbours had gathered under its then golden thatched roof to exchange news, play music
and tell stories. On special nights there was set dancing upon its
age smoothed flagstone floors while someone would have lilted
or played an old tune on a fiddle or accordion. The people who
once lived here and neighbours who once visited have all passed

on now but I sometimes sense a gentle echo of their lives when the hearth fire is lit. I had renamed the house *Teach Annie*, (Annie's House), after a grand aunt of my Mother's called Annie McGinley nee Mc Bride. She was a strong, resourceful and kind hearted woman. As the sound of Donal's lively accordion playing filled the hearth room I looked up at Annie's photo on the mantelpiece. In it she is seated on a chair outside her own front door with a content smile on her face and an accordion resting on her lap.

As I gazed once more into the fire and listened to the music I wasn't so sure anymore of the scientific certainty that time is like a straight ruler moving ever further forward and away from our past and present. Although time seems to be forever on the move maybe it spirals back on itself again and again, often without our knowing.

One of my last visits before leaving on the first leg of my journey was to call in and see Sister Nellie Mc Loughlin. She had helped set my journey in motion and I wanted to show her the disc that Charlie had made. Over tea, Nellie talked with great fondness about her time spent on the Northern Cheyenne Reservation in Montana. She told me how she had taken part in a retreat at a newly built womens' centre called Prayer Lodge and recommended I go there for a visit. She also talked fondly about Francis and Vonda Limpy who would be my hosts. I gathered from her that they managed the centre. She shared some funny stories from her time spent there but a tone of sadness entered her voice as she spoke about the many social problems on the reservation. As we said our farewells at her front door, Nellie handed me a small book on Native American Spirituality to read on the way.

THE JOURNEY BEGINS

My sister Donna met me in Dublin airport with my plane ticket. She was dressed very smartly in her aquamarine green Aer Lingus uniform and was looking very pretty as usual. "Are you sure you have everything with you now?", she asked with sisterly concern. Donna had been able to organise discount plane tickets for my travels. I was very grateful to her and jokingly shared my determination never to miss her birthday or Christmas gift for at least the next fifty years. As we hugged and said our goodbyes, rain droplets were gathering outside the departure lounge airport viewing glass. It was late summer and one of those rare days that you don't mind it raining in Ireland, only for the fact that you know you're about to board a plane.

Travelling at an average speed of 550 miles per hour and an average height of 35,000 feet above the deep Atlantic waters far below, our flight from Dublin to New York took just over six and a half hours. As we circled around JFK airport to land, the sun was setting a brilliant gold. I caught my first non-TV glimpse of the city skyline of Manhattan, far off in the distance. It looked for a moment like the Emerald City in the Wizard of Oz.

I queued at the immigration control centre with my passport clutched tightly in my sweaty palm. It was as if they pumped some invisible chemical into the air conditioning to make you think you might actually be a terrorist, deep-down. Seeing security personnel with high powered hand guns strapped to their belts didn't make me feel any more at ease. I had grown up with American popular culture and had happily watched the sit-coms, played the pop music tapes, worn the t-shirts, bought the action men and eaten the cereals. Now that I had finally arrived in the United States a part of me somehow expected a grand reception.

Were impossibly happy cheerleaders with brighter that white smiles waving blue and red pom poms too much to ask for? What about a colourful brass band playing "When the Saints Go Marching In"? Now that would have made a real impression on me! To have been showered at the airport arrival terminal with balloons and streamers, as a giant sized Uncle Sam character looking for all the world like Abraham Lincoln stooped down and in a warm gravely voice said, "hey there Keith, heck we're so glad you finally made it."

"Hello, excuse me sir, hello sir", boomed the security guard at me through a speaker mike at the booth I was cueing for. He then signalled me forward. "It says here that you are a teacher back home sir, is that right". "I am indeed", I replied. I had written that down as my occupation just to re-assure them that I'd be returning home again once my month was up. With a genuine look of gratitude that said, "I have three troublesome hyper active kids going to school at the moment", he stamped my passport and proclaimed "Okay you're in, welcome to the United States sir!"

There was no one waiting to collect me at the airport. I felt like a soldier dropped off at a beach head in unknown territory, wearing a bright neon uniform which proclaimed, 'raw recruit – just landed'. A half an hour later, I was standing outside a motel frantically negotiating down a one hundred dollar fare with an airport taxi driver from Iraq who had little English. The next day I hopped on the subway to explore New York. It was a little strange walking around Manhattan. Although I had never been there before every place I visited seemed to have a familiar quality. Rather than deja-vu, I put it down to the fact that I had probably seen a great deal of Manhattan before through movie and TV shows. One of the places I particularly wanted to see and experience for myself was Ground Zero, site of the infamous September 11th attacks. Through a high wire mesh perimeter fence I looked across a vast rubble and dust strewn site where the two World Trade Center Towers once stood. I could also make out a number of black gaping entrances to underground levels. It was difficult to comprehend that two huge skyscrapers full of people and office blocks once stood on this now derelict site. My mind played back the TV images of those jet liners crashing into the skyscrapers, just as the news channels had endlessly replayed them. It was still difficult for me to fully comprehend the terror and horror that was visited upon the people of New York that day. Thousands of lives had been extinguished in a just a few minutes and further fuel was added to a world already burning with more than enough hatred, fear and mindless violence.

On a late morning subway ride from lower Manhattan to Greenwich Village I heard the wailing cries of a young man coming from a nearby carriage. The wailing grew louder until a young man, no more than twenty-five years old, stumbled on two crutches into our carriage. He was of medium height and of strong build with neat jet black hair. As he steadied himself, military service dog tags swung around his neck. He was clearly distressed and looked intoxicated on either alcohol, drugs or both. Leaning on his crutches and standing at the centre of our carriage he reached down towards his knee and started fumbling with a strap. Everyone tried their hardest to pretend he wasn't there, including myself. Composing himself a little he released a false lower leg from his knee. Letting another wail to grab our attention, he held it up in the air while looking around desperately trying to grab peoples attention. "Can you please help me", he said, between short distressing breaths. "I got blown up by a roadside bomb over in Iraq. I need another operation as my insides are all messed up. I need some money to have another operation." He then lifted his prosthetic lower leg in the air again and cried out, "I'd like to see how George Bush would like it if he got his leg blown off by a bomb". At first everyone continued to look at their shoes and pretend that this person wasn't there. Then a young smartly dressed Latino woman sitting next to me opened her purse and with a look of genuine sympathy reached over and put a five dollar bill in his hand. One by one everyone in the carriage began rooting around in their pockets or purses for spare dollars to give this young broken down man. After what seemed an age, he managed to strap back on his false limb and stumbled quietly into the next carriage.

The next leg of my journey was from New York to Seattle where I was to spend a few days with a friend I met in Ireland. But for the kindness of a young lady on checkout I would have missed my flight. I hadn't realised there were seven terminals at JFK airport and involved my taxi driver in a frantic race against the clock. The disc that Charlie Gallagher had given me was now in my hand luggage to be carried on board my next flight. Security since September 11th was very tight and I worried would I be able to take it on board with me. Two white gloved security guards unwrapped it from the cloth and bubble wrap I was keeping it in and then asked me what it was. I explained that it was a cultural gift from the people of my part of Ireland to the Northern Cheyenne tribe who I was travelling to visit. Both guards looked at it in silent wonder and then carefully re-wrapped and re-taped it before handing it back to me and wishing me well. I felt great relief and excitement as I boarded the American Airways flight which would take me safely across the United States to the city of Seattle. The pilot came on the intercom before take-off and sounded like a frontier cowboy. You had to wonder was he wearing tanned brown embroidered snakeskin boots complete with spurs under his captains uniform. As we came into land he came back on the intercom in his gravely western drawl. "You all take care now do ya heeear and you all make sure and come back now and travel with us again reeeal soon." As the plane landed safely on the runway all the cabin crew and pilots got a rousing round of applause and cheers from passengers. I found myself warming to America like you would an enthusiastic and ever cheerful relative.

I was travelling across the United States to Seattle to visit a friend and from there I planned to take a bus to Montana. I had first met Meghan on the Derry to Galway Bus Éireann Express in Ireland on a bright cold January evening back in 2003. When I got on the bus in Donegal Town we were but perfect strangers. We had exchanged a brief mutually interested glance at one another as I passed up the aisle but we were seated on opposite ends of the bus until we stopped for a short break at Sligo station. When the bus arrived in Eyre Square, Galway City, we were sitting side by side and long past introductions. Meghan was of medium height and slim build with long blonde hair and large sparkling blue eyes. She was travelling through Europe at the time with a friend on a break from college studies.

Being too busy gazing in each others eyes we were last off the bus and I remember wishing I had enough money to bring her out for dinner. As I dragged my travel bag down from the overhead luggage space, I could scarcely believe it. On the seat opposite was a twenty pound note. Dinner became a wonderful romantic reality that night. I imagined a Zeus like God catching a cross glance from his Goddess wife Hera and him defending his action with the words, "c'mon will you, I was only trying to help the guy out a little."

Although our lives crossed but briefly on the magical road of travel , we had maintained a close friendship through e-mails and now I was going to meet Meghan again in her home town of Seattle. It was night time when our plane landed. Meghan met me at the airport with her boyfriend Lance and friend Gretchen. They had piles of question for me and seemed to take endless enjoyment from hearing me speak in my Donegal accent. A heavy travel tiredness came upon me which was temporarily lifted when Seattle's city skyline came into view. It was an dazzling spectacle with light studded skyscrapers and the landmark space needle tower which looked like a UFO resting on a tall landing pad.

The next few days were spent sight-seeing around Seattle with Meghan and her friend Gretchen. We saw giant sock-eye salmon swimming near one of Seattle's giant sluice gates. It was amazing to see such a timeless and natural upriver migration still occurring through the heart of a modern city.

Seattle is a booming high tech manufacturing city, home of Starbucks coffee and legendary guitarist Jimmy Hendrix. The city was more recently famous for being the epicentre of the Grunge music phenomenon of the early 1990's when bands like Pearl Jam, Nirvana and Sound Garden exploded unto the world music scene. Seattle is also the home town of billionaires Bill Gates and Paul Allen, co-founders of Microsoft who have become two of the richest men on the planet. While some wealthy people collect antiques or buy race horses, Paul Allen pioneered his own unique hobby. In fact he has taken to collecting memorabilia of a galaxy of rock stars such as Jimmy Hendrix, Jim Morrisson, Kurt Cobain and hundreds of other music artist, many of whom have thankfully managed to stay alive. Mr Allen then personally bankrolled the building of a multi-million dollar EMC Music centre in downtown Seattle to exhibit his personal hobby collections to the public. Built with suitable lavish gusto, the building resembles an electric guitar and is painted in crazy metallic colours.

Meghan had a job interview in upstate Washington on one of my days spent visiting her and she invited me to come along for the drive. We took the I-5 inter-state highway northbound out of Seattle on a hot sunny afternoon. I now got to experience U.S. car culture on a grand scale with 5 lanes of traffic going each way. It wasn't even rush hour and the highway was near grid-locked. The air was thick and hazy with carbon dioxide while car and truck horns released people's frustrations on each others ears. The traffic began to flow about a half an hour later just as we came across a brand new red Porsche sports car, crushed flat like a pancake. It had been dragged unto the hard shoulder by a tow truck. I wondered what had happened and thought about the driver who could not have survived such a devastating downward impact. Up ahead, a huge black cloud of smoke billowed high up into the stifled sky. A short time later we passed a truck cab consumed in tongues of yellow flames. A silence descended on both of us. There was a distinctly apocalyptic feeling about my first drive on an interstate American highway. When a long silver Buick then suddenly fender bended another car in the lane next to us the mood was somehow lightened. We both had to laugh to release the nervous tension.

Mercifully we soon veered off the highway and unto quiet tree shaded roads and lush green open farmland. As Meghan drove, we talked and caught up with each others lives over the last few years and our hopes and plans for the future. We arrived in the sleepy town of Emerson by early evening. Meghan pulled up outside the Mexican restaurant where she had applied for a job as a part-time waitress to help pay her way through college. Spotting a big inviting tree in a nearby park I told Meghan I would wait for her there and catch up on some reading. Before long three young Mexican boys around the ages of ten and twelve circled around me curiously on bikes. Soon we were involved in an animated and light hearted chat and began swapping stories about haunted houses, curses and spooky ghosts. They particularly liked hearing my story about the banshee or fairy woman. One of the Mexican boys said that his grandmother had once told them a similar story except the Mexican banshee carried a hand mirror rather than a comb to point in your direction and scare the life out of you.

That night back in Seattle I got a chance to talk with Meghan's parents, Mike and Mary. They were a kind, thoughtful and softly spoken couple. Mike was a bank manager. Although Mary had gone to college before they married she had made a decision to be a home maker for their two kids. There was an unmistakable air of sadness about them. I asked then about their son who's room I was staying in. On the wall there was a picture of him no older than twenty five years old and dressed in military uniform. They explained to me that despite receiving a college education their son had taken the surprise decision to join the army. He had willingly volunteered for active service in Afghanistan at the time of the U.S. invasion.

Being their only son, Mike and Mary seemed to have gone through a tough time. Although they accepted his decision it took a tremendous toll on them. They spoke of breaking down in tears during Sunday services at their local church. Although their son had returned safely and was now living and working in San Francisco as a civilian again, it seemed they were still dealing with the larger traumas of war. That night as we watched the news on TV a report came on in relation to the crash Meghan and I had seen earlier that day on the highway. The photo of the man who had been driving the red sports car flashed up on the screen. He had been driving behind a truck transporting large sheets of industrial weight metal. One of the sheets had come loose and flew off the back of the truck flattening the man in his car, killing him instantly. For some reason this news story had a deep impact on me. This man seemed to have everything going for him and yet a freak accident extinguished his life in a matter of moments. An emergency response team would have towed his car over to the hard shoulder to allow five lanes of traffic to flow freely once again. His now lifeless body would have been cut from the wreckage, placed on a stretcher and put in the back of an ambulance. Traffic flowed past and the world went on regardless with this man in it or passed on from it. The incident got me thinking on how fragile life is and yet how much we grasp unto things that are ultimately not such a big deal.

On my final day in Seattle I was invited by Meghan and her parents to attend a barbeque organised by their close friends. We drove about one hundred miles upstate to the San Juan Islands which Meghan informed were a playground for the rich. We arrived outside a tall two storey white washed wooden house which faced unto a picturesque inlet and wooded island about a mile out. Although still summer and in the mid 20's, Mount Baker rose like a glacier capped colossus on the Canadian-U.S. border to the north of us. I was introduced and warmly welcomed as a guest. We spent the afternoon eating, drinking and eating some more and then had a quietly competitive game of volleyball. The rest of the evening was spent relaxing on the waterfront, drinking sodas and watching seals watching us. Their shiny dark heads bobbed up and down in the choppy waters and surveyed us through coal black eyes. In passing conversation I had asked Valerie, our co-host for the evening, how long they had lived here. She replied in a deadpan mid-western drawl, "Oh well now, I guess we moved here with the house about ten years ago". Being a little puzzled I was compelled to enquire further. Valerie then willingly told me how she and her husband had hired a crack team of engineers to lift their house unto a giant barge and tow it more than thirty miles up Puget

Sound through sluice gates and open water. When the barge came to this lovely coastal site which they bought, they hired a crane and literally set it down where it now stood on the water's edge. I thought to myself, "America, the land where anything dreamed off is possible. Especially with enough spare dollars in the bank account!" Back at the Brunstadt household that night I presented them with a piece of polished bog oak taken from a peat bog in Inishowen, back in County Donegal. The bog oak had been given to me by a friend Brendan Farren. I explained that it was several thousand years old and gladly gifted it in gratitude and in thanks for their hospitality.

The next morning I boarded a greyhound bus bound for Billings, Montana where I was to be collected by my Northern Cheyenne hosts. An eighteen hour bus journey lay ahead of me which would take me across two time zones and the states of Washington, Idaho and Montana. On board for the bus voyage were students, elderly folk, army cadets, drifters, misfits, punks, a few Goths and a back-packer. Our bus driver was a zany and eccentric looking character. His bus uniform, a white shirt and navy blue trousers did little to normalise him. He had a large fuzzy head of air and thick black rimed glasses. He also wore white socks with black shoes which seems a standard dress code for bus drivers throughout the known world. Before he started up the engine he caught hold of an intercom microphone and lay down some bus rules for the journey ahead. "There is to be no food eaten on board, okay. We will be stopping along the way for food and toilet breaks. You are not allowed to drink alcohol or take drugs on this bus, do I make myself clear. If I'm not allowed to drink or take drugs while driving this bus then I sure as hell aint' going to allow you to." He seemed to really relish having a captive audience and an amplified microphone. He was always going to finish with a flourish, "if you feel nervous at any time while we are driving over some of the steeper mountain passes then my advice is to sit back and close your eyes, that's what I usually do anyhow." With the stand-up comic style lecture over our driver revved the bus into gear. On the daylight part of the journey we drove through an 'authentic' German Alpine village in the Cascade Mountains and passed by miles and miles of fruit orchards. By late evening we were winding our way through the Bitterroot Mountains of Northern Idaho. The landscape looked straight out of a scene from a Grizzly Adams movie. From my bus window I gawped out at frontier wilderness with seemingly endless pine clad steep mountain sides and just a few drive-thru service stations stretched out along river valleys. We crossed the Rocky Mountains in darkness. In Butte, Montana I woke up to see what looked like a space rocket hovering in the night sky. After a quick rub of my eyes and some hard staring out the misted bus window a giant glowing statue of the Virgin Mary came into focus. This real apparition was perched atop a steep mountain peak overlooking the town. During the late 19th and early 20th centuries, large numbers of Irish people came out West and ended up in Butte, Montana working in the nearby mines. They had evidently taken their strong Catholic faith with them On into the ink black night our bus drove along deserted roads. We arrived in Billings at the cruel hour of 5am. I wondered in sleep starved disbelief whether a sadistic bus clerk working undercover for General Motors made out the timetable. Our less than sympathetic bus driver woke his dozing cargo by turning the radio up full blast. He even had the audacity to smile at his own dastardly deed as a sorry procession of bleary eyed living dead slowly shuffled off his bus.

I spent the early morning walking around Billings waiting for a diner to open for breakfast. Billings was a large commercial town seemingly devoid of pedestrians. Pick-ups and SUVs clearly ruled out here. Drivers drove slowly past staring suspiciously at me and my misplaced back-pack. The streets were empty and treeless and mean in the glare of a blazing late morning sun. As I waited back by the bus station to be collected, a well built guy of medium height walked up to me. He was sporting a black stained vest, tattoos and a receding head of greasy black curls. "Hey", he exclaimed, "you're from Ireland aint you?" As I wasn't wearing clothes distinguishing myself as Irish I could only presume that I looked Irish and answered with a smile "I am indeed." He smiled back showing more gaps in his mouth than teeth, "I just knew it, my family is from Ireland man, my name's Thomas but my nickname is Shamrock." He then shook my hand with honest enthusiasm and went on to explain that most of his Irish relatives now live in England. He regarded them as traitors. "Have you ever been to Ireland", I enquired. "Nah, I got a couple of felonies and four federal assault charges which I did jail time for, I don't think they'd let me go." With an Irish storytelling gusto he then continued, "There was this one time I was in O'Hooligans bar, (I walked past this pub in Billings myself), and these big foreign looking blonde dudes came in right. Well I went right over and asked them where they were from. When they said they were from Sweden I said, 'why you fucking Vikings, you people raped, murdered and pillaged my people back in Ireland. Hell I sure showed them suckers what for."

Just then a stout lady with dark tightly cropped curly hair and glasses with a young boy in a baseball cap by her side, walked over to us. She asked me was my name Keith and gave my friend Shamrock a chilling stare that sent him backtracking down the street with a parting "hey, good luck Ireland." It was Vonda and her young grandson Smiley.

CHEYENNE DREAMS

My Northern Cheyenne contacts had arrived. I loaded my baggage in the back of their station wagon and we set off. I could scarcely believe it when she told me that they lived over one hundred miles away from Billings which was their nearest big town. I could see that Billings was built on a valley floor as the road climbed steeply out of town. There was no small chat after our initial introductions. As she drove, Vonda pointed out where a recent forest fire had ravaged the area and even crossed the highway in strong winds. Then as the road seemed to level off a huge sweeping landscape unfolded in front and all around us. It was my first sight of the Great Plains which had always enthralled me. They were just as expansive and awe inspiring as I had imagined they would be. Sandy yellow plains stretched off to the horizon on either side while up ahead the land began to separate into bench-lands of high prairie intersected by bluffs and hidden river creeks. A big unbounded deep blue sky overhead grew ever more expansive. We passed by the Little Bighorn visitor centre where the Sioux, Cheyenne and other Plains tribes led by Chief Sitting Bull and Crazy Horse had outsmarted and defeated a young U.S. Cavalry General by the name of George Armstrong Custer and his troops. As we passed the memorial site I caught a glimpse of a stars and stripes flag fluttering on a small distant hill. Vonda drove by without slowing down. She then broke the silence be saying, "do you know that we're now driving through the Crow Nation Reservation. Them Crows got a much bigger reservation than the Cheyennes because they sided and worked with the Government. Custer and the U.S. army employed Crows as scouts. Our people don't like visiting the monument at the Battle of the Little Big Horn as we think its glorified and biased. It was our people who fought so valiantly for our land and won a legendary victory." There was nothing for me to say in reply. I gazed silently out the window at this semi mythical landscape. Even today this land seemed unspoilt by human development. It was easy to sense the freedom of spirit that such a landscape invoked in the hearts of both Native American and later pioneers.

On the way we stopped off at the Crow Nation town of Harden to do Vonda's weekly shopping in a local supermarket. As I followed Vonda and Smiley through the automatic sliding doors a giant Crow man, at least six foot six inches tall with waist-length jet black hair nearly walked over me. On my map the Cheyenne Reservation looked about a quarter of the size of the Crow Nation Reservation and measures about 60 miles wide and 20 miles long. As we approached Cheyenne country the land began to change from high open plains to low sandstone hills. We dropped Smiley off at his parents house along the way. Before we left he showed me his horses which were corralled below their house within a tall wooden fence. Apparently Smiley was becoming an expert at breaking in horses. As we approached the small town of Lame Deer the sandstone ridges closed in to make a snug and sheltered valley with surrounding hills dotted with tall Colorado pines. "Our people fought long and hard for this piece of land and we're quite happy here", Vonda said, as if sensing that I was impressed with what I saw. Vonda and Francis lived two miles out of Lame Deer in a one storey wooden farmhouse with a basement nestled at the side of a small horseshoe valley cloaked by forests of tall pines. Piebald horses grazed peacefully beyond a large dark green corrugated shed. Francis was there to greet us at the door. He was a bespectacled man of about seventy years with a kind but life toughened wizened face and of medium height and wiry build. He wore brown boots, jeans and a chequered shirt and beneath a baseball cap flowed long silvery hair tied back in a ponytail, Indian style.

One of Vonda's grown up daughters was also visiting at the time with her three kids. Vonda made a tasty dinner of corn on the cob and mince beef burgers for us. I had to then deal with the culture shock that they not only didn't drink tea, they didn't even bother with an electric kettle. After dinner, Francis, Vonda and I sat around the living room area as the sun was setting and they asked me how was Nellie McLoughlin. They explained that she had stayed up at Prayer Lodge during her visit a few years back but that I would be staying with them. I then took the gifts I was carrying with me out of my shoulder bag and presented them to my hosts. Their faces lit up with wonder when I showed them the disc and they listened in silence as I explained the Native American and ancient Celtic symbolism associated with it. They asked me who made it and I showed them a photo of Charlie Gallagher. I told them that he had made it for me to take along on my journey as a cultural exchange gift. Frances then said, "well what about that, cause our medicine man is called Charles as well. His full name is Charles Little Old Man. I think we should show him this disc before you leave as he'd like to see it." I then passed the signed copies of Ted Hall's book and Eamonn Monaghan's collection of poetry. They seemed genuinely bowled over by the presents I had brought them. Vonda had mentioned over dinner that we would be working out in Prayer Lodge tomorrow and I asked her to tell me more about the place. "We built Prayer Lodge back in 1992 with the help of the Odenberg Franciscan Order as a safe and quiet place for people to meet and discuss their lives. It became a place to inspire, empower and educate ourselves. We liked the Franciscans because they are connected to the earth and understand the way the earth provides for us. St Francis of Assisi saw that everything has a spirit and we as a people have always tried to honour that through our beliefs. Vonda paused for a few seconds then continued, "you know with us Indians, there's always a prayer going in the back of our minds. We've got our own share of troubles here on the Reservation with alcohol, drugs, abuse, domestic violence and abandonment. When Prayer Lodge was open women were able to go there and leave there troubles behind them for a while. It has become a healing place for people to open up and relieve themselves of their troubles. Praying and doing sweats (sweat lodge purification ceremonies), has helped us all come through some tough times. I then asked Vonda to describe a sweat lodge ceremony to me. "It's like a womb, a space in darkness and covered over with canvass and blankets and originally buffalo and deer skins. Special stones are heated in a fire outside. We call these stones grandfather rocks. The hat keeper or medicine man is usually in charge of pouring cold water on the rocks inside the sweat lodge and sacred herbs are burnt. Hot steam builds up inside the lodge and our medicine man conducts the purification ceremony. After a sweat ceremony, you leave all your fears and regrets behind and you emerge newly cleansed and blessed every time."

Vonda then asked "Why are you here?". At first I was taken back by such a direct question. At the same time I felt relaxed and at ease in their company and after a moment answered. "I feel there is a lot of disconnection in modern life and in myself and wish to find a more real way of living with and being in the world. I also think re-building strong community based culture can solve a lot of our social problems. I have always carried a deep respect for Native American ways of relating to the earth and the natural world. I guess I am on a journey to see how I can better communicate all these concerns in a clear way."

Francis then asked me, "are there many people in Ireland who feel the same way as you do?"

"I believe there is a growing number. Many of my friends feel the same way but our culture has been changing very quickly for the past few generations although some changes have been very positive. I think more and more people back in Ireland feel that the past or time honoured traditions such as house visiting, storytelling or remembering local lore are not relevant to their lives anymore. If we forget who we are then what future have we?" Vonda then laughed unexpectedly as if to lighten my serious mood and then said, "do you know us Indians believe that visions or gifts are drawn from a higher power to help serve others?"

I woke the next morning feeling well rested. Before falling asleep I had heard Francis moving around the kitchen and then the hallway. As I drifted off into dreams a sweet incense like smell came through the room. Vonda informed me over breakfast that, "each night before retiring Francis heats some sweet cedar leaves over a hot pan and then carries the smoke around the house to bless and protect everyone through the night." I helped Francis load up his open back silver pick-up truck with tools and Vonda followed us out to Prayer Lodge. It was about a twenty minutes drive out of Lame Deer. Prayer Lodge was situated beneath the crest of a high treeless hill. It looked out over a wide valley of sun baked brown grassland which stretched off to a ridge of pine dotted sandstone hills far off in the distance. Vonda gave me a quick tour of the centre which included a state of the art kitchen, office, meeting room and three bedrooms. Francis and I were then put to work while Vonda did some office work. Francis was assigned general maintenance duties while I as an honoured guest was put in charge of pulling weeds out the front. Below the main building was a roofless shelter where a sweat lodge was set up for future use.

A few hours later Vonda called both of us in for lunch and we sat in the pleasantly cool kitchen and shared out juicy ripe water melon slices. I decided to ask Francis about the Little Big Horn visitor centre we passed by yesterday. After a pause to finish eating his slice of melon he began, "you see, every year the Oglala and Sioux ride from their Reservations over in the Dakotas which takes them three days on horseback. They are then joined by a party of Cheyennes. Myself and a group usually go up and sing and drum for them at the Little Big Horn." I then asked him about Chief Black Kettle who was a famous peace chief of the Cheyennes who I read about in books. Francis replied, "nearly all Black Kettle's band were wiped out when Custer charged the camp with his cavalry. The entire village was massacred... men, women and children. There was a great medicine man or hat keeper of the Cheyennes that lived up at Arrow Lodge at the time. Custer went up there a short time after the massacre and this powerful medicine man filled a pipe with tobacco for them to smoke as was the custom. When the pipe had been passed around and smoked and the medicine man was about to tip the ashes into the fire he turned and said to Custer, "see those ashes, if you ever fight the Cheyenne again that's what will become of you."

I then asked Francis had his own family been involved in the Battle of the Little Big Horn. He replied, "there was another major battle in an area called the Rosebud before Little Big Horn and my Great Great Grandfather took part in that. He was injured at that battle. That is how we got the family surname Limpey. His horse was shot from underneath him by a cavalry soldier and he was also shot. He tried to get away from the battle but he was injured and couldn't run very fast. He then remembered that the reins, (stirrup), was still on his horse. It was a great shame back then not to recover them so he turned back into the battle and got them. As he was retreating a second time and now badly wounded, a friend came back for him and they both managed to escape on his horse.

Our people know that battle as 'The Battle Where a Sister Saved Her Brother' as a sister rode straight into that battle and took her injured brother out of it". Later that evening Francis and I drove back to his house to collect a large singing drum as he had been asked to perform at a ceremony in Lame Deer to honour a recently deceased Korean war veteran. On the way Francis explained to me that were four main mens' societies on the Reservation. They were established by a prophet of their tribe called Sweet Medicine who lived over one hundred years ago. FrancIs belonged to the Kit Fox Society and it was with them that he would be singing. We drove up outside the entrance of the Northern Cheyenne Law Enforcement Centre. A large stars and stripes flag fluttered in an evening breeze on a tall stainless steel pole. Evenings were the nicest time on the Reservation when the hot Montana day cooled and the sinking sun cast golden and fiery red hues over the quiet land.

Beneath the flagpole the Police Chief Winifried Russel stood in full blue uniform complete with his rimmed hat and super white gloves. His commanding presence was slightly diminished by two prisoners dressed in bright orange jump suits who stood a short distance behind him, talking in hushed tones and sharing a cigarette. Police Chief Russell explained to the small crowd gathered that the flag had flown at full mast outside the police station to honour the memory of Joe, a well known Korean war veteran. The flag was now going to be taken down and given to his eldest son. Chief Leroy Pine then stepped forward in his ceremonial eagle feathers head dress and said a few quiet suitable words for the occasion.

Four small stools were produced for Francis and his three fellow Kit Fox Society members. They formed a circle around the drum and with cloth covered drum sticks began striking out a steady but slow muffled beat. They sang in unison, a high crying sound that was produced by singing from the top of the throat with their mouths wide open. Their singing cries rose and fell but their drumming remained constant. At first it sounded very strange on the ears but as I let the singing and drum beats wash over me it was clear that the songs they sang were rich in composition and meaning. There was an indescribable expression to it. Free from any contrivance or individual styles. This surely was music created from and for the heart of a tribal people. After the Kit Fox songs were finished, a Cheyenne police trooper stepped forward and played 'The Last Post' on his bugle.

Francis and I were then asked to join the deceased family for a meal. We drove a short distance across Lame Deer to a Menonite Church with a reception hall next to it. The majority of houses we passed along the way were one storey wooden dwellings. Some looking semi-derelict with doors and windows boarded up. As we waited outside in the last light of evening I got talking to Leroy Pine, one of the ceremonial Chiefs. He had put his eagle feathers and sash back in the car boot after the flag ceremony and asked that we talk at the meal. He was a soft spoken middle aged man with a face that seemed to have experienced its fair share of tragedy and more. We discussed everything from global warming and the rising price of car fuel to the Statue Of Liberty and the Northern Ireland Peace Process. He asked me what kind of music I was into and said he played in a rock band in his youth. We were then called inside where seating was laid out for about thirty people. The deceased veteran's son then got up and began to confidently speak. He was of stocky build and medium height with long brown wavy hair and a big drooping moustache.

He began, "as my children and brothers children are here today I think it is very important that the traditional heritage of my family and respect for who they are is passed on to the little ones. My father had a great respect for the military. This was a strong tradition in his family going back to the war chiefs Yellow Robe and Dull Knife who led our people back home from Oklahoma when the Government made us leave our traditional lands. With just a few rifles they protected our people from the army and hostile ranchers as they walked almost 1500 miles in the depth of winter. So we are very proud of these brave men. Although my father served in the United States military with honours he used to always tell us that war is bad and that people do bad things in war."

He then thanked everyone for coming and asked Chief Larry Pine to say a few words again. Larry spoke with great warmth about the deceased man. He recalled how they grew up together and how later he played an important part in his community and then concluded with a few words in English and the Cheyenne language. The eldest son then rose once more and asked Francis and I as honoured guests to serve ourselves first as everyone waited silently in their seats. Chief Leroy Pine sat with us as we ate and explained that it was part of their Native American tradition that the Chief always waited until everyone else was served and eating. He then leaned forward and added in a lower voice, "this is the way it is although my tummy always tells me that it is very hungry and I should really go first."

When the meal was over Francis and I were presented with a blanket each as honoured guests. I was struck by the kindness and quiet generosity of these people. When we got back Vonda was sitting in the rocking chair waiting to hear all the news. When she heard I got a blanket she laughed and said, "now you can go 'snagging' at the Pow Wow this weekend." Francis explained to me that snagging is a local slang word which means to go out looking for a girl to wrap your blanket around. A short time later the house phone rang and Vonda got up to answer it.

A heavy shadow seemed to pass over her face as she listened through the receiver. When she put down the phone she gave us the news that a young man by the name of Medicine Bull had taken his own life by shooting himself sometime late last night. As I settled down to sleep with the sound of crickets chirping noisily outside I felt a sense of steady sadness come over me that people on the Reservation must experience as a part of their lives.

I woke this morning to the sound of the TV blaring out CBS news in the living room next to where I slept. There was a brief report from Iraq where more U.S. soldiers were killed today in heavy fighting with insurgents in a violent chaotic climate of near civil war. A news flash later and a reporter excitedly revealed how actors Tom Cruise and Brooke Shields might be finally getting over their relationship rift and were on the brink of making up. The news channel changed and a Montana news anchorman talked in a frantic voice of how wild fires were still spreading across Western Montana engulfing farms and holiday homes in its relentless wake. So much drama and my head scarcely lifted of the pillow.

After breakfast I helped Francis find and then fold a teepee. It was for his daughter Brenda to take to the Labour Day Pow Wow over in Ashland. The Pow Wow is one of the biggest social events on the Reservation and these annual festivals have helped keep the traditions of dancing, singing and the custom of give-aways alive and well in modern Native American culture. Every tribe holds their Pow-Wows on different weekends over the summer months. This allows neighbouring tribes to visit one another and compete in competitions. An important part of the Pow Wow festival was the Give-Away which Vonda explained to me.

"During the year families save up blankets and food items as well as household accessories such as cutlery sets, cooking pots and toasters in preparation for the Pow Wow, especially if there is someone in your family you wish to honour. On the day of the Give-Away the MC calls up relations, friends or people who has helped the person they are honouring and gifts are presented and given away."

Francis garden was located to the back of the house and that's where Vonda sent us out to pull corn for our dinner. The tall waxy leaves of the Maize garden shone in the glare of the midday sun. Three eight foot tall sun flowers planted at the front of the crop smiled down on us as we approached. Francis worked silently checking what corn cobs were ripe and then threw them to me to fill up a plastic carrier bag. I then got the job of peeling the outer leafy skin and husking the strings from the sun yellow cobs.

With a few hours to spare before dinner I put on my boots and went exploring the pine forested hill to the back of their house. As I crossed some open ground the straw brown grass crumbled into a puff of dust underfoot while large grasshoppers sprang and scattered out of my way. The land was parched for even a drop of rain. The forest was quiet and pleasantly cool under its shaded canopy. Upon reaching the top of the hill I followed a ridge until I came across a magical outcrop of sandstone. Weather and time had sculpted the rock face and smaller outcrops into some fantastical shapes and circular holes of different sizes and depth. It felt like a citadel for the wee fairy people. I wondered were there any cousins to our mischievous lot living here out West in the minds and ancestral memories of their elders. On a high outcrop ahead I saw a tattered white cloth tied to the branch of a pine tree. These rags marked a place where persons had died in times past when the Cheyennes roamed freely through most of present day Eastern Montana and Wyoming. Back before the time of Christian burials, a cairn of stones was placed over the body to keep wild animals and scavenging birds at bay. The only sounds in the forest was the wind blowing gently through the tops of the pines and the machine gun taps of a woodpecker somewhere off in the distance. No fences or boundaries, no distant whirr of a chainsaw or rattle of a digger. A horse neighed somewhere in the valley below.

I arrived back for dinner to be greeted by Francis swaying contentedly in his rocking chair. "So you were up walking in the forests above?", he asked in a type of lead in questioning fashion.

"I was indeed and a nice walk it was," I replied back.

"You didn't see or hear anything strange up there by any chance?"

"No... apart from a horse and a woodpecker", I replied.

"Oh, that's fine...it's just a hungry mountain lion ate one of my neighbours horses up there a few months ago and I thought you might of come across him."

I looked over at Francis and pondered was he teasing or being serious. I guess I'll never know.

Saturday morning and the day of the Pow Wow came. After breakfast we started packing up the station wagon with goods as Vonda was planning a give-away. Francis was acting a little anxious. He had a long day of singing and drumming ahead. I was feeling excited about experiencing a Pow Wow and getting to meet Charles Little Old Man. On the way to Ashland we stopped by a place called Crazy Head Springs. Francis informed me that the tribe had recently managed to buy and reintroduce a small herd of three hundred buffalo back unto the Reservation. This was after many decades of persistent requests to Yellowstone Park officials to give them some surplus buffalo instead of shooting them. We waited a few minutes but despite their huge size and a lot of flat open prairie, the buffaloes had no intention to appear on request that afternoon. As we drove towards Ashland, Vonda consoled me with an old tribal story about the buffalo. "One day a young girl was sent from the village to collect firewood for her family," she began. "While away out fulfilling her task she heard a huge rumble coming closer from behind a ridge in the distance. Then the sky began to fill with a huge dark cloud of swirling dust. The frightened little girl climbed a tree as a noise like deafening thunder came ever nearer. It was a herd of buffalo so big that she held unto the tree for a full day and night until it finally passed by." Before the westward migration of white pioneer settlers in the later 19th century an estimated thirty million buffalo grazed the Great Plains. Horse tribes like the Cheyenne and Sioux lived a practically self sufficient existence from hunting them. The buffalo provided food, clothing, shelter, tools, drums and even fuel for the roaming tribes of Indians. When the buffalo was purposefully wiped out the possibility of maintaining their traditional way of life had become impossible. Perhaps the act of bringing some buffalo back though could help sustain their spirits through these times.

The Pow Wow ground was set up on a picturesque bend of the Tongue River, surrounded on three sides by groves of tall cottonwood trees. Some of the trees bark was scorched black from a wild fire that raged through the area the previous summer. A large numbers of cars and vans were already parked on the grounds. Thousands of people around the Reservation and neighbouring tribes were expected to attend the weekend festival. A large circular arbour had been constructed especially for the Pow Wow. The arbour was constructed with a wooden roof and open sides to let in any air. It also kept the relentless Montana sun of spectators who sat on a two tier circle of wooden benches. The inner arena was covered with a green carpet and in the centre stood a wooden pole on which hung eagle feathers. I carried in Francis's drum and felt like I was the only white man in a hundred miles. I was then introduced to Charles Little Old Man and his wife Marlene. Charles fitted the bill as a modern day medicine man without having to wear a single item of native regalia. He was of medium height with a strong round face and about sixty years of age. He wore shaded spectacles, jeans and a white shirt and moved with a walking stick and slight limp. There was a natural confidence about him that didn't require any acknowledgement. We got on straight away although he didn't say much. He expressed an interest in seeing the disc and asked would I look to take part in a sweat lodge ceremony before I left the Reservation. At that moment our attention was diverted by shouts and hollers as Chief Leroy Pine in full eagle feather head-dress went skidding on his heels across the Pow Wow ring. He looked for a moment like he was water-skiing but instead clutched a rope with two hands which had a mustang horse on the other end. The whole Pow Wow audience erupted in laughter. The give-aways had begun and the Chief had been gifted a half wild horse to get the fun started.

The MC for the day was a small bubbly character of about sixty five years of age who wore jeans, blue t-shirt, baseball cap and a claw necklace. Everyone called him Happy Herb and seldom did an Indian name or nickname suit anyone more. He started by explaining that he was the number one MC because he was the only one that did the proper preparation for it. He had the confidence of a black gangster rapper half his age. He continued, "I'd like to tell all you good people here today that I've travelled all around the world to MC at tribal gatherings, from London to Switzerland. While emceeing for my people and neighbouring tribes, other tribes from all over have been so impressed that they've asked me to represent them at their Pow Wows too". At this stage I was half expecting a group of sexy native Indian beauties in long black greased pig tails to perform a small dance routine around Happy Herb and smother him in kisses. Instead he held up an old time walking stick with an eagle head. He explained how a Swiss man had given him it as a gift when his leg went weak during a concert he was performing at. Happy Herb then began to pick out people from the crowd he knew and in a teasing yet non-hateful way began to tell very witty anecdotes about them. These stories had spectators in stitches of laughter with everybody seeming to know each other on the Reservation.

He finished by saying, "you've got to know that when a man is rolled up in the dirt in a foetal position, you've gone too far with the teasing." As well as joking and teasing, another favourite past-time of the Northern Cheyenne is eating. Unfortunately they seem to have to adopted some of the excesses of American junk food culture. Fast food vans parked around the Pow Wow ring served ever longer cues as the day went on. What separated this event from a big outdoor festival back in Ireland was the absence of alcohol. The Tribal Council had taking the decision to ban the sale of alcohol on the Reservation some years ago in an effort to counter-act the massive problems it has created and still visits upon communities here.

The Give-Aways went on through the afternoon and nobody seemed in any particular hurry as a hot Montana sun blazed down from above. A typical Give-Away started when a fold-up table was placed at the edge of the Pow Wow ring and stocked with eye-catching Indian blankets, food stuffs, electric appliances and pots containing cooked food. One particular Give-Away I witnessed was in honour of an elderly person who passed away the previous year. Immediate family members lined up behind the table as MC Happy Herb talked fondly about the deceased man and recalled personal stories about his life that vouched for his kindness and good standing. A song was then called for. The small group of five immediate relatives stepped forward unto the Pow Wow ring The women wore blankets wrapped around their shoulders. They slowly stepped clockwise around the ring to the beat of the drum and cries of the singers. One by one, cousins and friends walked out and shook hands with the Give-Away party before falling into line behind them. After one circle of the ring the procession and singing stopped. Happy Herb then called up people to receive gifts from the Give-Away table. Recipients of gifts included old childhood friends of the deceased man and a doctor and nurse who cared for him in hospital. With all the gifts cleared off the table, one of the relatives then walked over to Francis and Charle's singing group and handed them a twenty dollar bill for performing. A short civil discussion then ensued between the 'Tongue River Seniors' group before Charles went away to get change at a nearby take-away van. The 'Tongue River Seniors' were in steady demand throughout the day despite the fact there were seven to eight singing groups at the Pow Wow. One group comprising of four enterprising teenagers seemed to have about twenty younger brothers and friends hanging around their shoulders as they sang and drummed in the traditional style.

As the cool light of evening descended on the Pow Wow grounds a buzz of excitement grew. Every spare space around the arbour became filled with spectators. The traditional dancing competitions kicked off with a spectacular parade called the 'Grand Entry'. The MC's helped whip up the atmosphere amid the loud cries of singers and deep sounding thuds of drums. Leading the dancers into the Pow Wow Ring was a small group of Cheyenne men and women army officers dressed in full U.S. military uniform. They held the stars and stripes flag a high alongside their regiment colours and a tribal spear decorated with eagle feathers. The military escort was followed by a dazzling parade of male and female competition dancers in traditional costumes from the age of five upwards. The Pow Wow Ring was soon filled with dancers. The senior male dancers bobbed and swerved as they danced and tambourine like rattles attached to their legs filled the air with the sounds of jingles. Eagle feathers were woven into their long hair and fantastical fans of feather wings draped down their back which opened like eagles wings when they stretched out their arms in dance. On their feet they wore soft moccasins and in their hands they held their long handled sacred pipes. Around the medicine pole they danced, their feet rarely rising above ankle height. The women followed, dancing proud and upright in beautiful costumes of every hue of blue, green, violet, purple and yellow. Many of the dresses were made with rows of tassels and sparkling sequins. Their long dark hair was platted into pigtails and ponytails and decorated with down like feathers and ornamented head dresses. Some of the elder women carried a folded Indian blanket draped on their arm. Little princesses and miniature braves completed the procession, some of the smaller ones holding the hands of an adult. All evening and night the dancers competed in different age categories while the Pow Wow Ring echoed to the throat filled cries of singers and tribal thud of drums.

The MC's would call out the songs and dances to Senior competitors such as the Crow Hawk or Buffalo Dance. The dancer then took on some of the characteristics of that animal or bird as they moved in rhythm to the steady drum beats. The Native American people had recognised the animals and birds as brothers and sisters and all living creatures as sacred. Part of a great 'web of life'. Even the rocks and earth were believed to have spirit and revered as ancient grandparents. Their older culture had not voluntarily made the drastic and lonely path to separation, between 'us' and 'them' or 'it', between mankind and the natural world. These dances were surely part of a connection to a deeper, healthier relationship with the world. As this truth sank in I found myself relaxing more and more into the scene around me. Beside me Francis and Charles sang and beat the drum in unison, as I watched two senior traditional dancers immersed in movement, out on the Pow Wow Ring. Above the circular arbour the bunched leaves of the cottonwood trees shimmered and swayed in a gentle dance between the night breeze and bright moonlight. Everything seemed strangely familiar and re-assuring to me at that moment. I wondered had some ancient memory stored from my own culture been awakened. The half remembered words of an Irish poet and Celtic medicine man flowed into my mind

Is seabhac in aill mé,
I am a hawk on a cliff
Is déar gréine mé,
I am a dewdrop in the sun
Is bradán i linn,
I am a salmon in a pool
Is loch i magh,
I am a lake in a plain.

As we drove the thirty miles back to Lame Deer that night, they asked me had I any luck in 'snagging' a nice girl with a blanket for myself. When I answered with a slightly awkward 'nah'. Francis replied, "well Keith, you still have one more day to make your move."

The next day at the Pow Wow and under silent pressure from Francis I took a break from my cultural observations to go over and talk to a group of young white women who had travelled down from Myles City for the day. After a while I struck up a rapport with one of the girls. Her name was Tammy and she invited me to go on a walk with her around the nearby town of

Ashland. She listed off for me in impressive yet slightly unsettling style, a list of her hobbies, interests, likes and dislikes. She asked me where I was from and then informed me that she was planning to travel with a college gospel choir to Europe next Summer. As our walk was nearing an end and the Pow Wow grounds came back into sight I remembered my 'snagging mission' and asked Tammy would she like to meet up later. With a straight face she turned to me and said, "you could come to Church and pray with me if you liked". This wasn't the response I was hoping for but I somehow managed to lighten the situation by replying, "don't you think we're rushing things a little, I mean we barely know each other."

Deflated but not defeated I returned to my seat and a short time later was called by Vonda to attend a Native American ceremony. Charles Little Old Man was called to perform a naming ceremony for an eight year old lollipop sucking boy who waited by a marquee at the back of the grounds. His family and friends stood around as the little boy was put standing on a crate covered with a blanket. Charles Little Old Man then placed his hands on the boy's shoulders and turned him to face the four directions. He then asked his parents what name they were giving him. Taking a small bottle from his pocket he rubbed some green oil on the boys cheeks, forehead and crown of his head. The boy then had to suddenly divert his attention from his lollipop to landing on his feet safely as Charles gently pushed him off the crate, while announcing aloud his new Indian name as 'Black Bear'.

Back at the Pow Wow ring a young large framed Cheyenne man was given the microphone by an MC and began re-telling a story about one of his ancestors called 'Tall White Man'. Although this Cheyenne warrior had lived in the 19th Century, the young man spoke of him as if he had known him personally, such was the familiar tones he used. He began his story, "Tall White Man was a huge man in stature but also someone who would never turn anyone away empty handed who came to his lodge in need. Two of his sons Bobtail Horse and Crazy Wolf were two of the four warriors who had ridden out to the centre of the Little Big Horn River on the morning before the battle. His sons had prevented Custer and his cavalry from carrying out a devastating surprise attack on their villages of Tee Pees." The speaker continued and now had the attention of the audience, "after the Pine Ridge battle and surrender, Tall White Man and other prisoners of war were taken in chains over to a soldier fort in Myles City. There was one soldier there who kept on taunting Tall White Man and running up to him and staring him right up to his face. Tall White Man turned to one of his party who could speak English. He told him to tell that man to quit and stop taunting him like that or he would bite off his nose. The other warrior tried telling the soldier in English to stop taunting Tall White Man like that anymore as he was a very strong warrior and to watch out. On hearing this the soldier got even worse and ran back up to Tall White Man to do the same thing again. This time Tall White Man lunged between the guards, grabbed the soldier up of his feet and bit off his nose."

That story put me off my food for a while although I did feel obliged to try some fried buffalo strips when they were offered to me later. Francis and Charles were then busy once again singing and drumming while Vonda seemed to talk tirelessly with the endless stream of relations and friends who sat down beside her. Before sunset I got to see the Gourd Dancers initiate a new young member. Francis informed me that the Gourd Dancers were an ancient spiritual society who had died out among the Northern Cheyenne but had been re-introduced by their Southern Cheyenne cousins from down in Oklahoma some years back. The society belonged to the Arrow Lodge. While the Sacred Arrow is kept for safe-keeping down in Oklahoma, the Sacred Hat Keepers returned to Montana when the Northern Cheyenne were finally given a Reservation on their chosen homeland back in 1884.

In the early 1880's the U.S. Government had planned to send all the Northern Cheyenne down to Oklahoma, over fifteen hundred miles away. When Dull Knife and his band of around three hundred people walked back to Montana, they were sent back down to Oklahoma again. During their second escape half of Dull Knife's band were killed and again the U.S. Government ordered the survivors be sent back. This time a high ranking general by the name of George Crook refused orders saying that he had never fought against or dealt with a more honourable people. The politicians in Washington relented and a reservation of land was set aside for the tribe to live on. General Crook was later famously quoted as saying that the conquest of Montana on behalf of a handful of white farmers and pioneers was nothing short of sheer greed and avarice.

Two elder gourd dancers entered the Pow Wow Ring wearing jeans, shirts, white cowboy hats and a tribal sash. In their right hand they shook a sort of rattle, in their left they held an eagle feather while they stepped from foot to foot in rhythm with the drumming. A younger man in a white baseball cap entered the ring and began dancing with the two older men, one on each side. They danced slowly clockwise around the Pow Wow ring stopping for a few moments at the four directions, North, West, South and East and shaking their rattles above their head. They were then joined in a long side row by about 20 gourd dancers including Happy Herb and his little grandson, all shaking their gourds for what they were worth. One of the Gourd dancers was a white man who I was told later owned a ranch locally.

That night the Pow Wow Ring once again filled with the sight of dancers and sounds of singing and drumming. Every so often the MC would announce an inter-tribal dance which meant that visitors were invited to take to the arena. Two of Vonda's small grandchildren dragged me out along with them unto the parade ring and left me with no choice but to throw my shyness to the wind. I thought I was getting the hang of the steps until I spied the tears rolling down Vonda's and half the audience faces at my fancy footwork. There was nothing else for it but to break into a wee Irish jig for extra effect. This induced near hysterical laughter from the rows of spectators.

There were other white guests there besides myself. Three young men dressed in old world clothing and sporting 19th Century beards from a nearby Amish style community sat talking quietly among themselves and taking in the atmosphere. I also bumped into a big Indian guy called Dave who had travelled down from Alberta, Canada. Dave was built like a big Maoiri from New Zealand and wore a seemingly permanent smile on his face. He told me that he belonged to the Diné (pronounced Dinay) tribe in Canada. He had driven down with some mates who were taking part in the group singing competition. When he found out I was from Ireland he said half laughing, "Irish, heh, you're the wild crazy drinkers right? I've never been to Ireland myself but a few years back I travelled over to the House of Lords in London as part of a tribal delegation. Jeez but those Lords guys are really crazy. Man, I couldn't believe it when they started talking. Did you ever hear them speak?!" I then asked him how his tribe had come to visit the House Of Lords. Dave replied, "we gave Prince Charles the honorary Indian name 'Soaring Eagle' when he came to visit out where we live a few years ago. He seemed nice enough and asked us over to England. You know even though we gave him that Indian name we still know him as "Big Ears"! Dave then burst into a fit of laughter and so did I. Before we parted he handed me a cigarette. I told him I didn't smoke but his parting lines was, "we consider tobacco sacred so before you go on the next part of your journey leave it somewhere as an offering."

Just as the night was ending it was announced that a young man by the name of Jeff Parker from the Reservation had been shot dead in a dispute late yesterday evening. The MC then called for the 'Blanket Song' to be played to help out his family with the funeral arrangements. Four women each holding one corner of a blanket shuffled slowly around the floodlit Pow Wow Ring as people came forward and threw cash donations into it's fold.

The next morning I attended Jeff Parker's funeral with Francis and Vonda. The service was held in St. Labre Catholic Church. All funerals of a young person are distressing and deeply sad occasions and this was no exception. Jeffrey Parker had evidently touched the lives of many people in his twenty two years in this world. He had been a Little Big Horn Memorial rider and a small party of Sioux friends from Pine Ridge, South Dakota at-

38

tended the service. He was also a member of the Kit Fox Society and was descended from a long line of famous Cheyenne Chiefs. Mourners also heard how he had become a fireman at eighteen and how one of his favourite pastimes was cooking meals for his family. In fact it seemed that Jeff Parker had crammed a lot of living into his short lifetime as is often the case.

The funeral mass itself was a blend of Roman Catholic and Native tribal ritual. The service finished with a slide show of photos of Jeff, put together by his friends to the songs of his favourite hip-hop artists. Even as a visitor with no ties to the people caught up in this tragedy, I felt myself choking back the tears. We then drove out to a remote part of the Reservation where his remains were to be buried on a family plot on a piece of land known as 'Parker's Poor Farm'. The grave was dug next to an old wooden boundary fence, overlooking a small river creek. Behind and around stretched a wide expanse of open prairie. A strong sun beat down and the air was hot. We watched silently from inside the air-conditioned SUV as an open-top green wagon pulled by two horses appeared in the distance, followed in turn by a group of Sioux riders on horseback. Behind this a cavalcade of over 50 SUV's and cars wound their way slowly across a dusty dirt track. It was like watching a sombre procession of metallic buffaloes move against a hay coloured grassland and deep blue sky. At the graveside Jeff's family looked on disbelief as his remains were lowered into the earth. Francis and Charles carried a drum over to the graveside and sang the Kit Fox song for him as a final farewell. A Sioux rider held Jeff Parker's now rider-less mustang horse, fully fitted out with saddle and reins. His horse stood motionless looking in the direction of the grave as if sensing the sadness and loss of what had happened. After the service male relations were handed shovels and filled in the grave. A hawk cried out somewhere high overhead.

Mourners were then invited back to the cafeteria at Saint Labre Indian School where a meal was served. The priest who said mass sat at our table. His name was Father Paschal Siler and in conversation said he moved out to Ashland thirty years ago. Although originally from Minnesota. he had made the Reservation his home. An elderly Cheyenne farmer by the name of Nick Broken Nose set next to me. He had a weathered face which saw a lot of tough outdoor work in its time and yet his eyes were bright and still full of life. He recalled for me the tradition of holding 'wakes' among Indian families and how families still pass around cigarettes and stay up all night with the remains of a loved one. In a hoarse Montana drawl he then began telling a story, "I remember way back, going to a funeral of an old Indian cowboy who lived on the Res. As they were lowering down his coffin after the last funeral prayers one of the ropes snapped and the coffin crashed to the bottom of the grave. Well it wasn't the first time that old cowboy had landed on his head after being kicked off a wild bronco and everyone there knew it". He finished the story with a hoarse laugh before drying his eyes.

Although still early evening, no one was in the mood to attend the final night of the Pow Wow and we returned to Lame Deer.

The following morning Francis and Vonda had to attend yet another funeral of a young man in his mid-twenties who had taken his own life. I asked to be excused, which they understood and instead walked the two miles into Lame Deer. I was going to meet William Walks Along, a Director of the Northern Cheyenne Tribal Council which acted very much like our County Councils back in Ireland. A hot sun shone in a cloudless sky overhead as I approached the entrance to the Council buildings. A few official tribal lawn-mowing horses were contentedly munching some choice grassy verges.

The few snippets of conversation I picked up while waiting for my meeting left me in no doubt that local politics and bureaucracy operated here as it did everywhere else in the world. A secretary called my name and pointed me to an office where William Walks Along warmly welcomed me and gestured me to take a seat. He asked me about Northern Ireland and the Peace Process and also about Irish history in general. When I was finished answering him he paused for a moment before saying, "there is a great spirit among ethnic groups around the world who have experienced repression. Look at us for example, We are still here and have the determination to make a good future for our people." He asked me to write down my surname and then asked me to re-spell it. As a wry smile of recognition travelled across his face, he lifted his head from his writing pad and said, "Corcoran...I know a Burt Corcoran up in the Rocky Boy Indian Reservation. He was on the Tribal Council and as far as I can recall was Chairman for four years".

As I left the Tribal Council offices I wondered about this surname-sake, Burt Corcoran. My mind began to speculate about whether his ancestor had been a U.S. cavalry trooper of Irish descent. Had he decided after the Indian Wars to settle down in Montana on a piece of land and married a woman from some local tribe? Although tempted to try and find out, I also liked the idea of letting the mystery remain.

Later that evening after dinner Francis suggested we take the disc I brought with me over to Charles Little Old Man house so he could take a look at it. Francis looked physically and emotionally drained from the last few days as we walked out to his pick-up truck. On the way over Francis explained how Charles aunt had been a famous medicine woman of the tribe. There was clearly a strong connection and friendship between both men. From snippets of conversation I gathered that Francis seemed to be on some healing journey within himself, supported by Charles. We knocked on the door and Charles answered in a white vest and worn jeans and welcomed us in. I unwrapped the disc from some cloth and showed it to him. I wasn't as deluded to expect us all to be sitting around a dimly lit tee pee straight from the 'Dances with Wolves' movie set. I was a little annoyed, however, as I tried to compete with a blaring television and Charles Little Old Man's rapid barking terrier dog. The general commotion seemed to bother only me and Charles listened intently as I explained to him the disc's symbolism. Although reluctant at first to hold it he touched the red amethyst gem stone with his hands while touching his heart area back and forth and nodded his head as if understanding something. Charles then offered to hold a sweat ceremony tomorrow evening which lifted my spirits.

That night back in Frances and Vonda's house, a very vivid dream came to me as I slept. My guide was a beautiful young Indian woman with long shining black hair. She wore a long white deerskin dress and an ivory coloured bracelet type necklace. In her left hand she held a white roll of parchment on which she had embroidered a tapestry of bright multi-coloured symbols. She led me into a classroom where a voice told me to remember the kindness of my father.

I then jumped into a second dream which was much more sinister. It was set on an early 20th century American city streetscape and involved an animated half spider half man type creature with large bulging, cunning eyes. He held a stereo radio in one of his hands and a large loud speaker in another. I could not hear any music from the stereo or what he was saying into the loudspeaker but a throng of children, as if in a trance, appeared on the street and gathered around this character. He then led them into an old fashioned tenement building with a winding stairwell which he beckoned them up. I became extremely anxious and began shouting for everyone to stop before they went any further. The dream then switched back to the young Indian woman again who this time was standing in a forest clearing with sunlight streaming around her. I became immediately peaceful. Once again she held up a colourful parchment for me to see. I looked in genuine awe and told her that it was a very beautiful thing that she had made. She smiled warmly and then said, "thank you, but what I show you is a story you have yet to tell."

The next morning I greeted Francis with a few words of Cheyenne which he had taught me, saying, "*Aha Pueba Mey* (Hello, Rising Sun), which was his Indian name. Francis laughed hoarsely and replied "good morning Keith." Such a greeting was accompanied with an open palm pointed upwards. With as many as five hundred different Native American languages spoken at one time in North America, tribes had developed a universal sign language in order to communicate with each other. Francis had explained to me that although he had learnt Cheyenne from his parents while a young child, only a few mostly older people could now speak it fluently.

As I finished my breakfast I watched Francis and Vonda interact. I loved the way they still acted affectionately with each other although now well into their retirement years, sometimes fooling around like a couple of teenagers. A small photo of them hung on the living room from when they were very young. In it Frances looked very handsome and Vonda very pretty and they both looked very much in love. From what they told me I pieced together that they had left the Reservation shortly after getting married and lived in California and Utah where Frances had worked on a radar station. They had then decided to move back to their home area to raise a family and had bought the current house and land they owned. I spent the afternoon sitting outside on the backyard bench reading and updating my travel journal in the shade of some pine trees. After dinner Francis received a phone call to say that Charles had cancelled the 'Sweat' as yet another funeral had come up for which he had to prepare for. Although disappointed I realised the tragedy and sense of loss that visited this community during the space of my short stay. I resigned myself to the fact that it wasn't meant to be this time.

Just before sunset I climbed and clambered up a rocky slope on a ridge opposite the house and watched the sun sink like a fiery red globe beyond a line of distant pine clad rocky hills. As light faded, an intense chorus of chirping crickets filled the still dusky air as an impossibly large red harvest moon rose into the Montana night sky. The scene was a treasure to take home with me.

I rose before dawn the following morning to visit one final time the sandstone rocks along the back ridge. I sat cross-legged in meditation as the sun rose and cast its first rays of golden light through the sleepy forest below. I chose the foot of an ancient pine tree to bury the cigarette that Dave had given me at the Pow Wow. Kneeling on one knee, I said a silent prayer for a safe onwards journey and another in gratitude for having been able to come out here. Vonda was making breakfast when I returned to the house. Although excited about getting back on the road I had grown fond of both my hosts and knew I would miss them. My plan was to hitch-hike to Rapid City in South Dakota and catch a bus out to see the Black Hills. Another idea had been to visit Yellow Stone National Park. When asked by Francis how I intended to travel around the park I had replied, "walking I guess or maybe by bike". Francis had laughed heartily at my travel suggestion and then added, "boy that's a good one, do you happen to know that Yellowstone Park is about the size of Switzerland, complete with hungry wild animals, tee hee hee hee."

As I was packing up my things Francis presented me with a fringed Indian deerskin ceremonial pouch with a striking bead motif on its front. Inside he had put some dried bear root herb which he explained to me was good for sore throats if singing a lot. It had a pleasant fresh smell.

I said my fond farewells to Vonda, thanking her kindly for welcoming me into their home. Francis then drove me down to Ashland, close to the road I would take. We parted with a warm handshake and I promised to ring them in a few days and let them know I was safe and well.

ON THE ROAD AGAIN

An hour later and I felt like a mad Irishman under a hot midday sun, hitch-hiking along the Interstate Route 90 to Rapid City. As time passed so did the traffic. But my luck changed when a car pulled up with two men from the local Cheyenne Reservation. They were going as far as Broadus which they informed was about thirty miles further along the road. We soon got chatting and the driver told me his name was Richard Brady. When I told him that in Irish his surname was Ó Bradaigh which meant 'cattle hustler', he nearly swerved the car of the road from the amount of laughing he and his buddy did. Broadus seemed like one big lifeless main street built along the main interstate route. The place made the middle of nowhere feel cosmopolitan but my enthusiasm was still high. Two hours later and still hitching in the searing heat my enthusiasm was dipping into the red. Elderly men in white cowboy hats and shiny new pick-ups glared with seeming contempt as they drove slowly by while the road began to shimmer with a nauseous desert heat. Richard Ó Bradaigh then arrived back to see how I was doing. I told him I was hungry and thirsty and he gave me directions to a diner back up the town where I could get something to eat and sit down for a while.

Feeling weak and dazed from too much sun on the head I stumbled into a small diner, dragging my travel baggage awkwardly behind me. This was not the kind of peaceful haven I wished for to eat and re-recuperate a short while. A row of shiny off-white tables and red plastic chairs all bolted together occupied the centre of a bare tiled floor. Beside the entrance two middle-aged men sat at a high counter hunched over their coffee's. They stared up at a loud TV while a panel of American football commentators talked up a forthcoming feature match with manic excitement in their voices. Behind me a row of gold light flashing gambling machines communicated in some strange electronic sound language. A pale gaunt faced young man in a tracksuit and baseball cap was transfixed to one of the machines and seemed intent on deciphering its exotic code. A worldy wise waitress in her 50's with fading blonde highlights, took my order. She looked almost as weary as me, The heavy deep pan pepperoni pizza turned out to be the wrong choice and my stomach turned in on itself in protest. How did I manage to end up in this town and how was I going to get out of it were two questions I pondered anxiously and silently.

My mind even began to grasp at invisible straws such as the possibility of public transport. When the waitress returned to collect her bill I enquired with deluded optimism, "Excuse me please, do you know do any buses leave from here to Rapid City?" She took a step back and with one hand on her waist sized up my situation with savage reality, "honey, there's nothing for you but a whole lot of heartache between here and Rapid City." My spirits were less than raised.

I began hitch-hiking again on the edge of town and found a cool shaded spot under a tall cotton tree, right next to a motel. Evening shadows began to appear as drivers of lorries, pick-up trucks, SUV's and cars drove by with indifferent, suspicious or otherwise occupied eyes. I watched the Latino motel owner putting out his trash cans and pictured myself knocking on his door looking for work, unable to leave Broadus, Montana. I imagined that the owner had an only daughter with a little crying infant in her arms. In my despair and loneliness I would eventually turn to her for some comfort. There would be a hastily arranged Mexican style wedding and an awkward phone-calls back home. Dreams of ever making it to Rapid City would eventually fade away into memory and I would look forward to one day running the motel myself and renovating the back yard.

The honk of a car horn turned my head and I saw a dark blue SUV pull over on the hard shoulder as if stopped for me. I stared in disbelief for a few moments then quickly picked up my bags and sprinted. I opened the passenger door and asked the driver, a small thin woman in her early fifties with short brown hair where she was going. "Rapid City, Jump in!"

She introduced herself as Liz and explained that she was on her way to Nebraska to deliver a small golden retriever puppy to one of her grandchildren. The puppy introduced himself by licking my face frantically and then lying across my lap. I could scarcely believe my luck. Liz even stopped a few times along the way so that I could take some photos of the rolling plains of Eastern Montana. Most of the land had proved too poor for conventional ranch farming. Small herds of antelope and elk now dotted the vast straw coloured prairies which stretched off to meet low rolling hills in every direction. Conversation came easy between us. Liz told me about her job as a hospital intern and from other bits of her life that she shared, it seemed to me that she spend a lot of time helping family and friends through personal crises. She also told me that in two weeks time she was fulfilling a life long dream to visit Scotland with a group of friends. It was getting dark that late August evening by the time we drove off the high plains and down into Rapid City. Although driving out of her way Liz very kindly dropped me off next to a row of budget motels she recommended I stay at. We swapped email addresses and I invited her to visit me if she ever came to Ireland before thanking her for the lift. I tried sending Liz a thank you emailing a week later but the email was listed as invalid and strangely I never received a message from her either.

The next afternoon after a late morning lie-in, I walked into explore Rapid City. The town centre was built around a wide main boulevard and had retained some of its Old West buildings and charm. I passed a huge two storey gun store with large sale posters advertising 50% off selected ammunition. It was all a bit of a culture shock. Rapid City had a laid back atmosphere though despite its name. My main reason for coming here was to visit Cathedral Spires, a spectacular formation of red sandstone peaks which formed part of the Black Hills range. I had first seen Cathedral Spires on a TV documentary entitled 'The Wild West'. It was a fast sweeping aerial view of the red sandstone towers from a helicopter as the evening sun set over South

Dakota. I can recall being transfixed to the armchair in sheer wonder. I then came to understand why the Black Hills were considered so sacred to the Plains Indians and impossible to put a sale price on. At certain times of the year tribes people would make pilgrimage walks into the Black Hills to fast and pray as people still do to this day when they climb the pyramid shaped Croagh Patrick in Co Mayo.

Gold and precious metals were discovered in the Black Hills, however, during the late 19th Century. This was the era of the great migration west by white settlers and pioneers. The Washington Government broke yet another treaty and the Black Hills were grabbed despite a brave struggle by the Indian tribes led by such chiefs as Red Cloud and Sitting Bull.

In my late teens I had written a letter to the then U.S. Ambassador to Ireland Jean Kennedy Smith pleading that the Black Hills be returned to the Sioux Nation who consider them sacred and beyond the value of money. In 1980 the U.S. Supreme Court ruled that the Black Hills had been illegally taken and that remuneration of the original offer price plus interest be paid which amounted to $106 million dollars. The Lakota refused the settlement as they wanted the Black Hills returned to them. The sum remains in an interest bearing account which now amounts to over $700 million. The Lakota Sioux still refuse to accept the settlement despite their impoverished circumstances. I guess that in their hearts, to do so would validate the U.S. theft of the land they hold sacred beyond comprehension. It would be like a modern day mining corporation laying claim to the pilgrimage mountain of Croagh Patrick in the West of Ireland, relocating the people of West Mayo under threat of death and sending in the bulldozers.

Although Custer National Park and the Cathedral Spires were just forty five miles away, it soon became clear that it would be virtually impossible for me to get there without hiring a car. I even considered hiring a bicycle but the forecast was for rain and low cloud. Deciding to console myself with some ice-cream I met a young woman by the name of Andrea Steele walking down the street. She looked like a prairie bell with clear skin, blue eye and sandy curled hair. We got talking and she told me that some of her ancestors were originally from County Cork. She and her boyfriend Duke were travelling out to Mount Rushmore later that evening to watch the official lighting up ceremony for the autumn season. Andrea kindly invited me to come along. A few hours later Duke pulled up outside my motel in a high powered bright red sports-car. I was barely in the back seat when we sped off up the highway with a screech of tyres. Apparently we were late for the ceremony. On the way we picked up two Romanian girls called Patricia and Raluca who were working in a nearby hotel for the tourist season. The lights had been turned on by the time we arrived but no one seemed to mind. We stood at the viewing gallery and looked up at the giant heads of four former U.S Presidents, (Abraham Lincoln, Thomas Jefferson, Theodore Roosevelt and George Washington), all carved out of a solid granite mountain. Huge floodlights located somewhere deep in the natural pine forests which cloaked Mount Rushmore's lower slope gave the entire scene a surreal movie set feel. It felt sort of eerie and unnatural, especially the way the strong artificial lights cast dark shadows across the faces of the Presidents. I was glad when we left. As we waited outside a gift store I got talking briefly to Duke. He was a quiet and thoughtful young man. He spoke in a slow flat accent reflecting the vast open plains of the Dakotas. On his head he wore a white cowboy hat which he looked too young for. Although now working as a carpenter in Rapid City he told me he had served five years in the U.S. navy and had spent time over in Kosovo helping to re-build schools as part of a humanitarian effort in the wake of the last Balkan conflict. He and Andrea looked a good couple together. They told me on the way to Mount Rushmore how they enjoyed line dancing and how they often visited retirement homes where they would dance for the elderly residents and sit and talk with them a while. I admired them both. They were genuine and earthed.

After piling back into Duke's car again we drove through a nearby village, down a quiet side road and parked up outside an old world antique store. We stepped unto a creaky wooden veranda and past old lanterns, a stuffed bear, rocking chairs and a big old iron bed complete with a female mannequin sitting up dressed as granny smoking a pipe.

The antique store also doubled up as a sort of pub. It had a half bar, a fridge stocked with beer, a pool table and a karaoke room to the side. I was introduced by Duke to 'Wildcat' who owned the place. He was a tall gaunt man with thinning long dark hair and a drooping moustache. If 'Wildcat' was any more laid back he would have been in danger of falling over. To speak even seemed an unnecessary effort to this dude. The karaoke machine was switched on, cold beer cans were cracked open and an international line-up including two Romanian girls, an American couple and an Irish wanderer took to the stage. Wildcat sat perched on a bar stool at the back corner of the stage sipping a beer and operating the karaoke machine. Leanne got up first and sang the Tammy Wynette song 'Stand by Your Man'. The three girls then sang 'Girls just want to have fun' by Cindy Lauper. After Duke and Andrea performed a Country and Western duet, it was my turn to take to the stage. Thankfully a song came to me and Wildcat lined it up. First though I decided on a short introduction explaining my hitch-hiking adventure to Rapid City to laughs and cheers. The karaoke backing band started up and in my Donegal Willie Nelson accent started into, 'On the Road Again,

> Just can't wait to get on the road again,
> "The life I love is making music with my friends,
> And I can't wait to get on the road again.
> On the road again,
> Going places that I've never been,
> Seeing things that I may never see again,
> I can't wait to get on the road again."

I was now performing for the 'crowd' and followed up with a shakier but no less enjoyable version of 'Sweet Home Alabama' by those confederate rockers, Lynryd Synryd. There was something magically American about those few hours we spent that night at Wilcat's antique store with the wooden panelling, eccentric clientele and soft, old style lighting. It was like uncovering the fun carefree heart of America, the part that encourages you to dream the dream, sing your song, be yourself.

The next day I packed my bags and prepared to catch a bus back to Chicago. I rang Vonda and Francis to tell them I was alive and well and rang home to say much the same. My mother had received a phone call from an old friend of mine Jimmy Perri from New Jersey. When she told Jimmy I was out West he rang back with a contact for relations who lived on the Blackfeet Reservation up in Northern Montana close to the Canadian border. I had lost contact with Jimmy for about two years.

Jimmy was one of a kind. While working in Donegal Castle as a tour guide one summer afternoon, a well built man in his early fifties with long black Indian hair came bounding across the front lawn looking for a tour. He had a friendly open face and was wearing a pair of jeans and a dark grey sleeveless Harley Davidson t-shirt which showed off an Indian chief tattoo on one shoulder and an Irish Celtic High Cross on the other. He introduced himself as Jimmy Perri and we became instant buddies. Jimmy had been on his was on way to visit Gleanncolmcille. A week earlier he had packed his bags to the disbelief of his family and left his life in New Jersey to live in Ireland. He told me how he dreamt about Ireland from a young age but at the time didn't know where in the world his dreams were set. When he settled with his first wife in Pennsylvania he would visit a place called Donegal Springs and found out it was a place in Ireland. Then one day he visited a Celtic festival in Milwaukee which showed a video of the Irish landscape. He then knew where he had to go. It was Jimmy who told me that many Native tribes believe the practice of sweat lodges had been introduced to their people by the ancient Celts. Indeed he came across a restored *Teach Cuir Allais* or Sweat House building behind the folk village in Gleancolmcille when he went to visit. Very few Irish people know that sweat houses were common in the northern half of Ireland up until the mid 19th century and were used for a whole range of health treatments. Jimmy found work and eventually true love in Dublin but returned to Donegal on occasions to attend a number of house ceilís I hosted. He often brought his tribal eagle feathers and would play the Indian flute and sing traditional songs at the cultural nights by the hearth fire. The Indian flute music had a sad wild quality like the wind singing a lament for something lost.

One particular night that Jimmy came to visit stands out from the rest. It was a cold dark January night. Jimmy got off the Dublin bus at my home village of Laghey. As we walked up the darkened country road towards home, a bright white streak of light stretched across the starry roof of the night sky. From this bright wave of light, fainter curtains of stellar like streamers flowed downwards in every direction. I had never seen the Northern Lights put on such a spectacular show. For the next few days there were letters and phone-calls sent into local media enquiring about this strange natural phenomenon. On that night I remember Jimmy looked up, sighing in wonder and saying 'ahh, you know, that's a good sign my brother,'

Standing in a public phone booth in Rapid City, South Dakota I wondered if hearing from Jimmy was another sign to prolong my journey 'Out West'. Writing down the contact telephone number my Mother gave me, I decided to contact Jimmy's relatives right away. A man by the name of Angela Bull Plume answered the phone and welcomed me to come and visit. The following morning I boarded a bus for an epic seventeen hour bus journey back across South Dakota, Wyoming and up through Montana to the city of Great Falls. Instead of a Greyhound Inter-State luxury coach, however, an old red and yellow bus trundled apologetically into the bus station. It looked for all the world like it had escaped from a scrap-yard. As we boarded, a male passenger began verbally harassing our large female bus driver who looked like she was about to punch him. Someone shouted that they had called the cops. The man reacted by leaping from the bus and sprinting out of the station as fast as his legs could carry him.

Our bus was soon back up on the high open plains, this time in the state of Wyoming. The Plains of East Wyoming were brown and rippled like a gigantic sandy sea shore with the tide long past returning. A large car honked its horn suddenly as it passed slowly and kids in the back seat with jeering faces laughed and showed two fingers to everyone on the bus. As night fell the bus pulled up at a bus station near the town of Gillette. The bus reception area was a collection point for America's poor and marginalised. One scared wide eyed woman and her two children boarded a bus in their pyjamas, clutching plastic carrier bags of luggage to their chests. Another man hobbled around a row of public phone booths, begging for some spare change and checking empty coin slots. Rather than feel uncomfortable I felt strangely at home and at ease among these people, free from artificial social veneer. Perhaps these were a minority, the ones that the American dream somehow passed over. They were real people though in a real American that hasn't cared much until now for its own poor. It was just about prepared to tolerate them on the outside as long as they kept from stealing and dealing. Otherwise, a million plus prison cell reservations awaited their extended stay.

Dog Days in Browning

Our bus arrived at Great Falls, Montana the following evening as night fell and a yellow full moon rose in the East. We disembarked opposite a Salvation Army hostel. A large ghostly neon lit Christian cross dangled over the entrance. Great Falls looked grim, a large declining town lost to itself. One by one, passengers disembarked and dispersed. Having parked his car up in the compound, the bus driver pulled down the bus station metal shutters with a crashing bang. I was alone now and suddenly felt like a prime candidate to be robbed. The thirty six hour bus journey had taken its toll on my nerves. Picking up my hand luggage and hauling a heavy back-pack I picked a direction and set off at pace into the night. I didn't know where I was going but figured it best to stay on the move. Perhaps I had watched too many American reality TV crime shows in my youth. It didn't help recognising my location as definitely on the wrong side of the tracks. I found a gas station three blocks up and treated myself to a cup of coffee and an egg salad roll. With nervous energy exhausted the sensible part of my brain began working. My Blackfeet contacts could have been late and were possibly waiting for me back at the bus station as I munched my roadside supper. Picking up my travel baggage I rushed back the way I came and was extremely relieved to see an Indian man in jeans and black jacket sitting smoking a cigarette under a streetlight by the bus station.

It was my contact Angelo Bull Plume. We walked over to his Nephew's station wagon where a few other family relatives had been waiting. Angelo explained to me that his jeep had broken down and that's why they were late. They had travelled over one hundred miles to collect me. Soon we left the street lights of Great Falls and drove through a darkened table flat landscape, seemingly devoid of towns, villages or houses. Two hours had passed by when a small town of yellow and white twinkling lights appeared shining brilliantly against a pitch dark landscape. "That's Browning, our home", Angelo said. The electric lights soon separated out into street-lit rows of one storey wooden houses with estates separated by tall chain fences. I suddenly felt uneasy and was already having second thoughts about coming up here.

We pulled up outside Angelo's house and I thanked his Nephew for kindly driving the whole way to Great Falls and back to collect me. My mind wasn't put at rest when Angelo said, "you know there's still a lot of resentment on the reservation towards white people but you'll be safe enough staying with us here."

Angelo helped me take in my travel bags and his wife Leanne welcomed me made us up some supper. Their main living quarters was an open plan layout with the sitting room inside the front door and kitchen to the back. On the side wall of the living room hung a U.S. flag which had the profile of a Native American chief on the top right hand corner where the fifty blue stars of the States are usually printed. A TV stood in the far corner with a stack of video tapes underneath. Angelo sat down at the kitchen table to smoke a cigarette and invited me to join him. He was a tall broad shouldered man around 45 years old with dark brown skin and shoulder length jet black hair. He had a strong kind face but his eyes were sad and distant. Like most Indians I met he talked in a soft measured voice. His son Rueben sat watching videos and at eighteen years old was already a giant of a man over 6 foot 5 inches tall. As Leanne served us eggs and bacon I asked her how she and Jimmy were related. She told me that they simply decided on being brother and sister during one of Jimmy's visits to Browning. Jimmy's Mother had been born and raised on the Reservation before she moved to New Jersey. Leanne was much lighter skinned than Angelo with a rounder kind face and wore glasses. We ate supper and drank coffee together by the yellowish light of an old lamp.

Angelo then lit up another cigarette and told me a little about his life. 'This might sound strange Keith but I was a preacher some time back, an evangelical style Christian preacher." He pulled on his cigarette and waited for my predictably surprised reaction before he continued.

"I even spent years reading and studying the bible. Myself and some other members of our church group then decided to set up a charity to administer teachings and help poor people in need here in Browning. We began to restore old trailer homes and housed people in danger of becoming homeless. Soon the cops were driving around every day and carrying out surveillance on us. When I started making enquiries I was told that the cops and undercover FBI agents thought I was another David Koresh style Waco cult leader. When I heard this I became deeply concerned that they could frame me for something as they were deadly serious. Shortly after that I packed it in and the charity work folded."

Angelo then shook his head slowly as cigarette smoke billowed up around the lamp shade next to us. With an ironic smile he added, "can you believe that huh? I continued to preach though. One time when I was down in Great Falls attending a Church mission a white preacher came up to me. He was really worked up and angry and said, "do you know that all you're kind are going straight to hell?" I asked him calmly why he thought that.

He replied, "because Indians don't worship right. You worship animals and birds and trees which is akin to devil worship".

As a serious preacher I had studied the bible and quoted him a passage directly from the Book Of Job. "Ask the animals, and they will teach you, or the birds of the air and they will tell you; or speak to the earth and it will teach you." That white preacher was taken aback and lowering his voice said to me, "you're a preacher man aren't you" and turning his back, walked away." After that night I gave up preaching and made the decision to return to the ways of my own ancestors."

There was a real sense of loss in his voice and eyes as he told me how his Father had embraced Evangelical Christianity with religous fervour when Angelo was just a young boy. "One night he lit a big fire out the back and threw all the family heirlooms into the flames such as his sacred pipe and medicine bundles. These had been passed down from his Great Great Grandfather's time when we Blackfeet were still living in the old ways and out hunting the buffalo." Angelo then got up from the table and unfolded and pumped up an air mattress for me to sleep on. Before going to bed he shook my hand and looking me straight in the eye said, "any friend of Jimmy's is a good friend of mine."

Sleep didn't come as easy as it should have that night after forty hours travelling. Initial disbelief was followed by helpless frustration as I listened to a chaotic chorus of dogs barking all night in the street outside. After a while I was able to guess when someone was walking up from the bottom of the estate from the distant echoing of dog barks. As the brave or foolhardy walker continued up the street, the dog barks became louder and more aggressive. An occasional vicious snarl left me wondering was some late night pedestrian getting their leg chewed off.

Their was no stir in the Bull Plume household until well after noon the following day. Angelo laughed heartily over his cereal when I mentioned last night's local neighbourhood impromptu dog concert. "You see to the Blackfoot, dogs are revered animals never to be harmed or killed. That's why Browning is over-run with packs of dogs. Some of them defend their patch so fiercely that even we have to be cautious as to what streets we walk down."

It was warm and sunny outside but I was literally too frightened to venture outside the door. Angelo's black Mitsubishi SUV leaned on its side gathering dust with a dodgy gear box and two flat tyres. I was quite literally stranded and without a plan. We spent the whole day sitting around watching TV and videos and drinking sodas. The following afternoon I got a little more adventurous and stood leaning out from the safety of the front door. Across the street lay a vacant house. Its windows and front door were ominously boarded up with sheets of plywood while bushes, weeds and litter kept each other company in the front yard. On the front 'lawn' next door a boy of no more than ten years of age called Little Beaver sat playing with a pile of dust. He flung fistfuls of dry dirt up into the air which caught by the wind blew in dusty clouds back into his face. He stopped this game when it was clear he could no longer see. Rather than cry he just sat there trying to rub his eyes clean. When he could see again he repeated the dirt throwing. Later that evening there was a big row on the street between some neighbours. Angelo, Leanne and Rueben scrambled excitedly to the front door to get a good look at the public spectacle.

By the following day and with bleary eyes and white-head spots from marathon bouts of TV viewing and sodas I decided to take some initiative. With phone book in hand I rang Amtrak train company. An office clerk informed me there was a train station less that fifteen miles away called East Glacier from which I could buy a ticket to Chicago in two days time. I really wanted to see some of the area before I left and offered Angelo a few dollars to get his SUV back on the road again. Soon we were on a mission to walk into Browning to find a mechanic and do some shopping. With Angelo on one side and Leanne on the other of me we started off up the street. Angelo assured me that nobody would dare touch me although my confidence wasn't boosted by the fact that he walked with the aid of a stick due to a back injury. At the top of the street we surveyed the surrounding bleak looking estates like lost soldiers looking for a safe passage through hostile dog territory. Angelo stopped a local passer by who pointed to a gap in a torn silver wire fence. He recommended we follow the path on the far side into town and said we wouldn't have any trouble from the dogs there. Our first port of call was the post office. There were no postmen in Browning which for some reason didn't surprise me. Instead every household had a post office box locker at their local branch. Angelo then wanted to show me the new casino which was recently opened in Browning. The casino industry had become big business on many Native Reservations across America. Gambling was prohibited in most States but reservations were technically a separate country under federal law and many sought to attract tourists and their wallets. We walked across fresh smelling plush new carpets and around gambling machine suites and roulette tables. The casino owners had apparently given fifty dollars worth of free credit as a 'sweetener' to locals. Angelo shook his head as he pointed out people he knew from the Reservation playing slot machines in the new casino. He turned to me saying, "you know Keith I objected strongly to the plans for this casino. Many people from my Res are going to come down here after they receive their social security cheque. They are going to blow it on gambling instead of essentials like food, electricity and clothes for their children." As Angelo brought me around on his protest tour Leanne went off to enquire with the manager about putting her name down for a job. The bright glare of the afternoon sun pierced my eyes as we left the casino and walked through the parking lot. To our left the town of Browning began with its street clusters of one storey wooden houses. The town skyline was dominated by a silver metal water tower with the letters Browning painted across it in official writing. At a squint it looked like a spaceship straight from a 1950's B rated sci-fi movie. Behind the casino stretched a vast area of open high prairie, a patchy sea of brown grasses and tumbleweeds. Angelo informed me that winters' last six months up here and that cold northerly Arctic winds bring heavy snowfalls and freezing conditions to these exposed high plains. Dark blue mountains rose up starkly like giant jagged dinosaur teeth on the western horizon. Angelo pointed to them with his walking stick, "that's Glacier National Park, we can go there tomorrow if we get the jeep going." Leanne then spotted a relation leaving the car-park who gave us a lift back to the house. As we approached the top of their street, Angelo pointed to a group of men who were talking frantically on the porch of a house while two other young men were running towards a parked pick-up truck. It soon became clear what the commotion was about. Just a few yards further ahead a large framed young Indian man lay face down on the middle of the street. As we slowed down some of his relatives or neighbours ran over to him. Thankfully he began to move. He then made a sudden effort to get up on his feet but moments later collapsed back unto the street again. As we reached the house an ambulance sped by with full sirens blaring and lights flashing. Seconds later the pick-up truck we saw minutes before zoomed past in the opposite direction with a Reservation Police patrol car in hot pursuit.

Later that evening Leanne prepared a feast of Indian Taco and fried bread. In true custom she prepared a large pot before making a few phone-calls to invite some friends and relatives around to share the meal with us. Little Beaver from next door appeared in the kitchen almost instantaneously. A nephew of Leanne's called A.J. arrived carrying a satchel of study books. A.J. was in his early twenties and had a kind thoughtful face. Over dinner he announced to everyone that he had begun a one year course in Bio-Hazard Management through the local Browning college. He hoped to make as much as twenty dollars an hour when he qualified. I began to feel more at ease as we sat together and talked around the dinner table like people the world over. After we finished eating A.J. produced a guitar and sang some heartfelt songs he had written while in an alcohol treatment centre a few years back. Angelo then set up his keyboard and sang a song he wrote for Leanne when they were first going out together. The late evening sun shone in the kitchen window bathing us all in a soft golden light and for a while all the outside troubles of the world were forgotten. Angelo was a natural storyteller and everyone went quiet when he started telling a funny story about his great-grandfather. Old Bull Plume had been a revered and well loved medicine man of his Blackfeet tribe. "At the time back in the 1930's a Hollywood movie was being filmed over in Glacier National Park. It was a Shirley Temple feature called 'Susanna of the Mounties' as far as I know and in one scene the movie's director wanted to re-create an authentic Indian tribal ceremony. Someone came and fetched Old Bull Plume who was now an elderly man and asked him to dress up in his ceremonial head gear and clothing. The night scene was carefully prepared with a big Indian camp fire and loads of extras from the Reservation. When Old Bull Plume was asked what they wanted him to sing the movie director said in a big booming voice, "I don't know, how about a Rain Dance song". It was a clear starlit night as Old Bull Plume began chanting the Rain Dance. As he chanted and chanted, dark shower clouds suddenly appeared climbing over the high mountains. He continued to chant and began striking his medicine walking stick into the earth while the movie cameras rolled on. Before long there was a loud crash of thunder overhead. Old Bull Plume stopped chanting, looked up at the night sky and said, "thunder wants war". With that a torrential downpour and thunderstorm flooded the film set."

The following morning we began repairing Angelo's car in a rush of motivation. We spent quite a while re-fitting the newly repaired tyres. One thing was clear. Neither of us were Formula One racing cars support team material. This still left us the problem of how to fix the gear box. Angelo solved this technical hitch with a large handful of sawdust and a straight face. We set off for Glaciers National Park shortly after midday. Seldom was I more grateful for to be going for a drive in my life. The wind had turned around to the north bringing a chill to the air while high dark clouds began racing across the sky. As we neared Glaciers Park, the rolling brown barren plains gave way to valleys thickly forested with pine and punctured by towering mountain peaks. A light seemed to come back into Angelo's face. He began to tell jokes and said it was over a year since he was up in the mountains. He had lost his Blackfoot I.D. card though, which gave him and accompanying friends free entry into the park. He stopped the car and asked me how much money I had.

"Not much to be honest Angelo, I've enough put aside to get the train to Chicago", was my truthful reply. Restarting the ignition with a pensive frown he said more to himself than me, "Jeez I looked everywhere in the house for that I.D. card". When we drove up to the Glacier Park entrance pay booth Angelo rolled down his window, pinched the skin on his arm and said "see...Blackfoot". The lady warden looked a bit surprised at first but took it in good humour and with a short laugh replied, "so that's' how you guys are doing it now, go on, get out of here!"

Angelo had saved us fifty bucks which we didn't even have. This lifted our spirits even more and we laughed and hollered out loud at Angelo's quick thinking. The scenery in Glaciers National Park was simply breathtaking. We drove along the western shore of a large glacial lake which reflected jagged mountain peaks, lush pine forests, passing dark clouds and blue sky gaps in its crystal clear waters. Ahead of us rose the spectacular 'Going-to-the-Sun' Mountain. It got its name from local native Indians who on hearing that engineers were constructing a road west through the mountain range thought that the white men must be trying to reach the setting sun.

Beyond the lake road we drove through broadleaf woodlands and down into a sweeping valley where an old fashioned hotel was built at the shores of a lake. This remote hotel was built in the style of an Alpine wooden lodge and had provided the setting for the spine tingling horror movie 'The Shining' starring Jack Nicholson and Shelley Duvall.

As we both walked around the hotel grounds and gift shop, some of the holiday makers gave Angelo looks which seemed to me to range somewhere between embarrassment and annoyance. It was as if they would have preferred if he wasn't there at all. In some ways it reminded me of the way Irish people generally interact with ethnic Travellers. I also sensed that Angelo wasn't prepared to take much notice and in some ways was actually thriving on it. In the gift shop he picked up a large trekking stick which had a jingle bell tied to the top of it. He give it a few mischievously loud shakes as if to shake browsing shoppers to attention. He then turned to me and said in a tone loud enough for everyone to hear, "you know, nowadays trekkers roam these mountains with cameras and walking sticks like this one with a lunch bell tied to the end that says to the bears, "hey, dinner's ready, come and get it." In our culture we didn't hunt bear or other big predators like mountain lions or wolves. To the Blackfeet those animals were revered as useful teachers of important human qualities such as stealth, patience and fierceness. In our language we called bears our 'brother'. When we saw him out on the mountains at a distance we would say quietly "hello brother" and then make a path in the opposite direction. You know Keith, that's why Indians never got eaten by bears, even hungry ones."

The hotel lodge was a bit pricey so we sat on a wall next to the hotel car-park eating our pre-prepared sandwiches. As we gazed around at the awe inspiring scenery Angelo suddenly turned to me saying, 'you know Keith, this is all occupied territory, my people used to come here in the summer months to hunt, fish and gather wild berries." I couldn't think of anything to say and a long sad silence followed between us.

We finished our lunch and then walked up around the back of the hotel to where a group of men around retirement age were standing with a pair of binoculars. They offered the field binoculars to us with friendly smiles and pointed up to a high mountain ridge directly ahead. After a few moments and some directions as to where to exactly to look, Angelo exclaimed "yeah, I can see them now, they're feeding on berries." He then passed me the binoculars. After a few moments surveying the magnified mountain side I centred in on a large grizzly bear mother with two young cubs stocking up on food stores for the long winter ahead. It was a magical sight to behold. After passing back the binoculars we stopped and chatted cordially for a while with the men who said they were on vacation from Pennsylvania.

Back in Browning, Angelo and I excitedly shared the stories from our days adventure with Leanne and Rueben and finished off the rest of yesterday's Indian Taco. The following morning I packed my bags and prepared to catch a train to Chicago. Leanne was getting ready for her first day of work at the Browning casino. Before leaving the house Angelo clasped his two hands on my shoulders and pushed me out the door saying "I now give you your Indian name, Little Brother!" I was in fact, little compared to Blackfeet men such as Angelo and Rueben and was honoured to be thought of as a brother to them.

A silver two storey high Amtrak train pulled into East Glacier Station as a cold sleety rain began to fall from the lead coloured sky. I thanked Angelo and Leanne for their hospitality and we hugged and said our goodbyes. As I got my ticket and prepared to jump on board Angelo shouted across the station platform, "goodbye Little Brother, see you."

It was 9.30am and my train was not due in Chicago until 3.30pm the following afternoon. I managed to get a window seat on the top level but the landscape was endless high rolling plains and uninspiring to the eye. It appeared like a brown grassy dessert seemingly void for the most part of wildlife or even farmsteads. It was 6pm that evening before we left the state of Montana. All through the night our Amtrak train trundled ever eastwards over the even flatter prairies of North Dakota. The following morning I woke shortly after dawn. I had managed to sleep soundly for a continuous seven hours stretched out over two passenger seats. I went down to the lower deck to wash my face and scrub my teeth as the train began to slow down and pull up at our next stop. When I returned there was a man sitting in the seat next to mine. I smiled to myself and raised my eyes upwards thinking, "I bet this guy is someone I was supposed to meet on my journey isn't he."

He introduced himself as Hop Kleihaver. It was a great stroke of luck to meet him even for the fact that he had a bagful of cheeses, fresh bread, juice drinks and dried fruit and most importantly, a sharing nature. I guessed Hop was in his midfifties with cropped greying curly hair, glasses and a studious but open face and kind eyes. He wore wooden beads outside of a red woollen cardigan which sort of singled him out as somewhat of an alternative traveller. Hop was clearly on a journey also and from what he told me, he seemed to be making up for time he now felt he misused. He had spent most of his adult life as a successful chef working incredibly long hours in some of the top restaurants across America. He had in fact everything he thought he wished for. A few years ago personal circumstances came to a head for him. With his kids grown up, he had decided to make some major changes which included giving up the lifestyle he had grown accustomed to. Hop spoke in measured and thoughtfully articulated sentences.

"I came to realise I was living somebody else's life and not my own. A turning point occurred when I was flown over to India to chef for a rich client and his family. On one of my days off I went walking through the city streets. My mind was literally blown by the sense of how the spiritual seemed part of the everyday in their culture. I realised that I was looking for a more meaningful way of living in this world. I had come to realise that the window I have used to view the world had been much too small."

As we approached the outskirts of Chicago his advice to me was, "you should always acknowledge and honour your own ideas and creativity regardless as to whether they become reality or change into something different." He placed his hand on my shoulder as we parted and looking right into my eyes said, "it's been really great meeting and talking with you."

I waited on standby in Chicago's O'Hare Airport for a flight home to Ireland. Ireland was about to host the Ryder Cup golf tournament and the departure lounge was full of high spirited American tourists hoping to mix some golf, Guinness and sightseeing over in the Emerald Isle. With a five dollars bill left to my name I waited on standby praying against the odds for a seat on the flight home. At the same time I had to mentally prepare myself for a two night sleep over in some departure lounge corner with a chocolate and soda supper from a vending machine. Due to a last minute cancellation my name was called out on the intercom. I might as well have won the lotto such was my joy and I literally leapt in the air to the smiles of airport staff. My last glimpse of America was the Windy City stretching out along the dark blue shoreline of Lake Michigan. I was going home.

TO FIND YOURSELF AT HOME

Instead of following directly on with my travels to Asia I had returned home to Donegal for practical reasons. I had cut a year's supply of peat turf earlier in the summer. It was time to harvest and bring it home. The few months would also gave me time to reflect upon my experiences in North America. Yet still the journey continued, at first unbeknownst to myself. It was early October in Donegal, the golden month. I had left a few months previously with a restless heavy heart. It seemed that the very countryside itself was under attack from large diggers and rock breakers which echoed through the Drumlin hills like heavy machine gun fire. Hedgerows and trees bore the brunt of the destruction. Green farm fields were invaded and churned up into muddy battle-field style construction sites, most in the name of speculative house building. The broken relationship between man and his natural environment was reaching new levels of expression in this far flung corner of Europe. Up until then the Western seaboard of Ireland had escaped being tamed and broken by concrete and status symbol Celtic Tiger mansions. German bankers had released billions of euros to Irish banks. It was now an ugly credit 'free for all'. Once sane and grounded local people were visibly gripped in some kind of spell, like wild eyed junkies invited to a pop celebrity's party. Reality, sense and community good were simply uncool, past their sell-by date. Material dreams were now borrowed with no thought of how it all would be paid back. The financial gurus had brain washed an entire nation to think that the boom years could never end. To not dare to borrow huge sums on that new car, new apartment, two foreign holidays in the sun and keep up with the Jones's was to be a failure. Caution and modesty were for losers. The wealthy of course were the only ones with nothing to lose. Everyone else were encouraged to battle for the remaining spoils. It was never going to be pretty or end happily.

Early Gaelic poets had likened Ireland to a beautiful maiden. The ancient ones had known her as Fodla, Banbha or Éire. I felt deeply that we had scarred and disrespected her with the Celtic Tiger. It had somehow weighed heavy upon me as if I had partly internalised it. Travelling abroad had afforded me some precious time and space to put things in perspective. I could see that her landscape and essential beauty still remained, albeit tenuously for now. I saw her with a new freshness and appreciation upon returning and now understood how countless generations and waves of newcomers before me had grown to love her beyond words and endure her frequent grey sullen moods.

I would journey on to India and the Himalayas but first I felt the need to re-connect more with myself and the inheritance of my own unique ancient culture. Sitting by the hearth fire in my own cottage was as good a place to start as any. Just as my blacksmith friend Charlie Gallagher used fire to forge metal, my hearth would serve a similar purpose for an inner forging. A real Donegal fire required turf and my next mission was to get mine home. Before leaving for the States I had cut my own turf by hand with a special spade called a *slean*. My cousin Patrick had patiently showed me how to get started and prepared the area I would cut. The location was a mountain side known as Minchifin which in Irish meant *Mín Shuí Fionn* (the smooth high place of Finn's seat). I often marvelled at the poetic spirit of those simple farming folk who intimately named the world around them. My cousin Dermot had humorously knicknamed it 'Midgie- Fin' after the tiny bloodsucking flies which are the arch enemies of all bog-men on a breezeless day. The views from Minchifin were spectacular, with sweeping vistas of Donegal Bay, the striking table-top mountain of Ben Bulben, the Leitrim hills and West Fermanagh cloaked in high moors and lakes.

My spirit has always felt free in the high moorland bogs. To paraphrase the great Kerry philosopher John Moriarty, "there are no boundary ditches or fences to limit the mind up there." The skylark understood this magic realm and reflected it in its song and heavenward flight. The summer had been kind and with the help of family and friends I had managed to 'win' the turf by drying them by sun and wind, then filling them into empty plastic fertiliser bags. They were now ready to take home. My cousin Patrick again came to my assistance with a quad to drag them out of the bog and a tractor and trailer to transport them the five miles back to my own turf shed.

With the last of my turf home and the time of Halloween fast approaching I decided to celebrate with a house gathering and bonfire. In ancient times Halloween was known as *Samhain* in Irish which marked the beginning of the Celtic New Year on the first of November. It was a time when the people had gathered their fuel and food stuffs for the winter months ahead and could relax and celebrate together. The outdoor fires symbolise renewal where the past year's personal regrets, disappointments, resentments, hardships and other setbacks could be cast into the flames, to be released and transformed into ashes. It was also regarded as a time when the veil between our own world and other unseen dimensions could lift unexpectedly and spirits could pass easily between, an ancient acknowledgement that there are unseen forces which we cannot control. Nowadays it seemed our traditional festivals like Halloween, Christmas and Easter have had their meaning hollowed out and had become instead consumer orientated holidays. For many children though, there is still an element of magic and wonder in the rituals and costumes.

I got up early the morning of the bonfire and spent a few contented hours building up timber I had saved especially for it. The thought did occur to me as passing neighbours looked on slightly puzzled as to how did it fall to me to be at this activity. All I knew, is it felt right inside and that was enough to carry on. When I had finished building up the timber I left an opening near ground level to build a central core fire of twigs and turf to start the bonfire proper.

Jimmy Perri arrived on an afternoon bus. It was a fine, mild evening under a still overcast sky. Feeling a little apprehensive about how the night's party would go I suggested we take a short walk up to the water tower on the back hill. After a short trek we were rewarded with some great views of the area overlooking my home townland of Trummon. Jimmy gazed out in genuine awe at the circle of green Drumlin hills which enveloped the land in gentle valleys with a showpiece of two twin loughs fringed by wild bushes and tall rushes. "Ah, this is a really grand place to live", he said. On a high rounded hill to the south I pointed out Rath fort with its clearly visible earthen banks. I explained how distant ancestors had built farmsteads within its steep earthen ramparts and had farmed cattle on the surrounding land almost 2,000 years ago. Like the Native Americans, their forts and houses were built in a circular shape. Ancient people instinctively knew something we have almost lost about the power of the circle.

I had sent out email and texts to friends, neighbours and relations during that week inviting them to the *Ceili Samhain*. Some guests travelled hundreds of miles to attend and I rushed around trying to make up spare beds and announced a self service code regarding food and drink stocked in the kitchen. The rain mercifully held off and by early night it was time to light the bonfire. Before long there were twenty people forming a loose circle around the flames which leapt skywards in bright yellowy tongues. I suddenly realised that the majority of people present were under thirty years of age and thought it a good sign for the future. It seemed like a good time to welcome everyone and say a few words.

I then said a few words which came surprisingly easily from the heart. I thanked my cousins for allowing me have the bonfire in their field, my neighbours who transported timber for the bonfire and all the people in attendance who I was genuinely blessed to know and be host to. I spoke about my time visiting the Northern Cheyenne and Blackfeet Reservations. I talked of how the experience had renewed appreciation for my own unique culture and how it was great to see so many young people present as we were now custodians of traditions and customs thousands of years old. I also spoke a little about the ancient Celtic festival of Samhain and its potential for personal renewal symbolised by the hot phoenix-life flames of the bonfire. With the bonfire beginning to toast my face I wished everyone a Happy Celtic New Year to a round of laughs and cheers before we went back inside. The cottage was near bursting with traditional music, songs, stories, laughter and feasting that night until close to dawn. Our ancestors would have been proud of our celebrating and hopefully weren't light sleepers.

In early November my oil ran out and I began relying on turf and sticks alone to heat the cottage. This meant slowing my life right down to a new deeply grounded pace where tending the fire became a central focus. Books by Robert Bly, John Moriarty, John 0' Donoghue, Anthony De Mello and the poetry of Rumi became my everyday companions. Morning after morning I emptied out the ashes from the previous nights fire in silent respectful ritual before starting a new fire with a personal wishful prayer for it's continued heat and presence. Along with the ashes from the fire, I tipped out a lot of notions and delusions of what I had once believed would bring me happiness and fulfilment in this life. All through the winter the ash heap grew and so did a deeper acceptance and awareness. As the American poet Robert Bly revealed to me in his book 'Iron John', modern societies had all but pulled the plugs on this kind of personal work. In more recent generations, pharmaceutical corporations and criminal drug gangs had sadly stepped in to fill the vacuum.

As well as daily reading and tending to the fire I created a daily practice of sitting in silent meditation for a half an hour both morning and night. I had discovered mediation through a book that was lent to me by a friend and neighbour five years previously. It was a book on Tibetan Buddhism which had a profound influence on my life and helped give me my first glimpse of awareness. One of the chapters had outlined how to practice a form of simple *samatha* or 'watching the breath meditation'. I was intrigued and waited one afternoon for an opportunity when both my sister and parents were away to try it out. Like an earnest DIY enthusiast I found a way to keep the book propped open on the pages instructing me what to do. First I chose a chair with a straight back support to sit upon, as advised. Next I read the paragraph on assuming a correct sitting posture. At this stage I had to jump up again and go over to the book as I forgot what to do next. I was to relax and with mouth and eyes half open become mindful of my breath entering and leaving my body. This seemed a very strange thing to do at first but still I was determined to give it a go. The more I tried to relax and count my breaths the more I became aware of an incessant stream of thoughts racing through my mind. "How the heck is this supposed to relax me?", I asked myself in frustration. I jumped up once again out the chair to consult the book. The advice given by its author was to simply rest my attention on my breath while remaining spacious, whatever that meant. I was to remain relaxed and yet attentive, breathing naturally and yet be inspired. Determined to give it another chance, I sat back in a straight posture, looking straight ahead at my bedroom wall with hands resting on my kneecaps. I began to relax and again a constant stream of thoughts seemed to pass through my mind. These ranged from, "I wonder what's for dinner this evening? What time did will my sister say she would be home from work? to thoughts like, "my nose is itchy, maybe I should scratch it? I think I really am quite hungry now". I felt like any chance of mediation was about to be swamped in a sea of thoughts. "Just follow your breathing in and out and see what happens", I thought to myself for encouragement. Then something did happen. My entire body began to relax deeply. I gradually became aware that there was a part of me which was observing the steady flow of random thoughts streaming through my mind. As this understanding began to sink in, the stream of thoughts first quietly settled and then began to dissolve. The more I simply observed my mind while resting my attention gently on my breath, the more quiet and relaxed my mind became. Suddenly I became aware of the bright afternoon daylight which softly flooded my bedroom and could even sense my self sitting on a chair in my bedroom, in my parents house, in Trummon, in County Donegal, meditating.

For the first time in my life I realised deeply that I am a spiritual being and that this life is only one in a chain of lives that I had experienced. There was no point being fearful, worried, resentful or angry anymore. That was taking this short human existence way too seriously and personally. The path to a whole new life long journey and a quest for ultimate truth had revealed itself. I had found myself at home.

St. Brigid's Eve arrived to mark the month of February and the first tentative signs that spring was returning. To mark this ancient Celtic and Christian date I invited family, neighbours and friends around to make green rush crosses by the blaze of the kitchen hearth. I had been learning the Irish language over the winter and finally got the confidence to leave a phone message in Irish for one of my neighbours Pauric McIntyre, who was born and reared in a native Irish speaking area in the far west of Donegal. When he arrived at the door on the night of St Brigid's Eve he addressed me in Irish with the encouraging words, "*tá tú ag teacht ann leis an Gaeilge!*, (you are coming on well with the Irish!)" His words of praise were as good as an award to me. I felt like I had tapped into a deep ancestral wellspring that winter, one which I could and would return to, no matter where I roamed.

PART II

HERE AND NOW IN INDIA

After another week of blustery, wintry February weather in Donegal it was time to leave the protective and reflective space of my cottage in Trummon. Like countless seekers for at least the past three millennia before me, I headed East to India and the Himalayas. Once again my sister Donna had organised my flights while I concentrated on getting a six month visa through the Indian embassy in Dublin. This time I had no contacts to meet me and no travel plans except my flight destination, the city of Chennai on the eastern coast of India. I had learnt to travel light from my previous journey to the U.S. and this time took a much smaller backpack with essential clothing and a toiletry bag.

My first short flight was from Dublin to London's Heathrow airport to make a connecting flight with British Airways to Chennai in India, the following morning. It was a cold wet bleak Winter's night in 'airport land' as I tried to find a bus to the hotel I pre-booked overnight. The tower block style hotel was pricey by my wallet capacity and felt soulless. En suite room, breakfast optional extra, friendly conversation non-negotiable. A plush holding pen for air commuters who in John Wayne's own on-screen words were, "just passing through." I sat downstairs at the lounge bar for a while drinking a beer while three flashing wide-screen TV's vied for my attention. Feeling increasingly self conscious and flipping a beer-mat on the bar counter I thought to myself, "what a great way to start a six month adventure in Asia. Anything would have to be better than this."

The next morning I boarded my eight hour flight to Chennai. This time I would be travelling over the landmass of Europe and West Asia to India. I had gotten a window seat and was able to follow the route we were taking on my backseat video screen. Cloud cover cleared as we passed over Central Turkey and what surprised me most as I gazed down was the huge expanse of snow covered mountains which stretched from Turkey through

Armenia and across Northern Iran. Nightfall changed the landscape far below into a stark contrast of invisible darkened countryside and light jewelled towns and cities.

From the time of Alexander the Great until the early 20th century, travel from Europe to India involved a gruelling overland expedition or an epic voyage by ship or boat. It felt almost too easy to be travelling by jet airliner while flight attendants served us three meals. It was like taking a modern high speed time travel machine from one point on the globe to another without any journey in between.

My ears first filled with air pressure and then popped as our plane began to descend down into the sprawling lit up metropolis of Chennai, formely known as Madras in its British Colonial days. Dark smoky clouds illuminated by the city's erratic yellowish glow brushed past the side wing of our plane and a stuffy heat filled the air even before we landed.

After passing immigration control I managed to convert a hundred dollars into Indian rupees at a twenty-four hour Bureau Exchange. It was now 1am in the morning and I hadn't a clue where I was going to stay tonight or even where I was going. All the information desks were closed. For half an hour I just sat in the airport lobby sipping apprehensively from a bottle of water and marvelling at how many Indian people there were everywhere, this of course being India. With a population of 1.1 Billion people, there were high odds on me seeing a lot more during my stay. Thankfully it then came to me what to do next. Diving my hands into the bottom of my backpack I unearthed my travel book 'Lonely Planet Guide to India' which my sister Donna had bought for me as a going-away present. A shiny new blue glossy cover greeted my eyes and over 400 snow white pages packed with all kinds of travel information. My brain began to kick back into action again, this time in the survival mode 'inner type voice' of a U.S. drill sergeant. "Private Corcoran, d-o y-o-u k-n-o-w w-h-a-t T-H-I-S B-O-O-K I-S! This is your survival guide while in this country. You will travel with this book, EAT with this book, even SLEEP with this book. Do I make MYSELF CLEAR!"

The inner drill sergeant motivation programme evidently worked. Flicking to the index at the back of my travel book I found 'Chennai Accomodation' and scribbled down three hotel numbers on a piece of paper. A kindly airport official rang the numbers for me from his phone and on the third enquiry I managed to book a hotel with vacancies. I was then pointed in the direction of a taxi rank official outside the main entrance. A man of medium height in matching khaki brown trousers and shirt approached me with a novel pre-answered style approach, "you are looking for a taxi come follow me sir." We walked over to where a row of old fashioned ivory white Ambassador taxi cars were parked.

"This will be your taxi sir", the official looking uniformed man said. He then opened the back seat door where my driver to be was lying stretched out asleep showing us the surprisingly white soles of his feet. A few moments later and we were on the road. We drove for what seemed an age into the heart of Chennai city along near deserted roads faintly lit with random streetlights. My driver was no more than twenty five years old with a black mop of hair and a brooding appearance. Instead of a plastic Jesus on the dashboard of his car he had a whole collection of strange Hindu Gods which flashed bright purples, reds, greens and yellows. 'Do you like Hindi music', my driver said, not particularly waiting for my response. A few moments later and he was somehow swaying his shoulders to the rhythm of some Indian melody while managing to keep his hands on the steering wheel. A high pitched Indian songstress screeched out a love song on the radio while the taxi driver sang along to the chorus. There was nothing for it but smile and do the Irish slow clapping thing we instinctively do to lively music.

We arrived at the promised budget hotel just as my Lonely Planet travel bible had foretold. It was now after 3am yet the night air was still warm and stuffy. I was given a key and a friendly Indian porter carried my backpack and showed me to my room. I was feeling very tired at this stage and travel shocked yet my porter sat down cross legged on my bed and began to show me photos of his family and travel friends he met over the years. Subtle hints were followed by an outright declaration of my need to sleep. He finally left but not before he sold me a roll of toilet paper and a two litre bottle of water while also somehow managing to make me feel guilty for cutting short his visit.

Sleep turned out to be a greater challenge than I imagined. The switch for the ceiling fan situated directly over my head was broken and set to 'gale-force' speed. Two dogs barked in a small concrete yard below my bedroom window while Hindi Music blared downstairs in the hotel foyer. '"Oh for a boring Heathrow Hotel room now", I thought, perfectly happy to eat my words if it meant being miraculously transported back there.

I woke the next day with my room bathed in bright sunshine. I looked at my watch, it was 4pm and my stomach recognised me with an empty growl of disapproval. The hotel I was staying at was located just off a busy city market street. My senses were flooded as I began to take in my first impressions of India through this dusty bustling city world around me. Throngs of people were working, selling, haggling, eating, cooking, talking, begging and even sleeping on the street sidewalks and next to open shops fronts and various businesses. The streets were even more frantic with a continuous surge of bicycle rickshaws, auto rickshaws, taxi cars, vans, buses, lorries and even bullock carts, all zipping in and out of each other's way to a loud chorus of beeps, shouts and whistles. It looked like organised chaos in action with a few wandering holy cows thrown in for good measure. A heady mixture of incense, cooking spices, dust, petrol fumes and cow dung filled the air. Crossing one of Chennai's wide main city streets was another new experience. I soon discovered that Zebra crossings in India's cities are only a twenty perecent concession to take your chances if you dare. To a clueless foreigner like myself it seemed an impossible fete to cross the main thoroughfare safely as a constant river of traffic flowed steadily by. I was close to giving up when I noticed a small group of men, women and children gathering around me waiting for a gap in the traffic. I discreetly stepped back and left it to those with experience to make the first move. True to the natural law of safety in numbers, traffic slowed and temporarily stopped to our side as we 'flocked' our way to the far side of the boulevard and reached safety.

For two days I made short excursions from my hotel room, never venturing too far for fear of not finding my way back through the thronged streets ever again. My first meal in India was a local dish Masala Dosai. It was a potato and vegetable mixture in a delicious creamy sauce and served in an envelope of crispy light pastry. It just about qualified as a starter meal for me and I quickly understood why India doesn't have many overweight people walking around.

For luck on my journey I decided to leave in a new wool jumper that I had wore from Donegal to Dublin airport to a nearby hospice for the elderly. It would be t-shirts all the way for the next few months. Poverty in India was everywhere to be seen and on a level Ireland hasn't experienced for many decades now. Millions upon millions of people were clearly just getting by from day to day and many were even less fortunate than that. Although I intended to simply hand in the jumper at reception the nurse insisted I meet the manager and was escorted directly to his office. An officious man in his fifties with light rimmed glasses welcomed and invited me to sit down. He then produced a form and proceeded to take down my details and what items of clothes I had left in. Looking up from his writing pad he asked me, "you are from Ireland?". "I am indeed", I replied. He then tilted his head from side to side as Indians do as part of their body language and said, "Bless you".

As I walked back towards my hotel, the evening sun cast a hazy golden glow across the narrow city streets still pulsing with throngs of people and kids in smart school uniforms returning home from school. I stood a while and watched a group of women making baskets on the sidewalk amid the noise and din of traffic. A drum and brass band then seemed to appear out of nowhere. They quickly assembled on the far sidewalk dressed in shiny bright purple and satin costumes complete with glitzy turbans. While this was happening an open top lorry pulled up with a large sound system, speakers and an unsteady Bollywood style male singer with manicured big hair and waxed twisty moustache. A multi-coloured clown with red hair and a cake white face then emerged from somewhere and began to dance and jump energetically around the lorry. The singer began crooning into a microphone supported by a pulsing Hindi pop backing track. The drum and brass band started into its own festive music choice. The noise of passing traffic and busy street life somehow blended in with this spontaneous street carnival. It all seemed part of no particular pre-organised festival. Just a slice of archaic and funny chaos to simply enjoy.

The next day I decided to retreat down the coast of Tamil Nadu to the popular traveller hang out and fishing village of Mamallapuram. With cars beyond the purchasing reach of the majority of India's population, most people still rely on buses and trains for long distance journeys. I was soon to discover that buses are a basic but very cheap and reliable way to travel. Mossifuel bus station in Chennai is supposedly the largest bus station in Asia and therefore probably the world. Hundreds of buses seemed to be arriving and departing continuously and it was here I bought a ticket for my next destination. It felt like an age before our bus left behind the heavily polluted city air and fresh sea air rescued my lungs. Tall king coconut trees lined the road sides as we reached the city outskirts. Their large waxy green leaves swayed like elephants ears in the freshening afternoon breeze. We passed by mile upon mile of roadside dwellings and rubbish tips. Wilted brown thatched shacks were interspersed with bone white concrete slab houses. Some of the rubbish tips had smoke billowing from them while goats, dogs and cows scavenged through others. The roadsides were still alive with people walking, cycling, sleeping, selling goods or simply hanging out. Our bus got stuck in a traffic jam in the village of Kovalam where a lorry had apparently jack-knifed. In the midst of all the commotion a school bus with a giant garland of flowers hanging from below its windscreen began to edge past us before stopping. Suddenly all the schoolchildren on the bus started waving over and smiling at us. No road rage, no hateful finger salutes, just joyful looks on each face. At the same as this was happening a 'cool as ice' holy cow sauntered between the two buses, apparently going wherever the whim took her. "If cows back in Ireland caught wind of how their Indian sisters are treated", I thought to myself, "there would be big trouble and the threat of milk strikes."

Mamallapuram proved to be the perfect place to stop and acclimatise for a few days. Set inside a series of small sheltered bays along the Bay Of Bengal, the area was effected by the 2004 Tsunami but did not experience the same devastation as coastal communities further South. I found a peaceful budget hotel called the Ramkrishna with a cool central courtyard, just a few minutes walk from the beach. Due possibly to the humidity and sudden change of climate I developed a chesty cough and congested sinuses and took to my bed for a few days rest and recovery.

Mamallapuram is famous for its magnificently carved ancient temples, many dating from 1,300 years ago. The amazing fact is that this ancient craft of stone carving is still alive and thriving in the area. Finished pieces are exported all over India and in more recent years to Europe and North America. Every morning I would wake to the tip tap of local artisans' wooden mallets on chisels although I also sometimes heard the unmistakable whine of electrically powered angle grinders coming from back-street workshops.

Feeling much better and with my jet lag also shaken I walked across town to visit some of the temples. The entrance to the Five Rathas temple complex was preceded by a walk along a shaded tree lined avenue where traders hustled intensely with tourists to buy everything from t-shirts to Indian flutes. There was a sizeable admission charge, by Indian money standards, but it was well worth it. Five small temples had been beautifully carved quite literally out of five massive granite boulders of a light brown colour. The intricate detail was simply mind boggling, considering the tools used and the time it must have taken to transform the rock faces. The World Heritage site had been rediscovered two hundred years ago by a team of British archaeologists who uncovered it from the shoreline sand. The site looked like some fantastical Indian version of Disneyland. The monumentally shaped Rathas were guarded by a larger than life elephant and bull, both figures again carved out of solid rock. Together they seemed to watch stoically over the steady flow of tourists.

On the way back into Mamallapuram I stopped off at Krishna's Butter Bowl, a massive circular boulder perched on a bare rocky outcrop of bedrock overlooking downtown. It appeared to be defying gravity and seemed at any moment ready to roll and crash down on to the busy street below if anyone as much as dared breathe heavily or sneeze as they walked past. A young Indian family were happily enjoying a picnic beneath its cool shaded underside, obviously convinced it was not about to move anytime soon. Tourism has brought huge changes in recent years and many of the locals have been moved out of the town centre to accommodate this influx. One young local man told me that the elders who now live in the back-streets often cry at the huge changes that have come to their small town.

Just a few doors up from the hotel where I was staying was an elderly man from Norwich in East England. His name was Felix and he explained to me that every year during the winter months, he and his son rent their home in Norwich and move out to India for a fraction of what a normal sun holiday would cost to Spain or the South of France. It turned out that Felix was a sprightly eighty eight years of age.

By the following afternoon I felt fully recovered and decided to go for an afternoon swim at the nearby beach. Mamallapuram boasts a long white sandy strand several miles long. As well as being popular with sun seeking tourists, the beach also served as a working shore for local fisherman whose small boats bobbed a short distance out on the bay in choppy waters. The ocean looked a light turquoise as large foamy waves crashed unto the beach. I walked over near to where a young couple were swimming and jumped into the water close by. The water felt invigorating and deeply refreshing under a hot midday sun. After a few leisurely minutes spent splashing and swimming close to the shoreline, I felt rough coral wash up under my feet and decided to try and dive down and grab some. When I emerged I was some metres out from the beach and felt a pressure of water around my waist dragging me out further. I was caught in a current and tried in vain to swim against it in an effort to reach shallow water again. My limbs began to tire and waves crashing and breaking around me drained me further of energy. Panic began to set in and although I shouted out, neither sunbathers nor the young couple swimming close by seemed to notice I was in trouble. The correct thing to do would have been to swim across the backwash current towards the shore but panic had overridden any judgement or wise inner advice. I felt locked in a struggle with the sea for what seemed like an eternity. My whole body was pumping with adrenaline and a part of my mind went into a frenzied spin of fear. After a few more futile attempts I decided to try floating on my back in the hope that an incoming wave would catch me. I began swimming the backstroke like my life depended on it. Mercifully, It worked. I was carried in on the crest of a large wave and found myself back in waist high water. As I made for the shore the outwash still tried to drag me out again as if the ocean was still hungrily grasping for me.

With shaken legs and in some shock I collected my clothes, warned the young couple of bathers to be careful and walked back up the beach. There were no warning signs and no life guards to complain to about my own carelessness and poor judgement. I felt like crying with relief, not sure how close I came to drowning.

A fishing boat had just landed back on the beach. Women were busy filling red plastic buckets and baskets from a large wriggling silvery net-full of fish. They brushed past me and rushed up towards the village with their haul, balanced on supple bony shoulders. Two elderly fishermen with greying hair and sun blackened faces sat cross-legged opposite each other on the bow of their beached boat sharing a cigarette. As I observed this scene of life feeling like a ghost come back from the dead, an understanding struck me that the world and every living thing in it would and will go on regardless without me in it. If I had drowned, my washed up body would have been flown home, perhaps along with my belongings. My drowning would have made the local newspapers back home, maybe even a national media mention or two especially as it had happened out in India. News would quickly become old and someone would use the page with my tragic story on it to light their fire some morning or to dry up a floor spill. My dear parents, sister, relations and friends would have grieved for my death but life would have moved on. I could hear my inner ego saying, "stop that silly nonsense chat, what would you do without ME. We got through this together now forget about it and lets get back to normal."

I simply had to tell someone what happened and so chose my hotel manager Mr Prakash. "You know, I was caught in a current and nearly drowned while swimming close to the beach today", I proclaimed in a low earnest tone. With a matter of fact-ness bordering on the surreal Mr Prakash tilted his head slightly sideways and answered, "Oh yes Mr. Keith, we lose some tourists and visitors every year from drowning mishaps, it is always very unfortunate."

I walked with unsteady legs up the stairs to my room and drifted into a deep sleep for a few hours. I awoke to the softer light of early evening like a man given a new life. Felix from Norwich had told me about an Eagle Temple located about fifteen kilometres inland. With a few hours daylight still remaining I decided to hire an old black Raleigh bicycle like my Grandfather in Donegal used to ride. With a local tourist map as my guide I set off at a steady pace. I passed through rural villages and along country roads with thatched houses and haystacks in the front yard. One elderly woman in a bright yellow sari herded goats through thorny scrubland shouting orders at her flock and shaking a stick above her head. Locals smiled and waved as I passed and I felt some sort of connection with the land and people of Tamil Nadu. I would agree with W.B. Yeats who believed that prior to the Battle of the Boyne in 1690, the Indian cultural world had stretched from the Bay of Bengal right across to Galway Bay in an Indo-European arc. The people of Tamil

Nadu have holy trees and thorn bushes beside wells where they tie prayer rags and see hospitality as the highest social custom. As I was cycling along a cool tree shaded stretch of road a fellow jumped expertly on to my bike carrier while I was moving at a good speed. When I turned around in surprise he smiled and pointed enthusiastically down the road at some invisible destination. About two miles further and after an upward hilly stretch I got a bit cross with my passenger but we parted company on good terms at a roadside wine bar.

I reached the small town of Tirrikalikundum just before sunset and perched on a steep rocky hill-top clad with thick forest was the striking Hindu Eagle Temple. Its walls were painted in stripes of red and white like a barbers pole while on top a golden domed roof gleamed in the soft light. Upon paying a small donation to the official temple beggar, admission man, cloakroom attendant to keep my sandals and compulsory banana rations seller, I walked up the still sun hot three hundred and fifty steps in my shoe softened bare feet. I was rewarded with a very special view. A small cluster of rocky peaks of different sizes rose sharply around Tirrikalikundum amidst a table flat patchwork of fields, some flooded for growing rice. It was as if the peaks of hidden underground mountains had magically thrust upwards into the surrounding plains and I was now standing on one of these peaks. The sound of evening prayer from Muslim mosques and Hindu temples far below drifted upwards in the still twilight. Far to the West a small bright red sun set in a purple and crimson dusty horizon.

Inside the temple the air was full of clouds of incense smoke. Offerings of food, money and lotus flowers, lay before exotic looking Hindu Gods such as Shiva and Ganesh. I received a blessing and a young priest in a white lungi (Indian male skirt), with long black hair smeared a thumb of red tumeric paint in the centre of my forehead and asked me to repeat three times, 'Saiyee Saiyee Shiva Shiva'. I gave a fifty rupee note as a donation equivalent to about one dollar. He then asked, "are you married?", to which I replied "no". "You will be soon be after you return home", he said in definite tones. I wondered about asking for my donation back but said nothing and instead did my rounds of the temple with a very nice elderly Indian man called Doryan.

Being the last visitor of the day in true Irish timekeeping tradition, the priests offered to share their meal of freshly cooked rice and water with me which I gratefully accepted. In the Hindu religion it is quite acceptable for priests to marry and have families which they support through temple donations. One of the older priests explained to me why it was called the Eagle Temple.

"It is believed that on certain evenings a sacred eagle flew down from the holy city of Varinassi to visit this temple from many thousands of miles to the North. He then added, "this eagle has not been seen for a long time now and Varinassi is a very long way from here."

As we walked back down the temple steps some of the priest answered calls from family on their mobile phones. Ancient and time honoured customs and rituals seem to be woven effortlessly with new modern lifestyle changes. It occurred to me that their culture seems much richer and more grounded for having the confidence to do this. I cycled the fifteen kilometres back to Mamallapuram in virtual darkness using a mixture of gut instinct and bicycle bell sonar to avoid other locals as well as night rambling holy cows. As I passed some farm houses I could see the unmistakable flickering shadows of television sets through open windows and doors. Electricity had recently come to these rural areas and would surely bring with it profound changes both good and bad.

Super Tailor's Shirt

After a week it was time to move on from Mamallapuram so I booked a very cheap train ticket to the city of Trichipalli in the heart of Tamil Nadu State. While visiting the market area of Mamallapuram on my last evening I took a notion of buying a new shirt for travelling. I noticed that although a lot of Western travellers wore ragged technicolour pseudo ethnic Indian clothes, the majority of Indian men wore smart slacks and chequered cotton shirts of different colours. I passed a tailor shop selling shirts and decided to go in and try on a few. A bright friendly young man in his early twenties called Canaan managed the shop and had some friends working along with him as assistants. I was reluctantly encouraged to try on a few shirts as there were no dressing rooms. Canaan's assistants had to act like a human screen to save the blushes of passing sari clad Indian women...and myself. Despite my best efforts I couldn't find a shirt that I was happy with. As I turned to leave Canaan burst into a sale pitch, "No No Mr. Keith, you don't understand, we will m-a-k-e you a shirt of finest workmanship." Someone then shouted, "quick go get Super Tailor", while Canaan encouraged me to select a choice of bright shirt materials displayed behind the counter. Super Tailor arrived on the scene in suitable guise with a measuring tape draped around his neck. About the same age as Canaan, he was the happiest looking person I had ever met in my life. He stood there with a blissful smile so wide it made his eyes close slightly. His forehead was lined with different colour temple paints and he nodded his head from side to side continuously. There was no way of backing out now. After selecting a preferred material it was time to bargain hard with Canaan who of course started with a crazy asking price. Soon a small crowd had gathered inside the doorway in a buzz of self generated excitement. The bargaining continued and tension was mounting when suddenly a young boy burst through the door banging a drum. Everyone, including myself, jumped and danced around the tailor shop for a pantomime minute. The drummer boy then stopped in mid dance and thrust out his open hand to me to place a few rupees upon. After due payment, he quick marched back out the door, drum banging once more. A few minutes later and the now theatrical like bargaining for my shirt, yet to be made, was almost completed. I thought it time to ask for a luck's rupee back on the deal protesting in high spirits that it was a long standing tradition in my home country of Ireland. Canann conceded a further rupee and we shook on the deal. Super Tailor measured me up while Canaan assured me that my new shirt would be ready by 10am the next morning.

The following morning I arrived back to the tailor shop and sure enough... my shirt wasn't ready. I reminded Canaann of my deposit and the fact that I had a connecting bus and train to catch. "There is no problem Mr Keith", he assured me confidently with a beaming enthusiastic smile. "Come, we will go directly and collect your shirt from Super Tailor, you will see it is ready for you". Canaan had a sparkling clean Suzuki 125 motorbike parked outside the shop and beckoned me to hop on the back. Through the side streets of Mamallapuram we drove at breakneck speed swerving to avoid pedestrians, street vendors carts and wandering cows. We pulled up outside a workshop and waiting by the street side was Super Tailor still in top form. In his outstretched arms he held a neatly wrapped brown paper package containing my shirt. I thanked Super Tailor who simply beamed smilingly back with head nodding sideways. Canaan remarked he hadn't any English but I wasn't so sure. Maybe Super Tailor had just decided to stop talking altogether as it only got in the way of his inner brimming-over happiness.

We climbed back unto Canaan's motorbike and narrowly missed a droopy-eared goat sniffing a chocolate wrapper off the road before we made it safely back to the tailor shop. In quiet excitement I tore open the brown paper wrapping. It was a lemon green chequered white shirt as I had asked for. As I tried it on over my t-shirt, a small audience seemed to once again spontaneously gather. It felt a good fit around my shoulders and the stitching and seaming was excellent. But as I went to close the button on my wrist cuffs it became apparent...the right hand sleeve stopped 3 inches above my wrist. The awkward silence that follows disappointment began to take hold of me and I felt the surrounding crowd take a collective inward breadth. Seizing the moment Canaan walked quickly forward, unbuttoned the cuff links again and folded both shirt sleeves neatly back to my forearm. "See, this is how Indian men wear shirt Mister Keith...proper style", he said, smiling and holding a thumbs up to his inside finger in a quality loop sign. I turned to the tailor shop audience. They were smiling and giving me the thumbs up and nods of approval. I paused a moment then smiled myself saying, "the shirt is good, I will take it!"

My last lunch in Mamallapuram was on the roof top terrace restaurant of the hotel I was staying at. While waiting for my meal I watched a chipmunk hop down from an overhanging palm tree unto a vacant diner table and made a beeline for the sugar bowl. He gathered up a paw-full of sugar grains and gnawed them nervously keeping one eye on the kitchen door. The restaurant owner Robin was an intense man in his fifties with heavy rimmed glasses and untidy black thinning hair. When I told him I was leaving he handed me a card while he served up lunch. The card was the contact details of a nearby orphanage. "Both my wife and daughter were killed in the tsunami. I helped set up this orphanage in memory of them and we currently have fifty children being cared for there." Robin explained that because many fishermen further down the coast died in the tsunami, the family lost their sole breadwinner and many mothers were no longer able to support their children. I then asked Robin did these people receive financial assistance from the international funds raised by millions of people worldwide after the disaster. "Yes, money was sent to India but by the time officials from New Delhi to local Government took their share there was very little left for survivors and their families." Felix from Norwich confirmed Robins tragic family story and I felt compelled to leave a donation before I left.

I collected my reserved train ticket in Mamallapuram, then got a public bus to Ckikalpatu where my train to Trichipalli was to stop. My plan was to stay in Trichipalli a few days and organise a flight to Sri Lanka to meet up with some friends from Ireland. I waited on the platform in the baking heat as what seemed like a mile long passenger train snaked its way into the station. It then slowly dawned on me why my train ticket was so cheap. I was booked to travel in the 'second class unreserved' carriages. Too late to change my ticket, I squeezed my way past passengers literally hanging out of the carriage doors. The train was packed but I managed to find a space on the floor between two seats to sit with my knees tucked up. The air felt thin for lack of fans and the mill of people. It was two hours to the next station. I stopped myself from panicking by remembering that it was as uncomfortable for everyone else as it was for me and that there was no point making a personal drama out of it. At the next station stop I was relieved to be offered a seat by a young man called Balla. He was on his way home to Trichipalli after a week's work in Chennai. Balla was broad shouldered in stature with a large crescent shaped moustache and round kind face. He wore glasses and I guessed was in his early thirties. An older man with a strong head of grey hair and wizened face carved from years of hard labour, asked Balla in his native Tamil language a question as he glanced over at me. Balla translated for me and said, "he wants to know why as a Westerner are you travelling in this carriage". I replied "Tell him if I wasn't travelling in this carriage I wouldn't have got a chance to meet you all." The old man listened attentively to Balla's Tamil translation of my reply and then smiled and waved his hand as if to politely pass off my comment.

Balla was highly articulate and a great conversationalist. He informed me that he worked as a Government civil servant in a department dealing with national statistics such as incomes and expenditure.

He explained, "although India has a per capita average daily wage of three hundred and fifty rupees (seven euros), the majority of people survive on less than fifty rupees per day. This will give you an indication of the gap between rich and poor. I can assure you that this gap is widening every year and causing growing unrest, especially among a young and increasingly educated workforce. My wages as a civil servant simply do not cover my basic economic responsibilities to my family even though I have a college degree." Balla put his points across very passionately and others sitting around nodded their heads in agreement with him.

Balla and I talked the whole way to Trichipalli Junction Station where he then kindly offered to help me find accommodation. It was the wedding season in Tamil Nadu and every hotel on my Travel Guide Book hit-list was booked up but Balla walked around town with me until I finally found a hotel room for the night. Before we parted he gave me his mobile number and invited me around some evening to visit his family house for dinner. I spent the next few days visiting Hindu temples around Trichipalli and learning some basic Tamil phrases such as *wanakam* which is the standard greeting and *nandri* which means 'thank you'. The city had an excellent bus service and most journeys cost five rupees or the equivalent of ten cents. Every bus driver had a dashboard shrine devoted to his own favourite Hindu Gods. Flowers and prayer beads often hung from the front mirror while Hindi music tapes blasted loudly over the speakers. Bus drivers seemed to operate on the chaotic crowded streets by beeping each other loudly when cutting in and out between traffic. Skinny whistling ticket conductors seemed to defy the laws of gravity by somehow balancing on two feet while issuing tickets. No one seemed the least bit offended or even annoyed at the overuse of car or bus horns or aggressive driving manoeuvres. In rural Ireland such behaviour would lead to a family spite taken against the offending driver for at least two generations.

While walking up the polished stairways to my fifth floor room in the Hotel Chittra one evening I felt the atmosphere a little strange and chilly despite the pervading heat elsewhere. There was a long dark corridor to the left of my room and although the hotel was supposedly fully booked it felt uncomfortably quiet. A few nights later I experienced the most intense supernatural experience of my life. Sometime closer to dawn than midnight I woke up to find my arms pinned down in a deathlike grip from behind as I slept by someone or something. The room was ink black dark. My whole body felt paralysed as this being in the grating breathless voice of an old hag began to speak slowly close up to one of my ears. When it occured to me that this voice was clearly coming outside my own head I was struck with fear. She spoke in riddles and was giving me advice and predictions about my life ahead and other matters. I was in total shock at what I was experiencing but I had no choice but to listen. My mind simply blanked the first few riddles out of sheer disbelief. I can only hope it wasn't something profoundly important as there was no chance of requesting a repeat. One riddle was, "you will see yourself soon as you once were". Another stated, "you will carry a sword as you go by your side, a sword to cut through everything and yet nothing." There was another riddle that I can distinctly remember but it is to remain my mystery, at least for now. When she finished speaking her voice faded into a death like throat rattle and I felt my cold rigid limbs relax a little.

After a few minutes I gathered the courage to move from the bed and switch on all the lights and open the curtains to the night outside. I looked around the room and wondered if a chemical in the electric mosquito repellent plugged into a wall next to my bed had triggered off some kind of hallucinogenic episode. It may have been a possibility yet the experience seemed so real and the entity spoke so clearly and with intent that it made some sense to me and I felt clear minded directly after it. I spent the next day in a state of shock, trying desperately but in vain to find another hotel or guesthouse to stay in. Everywhere was booked up and my flight to Colombo in Sri Lanka was still two days away. The next night I eventually fell asleep with all the lights on. I had considered leaving the television on until I remembered the scene in the Poltergeist horror movie when spooky voices came from the TV.

The following day I rang Balla who invited me around to visit his parents and sisters. He collected me from the hotel on his motorbike after work and we drove to a suburb of Trichipalli where they lived in an apartment block. On the way he told me about his girlfriend Wassindra and how he was keeping her secret from his parents for the time being. I was naturally glad to be away from the Hotel Chittra for a few hours. We were welcomed by Balla's family into a small three room apartment and adjoining kitchen. Balla, his Father and I chatted in the living room while his mother and one of his sisters began cooking and preparing a meal for us. He had three pretty sisters, one of which was married. It turned out to be a special night. First Balla and I were served a feast of noodles and then the nicest masala dosai I have ever eaten. Afterwards we all sat around and they sang some traditional Tamil songs for me. Thankfully I had brought a few small gifts which I presented to Balla's niece before leaving. I felt privileged to have been brought back to an Indian home and to have experienced the natural hospitality of these warm and big hearted people. It was near midnight when I arrived back to the spooky Hotel Chittra and promised Balla I would send him some books when I returned to Ireland. I decided to stay up and pack my backpack as I needed to catch an early flight to Sri Lanka. I was looking forward to leaving India for a few weeks and meeting up with a good Irish friend John Ahern and his soon wife to be Maria. I was also relieved at how quickly I recovered from my intense supernatural encounter with no one to talk to about it. In a way my belief in spirits and ghosts and previous unexplained experiences helped me accept and remain open to what had happened and to simply accept it.

JOURNEY THROUGH SRI LANKA

I landed in Colombo less that two hours later. My first impressions were that Sri Lanka was a lot less hectic and more sedate than India despite the fact the country was on military alert with a full blown civil war still raging in the Northeast. Anti-aircraft guns and sandbag bunkers manned with nervous looking soldiers lined the runway as we landed. The airport was awash with military checkpoints and yet somehow the overall atmospheres was that of calm. I had moved from a predominantly Hindu culture to a land where over eighty percent of its people practice Buddhism. Tropical Sri Lanka, also known as 'Pearl of the Indian Ocean', is situated off the southern coast of India. From an on-board glossy brochure on my short flight I had read that Sri Lanka is a developing country about the same size as Ireland. With a population of eighteen million people it is incredible to think that there are still leopards, wild elephants, bears, crocodiles and giant lizards still thriving in parts of the countryside not to mention a dwindling number of native hunter gatherers called Vedhas. I could just imagine Joe Duffy's Live-Line radio show back in Ireland if we had a similar array of wildlife. "Joan in Offaly is calling up to complain about wild elephants tramping across her manicured lawns. Tony in Leitrim has a nuisance bear taking up residence in his tool shed and eating his garbage." Sooner or later a caller would proclaim on the national airwaves, "surely the should we call out the army and declare a state of emergency Joe."

My first port of call was Negombo town and beach resort. Negombo is home to a number of picturesque Catholic churches and grottos dedicated to the Virgin Mary. The town owes its strong Catholic heritage to the Portugese who colonised parts of the west coast of Sri Lanka from the 16th Century. Negombo had the look of a holiday resort in slow decline. The ongoing conflict between Tamil Tiger guerrilla armies and Government forces, mainly in the far Northeast of the island had taken its toll. Sporadic bombings around the capital Colombo in recent years had scared off a lot of affluent European holiday makers. The weather in Sri Lanka was a lot more changeable than India. Cloud and humidity would increase during the afternoon so that by late evening thunderstorms rumbled and flashed out to sea followed close behind by heavy torrential downpours. The local drink is called *arrak,* a strong clear coconut rum usually mixed with soda. My arm was twisted to have a few drinks one evening by a group of local businessmen that I met in a local cafe. My hosts were generous enough with their rounds of *arrak* but their conversations in English suggested that things were not so good. The tourist were simply not coming anymore in big numbers and it was beginning to have a knock on effect on most areas of the Sri Lankan economy. Our few quiet drinks at the bar were followed by 'one more' in a nearby pool-room bar and 'one final small drink' in some disco bar. Some kind Samaritan auto rickshaw driver ferried me back to my hotel room that night where I slept off my first 'arrak-attack'.

The next morning brought a day of self inflicted suffering, mostly in the region above my eyes. Experience told me that fresh air was my best bet for a quick recovery. I decided on hiring a mountain bike from a nearby bicycle shop and set off in the hope of seeing some countryside to the north of Negombo.

I cycled along the beach road lined with budget and five star luxury hotels. As the buildings thinned out I spotted katamarang fishing boats off the coast, bobbing in choppy dark blue waters. Their tall traditional square sails bulged out in the middle, catching a brisk sea breeze. The landscape then changed to tree sheltered narrow roads with small concrete houses peering through dense tropical foliage. I soon reached the outlying village of Koch-chikade where small yellow and black auto rickshaws with buzzing engines darted along the sleepy Sunday evening streets. I stopped a local man on the street to ask for directions. He introduced himself as Cedrick and pointed out the road I wished to take. He wore a brown and orange baseball cap on his head. The lines on his face spoke of an interesting life which he projected with a contented unassuming smile. I was a little sarcastic with him for some reason when he invited me to visit. He simply brushed it off and pointed to where he lived if I changed my mind and wanted to call later. About a mile out of town I came to a wide deep looking river, one of many large rivers in Sri Lanka that flow down from the Central Highlands. Huge luxuriant trees straddled the river banks. The idea came to me to go for a refreshing swim until I remembered that Sri Lanka's waterways are well stocked with crocodiles, giant monitor lizards, snakes and leaches for good measure. I decided instead to cycle a little further but was forced to change my plans when the saddle literally snapped off my hired bike. Placing the saddle in my backpack I turned my bike around and started cycling while standing on the pedals. I headed back in the direction of Koch-chicade making a strong mental note not to forget I no longer had a saddle to sit on. Upon reaching Koch-chicade again I cycled towards the street Cedrick told me he lived on. I stopped a wild looking man with long spiky grey hair and asked him did he know a man called Cedrick. His eyes lit up and he beckoned me to follow him. Cedrick was sitting on a red Coca-Cola crate at the top of a narrow street in conversation with another local. The wild looking man's name was Anthony and it turned out he was one of Cedrick's best friends. The other locals joked that Cedrick had given a blood transfusion to Anthony one time when he was critically ill in hospital. Cedrick took a look at my bike and asked what happened to my saddle. A few local teenagers arrived on bikes and Cedrick started talking to them in Sinhalese. He asked me to give him five hundred rupees and one of the boys would try and buy a new saddle for me up town. At first I thought they were pulling a scam and assured them I was happy to take the bike and broken saddle back to Negombo. Anthony then produced a tattered wallet and counted out five one hundred rupee notes which he went to give the teenagers. It might well have been his life savings. I thanked Anthony and told him to put back his money back in his wallet before handing over a five hundred rupee note, reminding myself it was less than four euros.

One of the teenagers then sped off up the main street on my hired bike with the saddle in his hand. Someone produced a plastic chair for me to sit on and Cedrick began talking.

"You know at one time I was a tourist guide here in Sri Lanka. I can speak five languages fluently. I did very well and a lot of tourists came to me. I made friends and contacts from all around the world. One particular group of Saudi businessmen invited me to come and visit them which I did. When my two sons and daughter grew up I was able to set them up with good jobs in Dubai and Saudi Arabia."

He paused for a moment and then looked at me with an ironic smile. "Would you believe me if I told you that now I don't even have a home. I don't know where my next meal is coming from or even where I will put down my head tonight. Is it not funny how life can bring you into situations you never dreamt possible? Yet I refuse to worry, all the people here respect me and sometimes even ask for my advice. I know that somehow there will be a meal for me this evening. I don't want any charity but if you wish to help me get a clean pillow and mattress it will cost me three hundred rupees. They are the only items in the world I wish for."

I gladly handed him three hundred rupees and we shook hands as friends. A short time later the teenage boy arrived back with my hired bike and broken saddle. Cedrick translated for the teenager that no bike shops were open before he handed me back my five hundred rupee note.

The next day I had to venture into the capital city of Colombo. All around the downtown Port Area there were sigs of economic development. Recently built glass and white concrete skyscrapers brashly proclaimed a new level of wealth yet the main river running through the city stank like a giant sewer. My destination was the Sri Lankan Airways office to change the date of my return flight. Located in the towering World Trade Centre Building, security was extremely tight with checkpoints, metal detector screens and compulsory baggage searches. The World Trade Centre was like a modern Sri Lankan Palace. Bright tropical sunlight poured in through its giant glass exterior. A huge water fountain seemed to take up most of the ground and first floor. Young businessmen in smart suits and beautiful Sri Lankan princesses in traditional dresses walked proudly around the multi-level skyscraper in air conditioned comfort.

Colombo Railway Station was a different world, bustling with thousands of commuters. Its tall shed-like platforms cruelly trapped the afternoon heat and fumes from the old petrol train engines. A stream of sweat trickled down my back as I joined a mad scramble to get a seat on a train heading down the west coast to Aluthgama. While waiting on the platform a tourist tout by the name of Ananda befriended me. He was returning home to his village and convinced me to stay a night of two at a nearby guesthouse along the coast. With no pre-made plans I accepted and he shared a Sri Lankan travel secret of throwing your luggage in the train window to secure a seat. I sat next to Ananda during the journey. He was a small thin nervous looking man in his forties with a sparse comb-over of black hair. He rubbed the beads of sweat of his brow with a white handkerchief and scanned the carriage as it looking for somebody he knew but never found. After a time our train mercifully pulled out of the boiling station and a refreshing sea breeze blew through our carriage. Office blocks and grey concrete suburbs gave way to rows of shanty town style huts roofed with wilted brown palm leaves. Long lines of washing hung between available tall coconut trees. After a few hours trundling and clattering down the west coast rail-line we reached the station and small town of Ambalangoda. Ananda helped me carry my spare hand luggage and we got an auto rickshaw along the coast road to 'Sunny's Guesthouse'. On the jungle side of the road we passed by passed by scores of houses which looked like bombed out ruins from World War II archive movies. Ananda explained that this part of the coastline had bore the brunt of the devastating tsunami that struck back in 2004. On that fateful day during the late morning of December 26th, 30,000 people lost their lives when the tsunami struck Sri Lanka. Indonesia suffered worse where the tsunami claimed 200,000 lives.

We drove up a small laneway and stopped in front of a large two storey guesthouse with bright red roof tiles which belonged to a German man called Sunny. I had told Ananda about my swimming experience in India and he brought me to a sheltered cove where he assured me was a safe place to swim. The beach looked straight out of a holiday brochure with tall thin coconut trees, white coral sand and clear turquoise blue water which was deeply refreshing after the sweaty train journey. Ananda stood a short distance off signalling at passing traffic and smoking a cigarette.

Sunny was a big softly spoken German man, over 6 feet tall with blonde hair and moustache and wore light rim glasses. He explained to me that he worked as a taxi man in his native city of Dusseldorf for half the year, then rented his tax plate and spent another six months out here managing the guesthouse he bought ten years ago. His son was out staying with him at the moment and he further explained that his family came and went during the year. He employed local people to run the guesthouse and seemed to be a fair sort of boss as there was a nice relaxing atmosphere. Over dinner on my second night's stay I asked Sunny and Ananda about how the tsunami affected the local area. Sunny explained that he was back in Germany when he first heard news reports about the tsunami which struck the Indian Ocean coastlines of Sri Lanka, India and Indonesia. He then turned to Ananda as a cue for him to talk. Ananda smiled nervously while shaking his head and signalled Sunny to continue with a forward wave of his hand. Sunny continued, "I am sure that you saw the destroyed buildings on your way here which gives you some idea of the scale of the devastation caused. As I said I was in Germany at the time but I had rebuilt this two storey guesthouse just a few years prior to the tsunami. By all accounts, the first wave struck the coast during the mid morning when communities were mercifully up and about. The first warning locals here got was when people started shouting and pointing out to the ocean horizon where a large wall of water was growing in alarming height. You can just imagine the panic. As my guesthouse was the tallest building in the area, parents grabbed their infants and children and ran for their lives towatrds the guesthouse here. People managed to hauled each other up on top of the roof just before the first wave struck. Ananda lost three of his relatives in the first wave. As the water surged back out to sea, one of Ananda's neighbours ignored pleas to wait and instead climbed down to search for two of his missing grandchildren who had been swept away. The second wave was apparently much more devastating than the first. Locals alter described to me how it ripped through concrete houses and twisted nearby rail tracks together like pieces of rope. The second wave carried with it a hot tar like substance which combined with the salt water burnt every last piece of vegetation a quarter of a mile in from the coastline. The only thing left standing was the tall coconut trees."

Ananda who had remained silent then explained in broken English how another neighbour and his two sons were setting off walking along the coast road to Ambalangoda. They heard the shouts of people running to Sunny's guesthouse and managed to run back just in time to save themselves. Ananda then mentioned that when President Clinton came to visit, the locals brought him to see small Buddhist shrines made from bricks and white plaster which had also miraculously survived the impact of both tsunami waves. The Sri Lankan peoples Buddhist faith with it's philosophy of impermanence and rebirth had clearly helped them overcome this immense human tragedy. We continued to talk and I explained to Ananda how the tragedy had captured the hearts of people throughout the world and how in my native Donegal, schoolchildren, businesses and community groups had raised hundreds of thousands of euros' for Aid Organisations. Ananda then pointed across the courtyard to a newly built red brick house next to the guesthouse and explained that he had received a full grant from a Foreign Aid fund to rebuild his parents house. The next day I got the bus into town, bought a wedding card, and sent an email to my friend John Ahern from Cork explaining that I was staying close by. He was staying with his girlfriend Maria at a beachside resort near the town of Aluthgama. They were to get married at a private ceremony in two days time and then planned to spend their honeymoon touring around Sri Lanka.

I had promised Ananda that I would go an a half day tour with him and we arranged a price. Our first stop was Kosgoda Turtle Sanctuary. A bored looking tour guide explained to us how turtle eggs are gathered from nearby beaches, hatched and then reared in special water tanks until they are a few weeks old. With this protected start in life the baby turtles are then released into the ocean in an effort to boost declining sea turtle numbers. Ananda brought along an older friend Arrah who kept asking would I marry one of his daughters. I passed it off the first few times as a bit of joking until I realised the man was one hundred percent serious. Ananda and Arrah were a right pair of rogues and chancers. I soon figured out that they were bringing me to places such as temples and craft shops where I had to pay a steep admission price. This guaranteed them a commission as well as what I had agreed for the tour. I decided to cut my losses and return to Sunny's Guesthouse early. Ananda and Arrah then took an auto-rickshaw into Ambalagoda to go drinking beer for the day on my twenty five dollars. I was to meet with John and Maria in Aluthgama later that evening and before I left the house Sunny handed me his card with the guesthouse address in case I got lost. As I waited by the roadside for a bus who should stumble up the road but Ananda and Arrah who were quite obviously both 'drunk as lords' on my sponsored tour money. When I mentioned I was going to Aluthgama, Ananda announced that he had a sister living there and they would join me for the journey. All I could do was bite my tongue and proclaim "you're some pair of buckos." They sang traditional songs along the way and taught me some rude words in their native Sinhalese language. Amid the general revelry Arrah somehow knocked Sunny's business card out of my shirt pocket where it lodged between the inside seat and side of the bus just as I was coming up to my bus stop. I tried in vain to prise it out with my fingers. Hopping off the bus I consoled myself with the notion that I knew where Sunny's Guesthouse was anyhow.

I met up with John and Maria in the Riverina Beach Hotel where they were to get married the following day. Although I was only a few weeks on the road, it was still great to meet up with people from back home in Ireland. After a refreshing beer they invited me to join them for a massive buffet dinner and dessert table. I felt like I was stocking up in survival mode for some unforeseen food shortage. After dinner we sat outside in the balmy night air until late chatting with warm informality and sharing travel stories. When I mentioned that I planned to travel to Nepal John's eyes lit up and in his soft Cork brogue, he recommended that I check out a meditation retreat centre called Kopan situated outside Katmandu. He also recommended that I go on a trek into a remote region of Nepal called the 'Solu-Khumbu' which he had thoroughly enjoyed a number of years back. I expressed genuine interest and John promised to email me on some more information. I wished them a very happy wedding day and thanked them for kindly inviting me to dinner at the hotel. They were a great couple and I admired them for doing there own thing by getting married and spending their honeymoon in Sri Lanka.

It was a mad dash to catch a late mini-bus back down the Coast Road. No sooner had I found a seat when a charismatic Government tourist lecturer called Sidath introduced himself. He then began furtively explaining to me about a major tourist project he was working on. He persuaded me to meet him to-morrow and discuss his jungle theme park further, pushing his card into my hand as he got off in Ambalangoda. I knew that Sunny's guesthouse was just a few miles further on up the road but it was dark and I had a few drinks too many and couldn't find any landmarks. Like an uncertain parachute jumper I stood shiftily by the bus door and asked the driver to stop and drop me off at what turned out to be somewhere other than the driveway into Sunny's guesthouse. I turned my quiet frustrations towards Ananda and Arrah who were now very probably sleeping off their full day's drinking session. I was lost, but consoled myself with the fact that the guesthouse I was looking for was definite-ly somewhere along the Coast Road. "How long is the Coast

Road?" was a philosophical type question I posed to myself. I walked for a while in the hope of spotting a familiar landmark. A bright tropical full moon cast silvery shadows through the coconut trees overhead and bats as big as cats with see-through wings swooshed down from above. Some unfortunate young fellow driving home on his motorbike, probably happy and content after a midnight rendezvous with his sweetheart, was suddenly flagged down by a tipsy lost Irishman. For the next hour we drove up the Coast Road and back down the Coast Road and up it a short distance again until I finally recognised the laneway into Sunny's guesthouse. Wishing my reluctant motorbike rider happiness and good fortune in life and love I retired for the night pushing some dollars into his hand.

The next morning I rang the charismatic tourist lecturer Sidath to come and collect me. He was a jovial large man with a full head of neat jet black and matching black groomed moustache, common among professional Sri Lankan men of a married age. Sunny came out to say farewell and a charismatic introduction later, both he and Sidath were excitedly exchanging business cards. We drove back to Sidath's house where his wife had prepared a large breakfast feast. We spent half the morning leisurely eating and chatting. When his two young kids arrived back from school for lunch his daughter shyly asked her Mother in Sinhalese, "why has Daddy brought a white skinned ghost home with him?" After school I played and hung out with their son and daughter who tried communicating with me by asking me questions slowly over and over in Sinhalese so that I should u-n-d-e-r-s-t-a-n-d what they were saying. They would then stare at me deeply puzzled at my complete lack of comprehension. They showed me around their garden and I was amazed to see so many fruit trees growing there. They had banana and papaya fruit trees growing next to the clothes line while prickly dark green jack fruits, twice the size of a football, hung from a large perimeter tree. In Ireland the Health and Safety inspectors would close off the garden as a 'jack fruit hazard drop zone' but adults and children here seem to possess the natural sense not to stand under one.

The climate in Sri Lanka's coastal lowlands for most of the year is akin to living in a giant invisible glass house. Lush jungle type vegetation covers much of the land not cultivated or built upon. Fruit bats with one metre wing spans glide over your head at night. Later that evening Sidath brought me to watch his two kids rehearsing for a forthcoming school play. We then went to visit the chief Buddhist priest who lived a short distance away. An elderly shaven headed man with a grounded presence stepped out to greet and shake hands with us. It was difficult to guess his age as his face was free of lines or wrinkles. He was perhaps close to seventy years old. He wore no sandals, watch or jewellery of any sort, just a long bright orange toga-like robe which was tied in a knot at one shoulder. Sidath introduced me and told the chief monk where I was from and that I was on a journey through Asia. The orange robed chief priest nodded slowly while looking at me without any visible expression. Instead he turned on his heels and walked back into his house before returning with a book in his arms which he handed to me as a gift. The cover title was 'Why Worry?; How to live without fear and worry', by K. Sri Dhammananda. I was taken back by his spontaneous generosity and matter of fact kindness towards me. Having picked up a few words of Sinhalese out of respect for my host culture I thanked the chief monk with my two palms placed together "Boma estudtee' He paused with me while Sidath took a photo and then left to attend some other locals waiting to see him.

Back at the house another big meal was prepared for supper and Sidath and I sat around for hours talking, to the background sound of crickets chirping noisily outside. The night air was balmy and sticky, as if some grand cosmic caretaker had forgotten to turn on the cooling system once the sun had set. Sidath talked passionately about how important the family is in Sinhalese culture. He talked about his time spent studying and working in Moscow and how cold the winters there were. He could still speak Russian fluently. Sidath was also interested to hear about the success of the Northern Ireland Peace Process. We discovered that both the conflict in Northern Ireland

and Sri Lanka had some similarities in its origin. Both conflicts were for the most part localised in the Northeast regions of both islands. The conflict in Sri Lanka stemmed from the British policy of transplanting hundreds of thousands of Tamil people from Southern India to work on the tea plantations. The Tamil people brought with them their own culture, religion and language from mainland India. They have been fighting a twenty-six year guerrilla war campaign for a recognised Tamil homeland in the North of Sri Lanka. Over eighty thousand people have lost their lives since the conflict began. During our discussions Sidath asked me what was the main factor that helped create peace in Northern Ireland. I shared with him my own opinion that the keystone success of the process was that both sides involved in the conflict were willing to make difficult compromises which created the space for dialogue and initial trust. Sidath then shared with me his grand plans for a theme park but it was getting late and we both ran out of conversational steam. Before retiring for the night I asked Sidath was there a mosquito net for over my bed as there was already a small squadron of mosquitoes circling the room I was staying in. Sidath smiled widely then gesturing with his palms held apart replied, "our family does not use mosquito nets. Each evening we include mosquitoes in our *metta* (loving kindness) practice towards all living beings. As a result we rarely get bitten." That night as I wrapped myself in a cotton sheet I prayed to all the saints of all the religions I knew and wished all mosquitoes happy and contented lives but not at my blood's expense. I was woken suddenly at six the following morning by the start of a Buddhist mass turned up loudly on the kitchen radio. A male voice was chanting in hypnotic nasal tones from the radio speakers. Each morning Sidath and all the family listened to the radio Mass while showering, dressing and having breakfast. I was relieved to find just one mosquito bite on my right ankle.

I said my goodbyes and heartfelt thanks to all the family before catching a bus to Colombo with Sidath. He was commuting to his work and had lectures to attend to later that afternoon. We parted company at the train station and I wished him well with his work and business idea, thanking him again for inviting me to stay with his family. "Maybe I shall come to Ireland someday Keith and you can show me the Cliffs of Moher," he joked as we parted and went our separate ways. As I studied a map of Sri Lanka in the window of a tourist office I noticed that all Sri Lanka's mountains are clumped together in the centre of the island while In Ireland most of our mountains circle the coastline. I decided to travel to the inland mountains next for a welcome respite from the humidity and heat and bought a ticket to the city of Kandy. Again I took my chances on the train and was rewarded with some very fine scenery. One of the positive legacies of British rule was that the new Sri Lankan State inherited a comprehensive railway system built through the Central Highlands, West and South of the country. The railways had originally been built to transport spices, tropical hardwoods, fruit and most famously tea from the hill country down to the busy ports at Colombo. They had also opened up the highlands to Victorian era tourism.

For the first hour of the journey our train trundled lazily along Colombo's suburbs and then out into a countryside of lush tall grassland fringed by thick stands of forest. Just when I began wondering if the highlands were a tourist gimmick our train began to slow down and wind its way through forest clad foothills. An hour later and our train slowed to a crawl of fifteen miles per hour. It dragged its way up ever steeper gradients through dense jungle, belching thick black clouds of petrol smoke from its engine. On the occasions that our train passed through a tunnel, all of the carriages went from bright sunlight into pitch black darkness. Kids of all ages made universal ghost sounds, oooooh..oooOOOH!, with a few ghoulish screams thrown in for extra effect. This 'Ghost Ride' came included free in the ticket price. It was all good fun and brought spontaneous smile to everyone's face when bright daylight and fresh mountain air once again filled the carriages. Our train snaked beneath towering rock cliff faces and on occasions, the tree cover cleared to reveal deep river valleys below us with traditional farming villages and sunny green cultivated fields. Smokey blue mountain tops appeared above the distant jungle cloaked horizon. My spirit soared with the sense of adventure of it all.

As our train pulled into Kandy station a huge castle of dark cloud rose above a steep hill overlooking the small city. The air felt heavy and thick. A silver haired man sitting across from me saw me weather watching and raised his two hands up with fingers outstretched and then dropped them several times as if unto an imaginary piano. He was either highly eccentric or making the universal sign language for heavy rain coming. No sooner had I jumped into an auto rickshaw than the skies darkened overhead and then burst with a torrential downpour. Soon the streets of Kandy were rivers of water as people dashed to and fro along sidewalks seeking out shelter. I had the address and name of a guesthouse called the Pink House. It was run by a woman called Eva who a young couple from back home had recommended I visit. Finding the address, I made a run from the auto-rickshaw to the front porch and was relieved to hear they had a room for me. The rooms were sparse but there was an unmistakably relaxed atmosphere about the place. It was in fact the perfect spot to stop a while. When the rain cleared I took the opportunity to climb a steep road behind my guesthouse to get a better look and perspective of Kandy. Set within a bowl of steep forest clad hills Kandy looked like the most picturesque setting for a small city I had ever seen. The central landmark of the city is a huge lake which was constructed under the orders of an Indian tyrant king called Sri Wickram Rajasinha in 1807. He was the last ruler of the Kingdom of Kandy before the British army finally managed to conquer the area. By all accounts few locals mourned the passing of the king, especially those he made dig out the lake with their bare hands and basic shovels. The guesthouses and hotels were situated on the right side of the lake. Across the lake stretched the awe inspiring Temple of the Tooth Relic, Sri Lanka's holiest Buddhist shrine. Legend has it that a tooth was snatched from the flames of the Buddha's funeral pyre in Northern India in 543 BC. It was supposedly was smuggled into Sri Lanka in the 4th Century AD when the majority of the island's people became Buddhist.

I met Eva for the first time when I returned to the Pink House. She had prepared pots of rice and curried vegetables for all the staying guests and her own daughters and grandchildren. Although in her mid fifties, Eva had retained a youthful essence. She had long dark curly hair with grey strands through it and seemed always close to a mischievous smile and witty comment. There were no formalities with her which was also refreshing. The famous dining room was a long black wooden table and chairs situated in the back garden between kitchen and guest rooms. It had a simple wooden roof to keep the rain off and was a focal point each evening for backpackers and longer term guests to talk and exchange travel stories. At the top of the table as if holding daily court sat Jimmy Gilchrist, a tall lean silver haired man. Jimmy's parents had moved to Zimbabwe from Scotland when he was a young child. He was forced to leave when a young man along with thousands of fellow white farmers with the rise of black nationalism in the country stoked by Robert Mugabe. Jimmy had married in Malaysia and spent a number of years working as an engineer out in Papua New Guinea. At the ripe old age of seventy eight he was still working as an engineer in Malaysia on road building projects for six months of the year and then spent another three month residing at the Pink House, "to keep an eye on my dear Eva", as he put it.

Everyone in Kandy went to bed early and after a wash up I retired to set up my mosquito net. It had become a nightly ritual of finding hooks to tie up the net and then making sure to tuck it carefully underneath the mattress. With lights switched off and safely inside, my final mission each night was to scan the mosquito net interior with the light beam of a small hand torch to search for mosquito intruders or holes in the nets which I tied or taped up. It resembled a scene from the London Blitz with anti aircraft lights searching out enemy bombers circling above. With my hand torch still on I decided to read for a short while from the book the Buddhist priest had given me, entitled 'Why Worry?'. One of the opening paragraphs made the wise pitch that worry is in fact useless. "If we can do something about a situation", it read, 'then why worry and get upset over it – just change it. If there is nothing we can do about a situation, again, why worry and get upset over it? Things will never get better with anger and worry." At around three in the morning I woke up to the sound of monks chanting which was drifting across the lake from the Tooth Temple. I dressed and walked out to the back garden. All was quiet and still. Wisps of silvery cloud sailed across the face of a bright full moon flanked by two tall coconut trees. For a few moments I felt the wonder of gazing up at the moon as a child, my mind quiet and happy to simply enjoy and appreciate the scene.

I had just a few days left before my flight back to India. With one day already spent catching up on emails and washing my laundry I set off for the world heritage rock palace of Sigria, a half day away by bus from Kandy.

The first rule about a limit to passenger numbers on Sri Lanka buses is that there clearly are no limits. In fact it seemed to me that the bus conductor was aiming to smash any existing world record for the greatest amount of people squashed on to one bus. With seats full and people standing three abreast on the passageway, seat passengers were then forced to double up and allow other strangers sit on their knees. Our bus eventually left Kandy with barely a square inch of unoccupied space on board. If someone fainted from the stuffy heat they would simply remain wedged in position. An hour later and passenger numbers were mercifully bearable again. Our bus driver, however, then began passing out traffic at an alarming speed, even overtaking a lorry on a blind bend. Sitting in the front seat as I was, no longer seemed like a good idea. As we were taking off from another roadside bus-stop, a white Toyota van suddenly screeched in front of our bus compelling our driver to slam on the brakes. A large angry Sri Lankan man with fists clenched tightly then jumped out and caught our driver with a glancing punch as he leapt from the bus and set off running down the road at an impressive speed. Half the bus passengers piled out and cross words were exchanged between the clearly irate Toyota van driver and our bus conductor. At the same time another group of men tried to persuading our bus driver to return to his duties. It was over as quick as it began and we set off down the road again, this time at a less frantic speed.

As we approached Sigriya the landscape appeared almost English in nature with large open fields and tree lined hedges. The exception being local farmers here were growing rice in the dry clay ridges and waiting for monsoon rains to arrive.

The sun was setting and I realised it was too late to visit Sigriya today. I met another back-packer on the bus called Michael from Malaysia and together we went in search of overnight accommodation. It was an active education to watch Michael bargaining with the locals for anything from a bread roll to an auto-rickshaw fare. Sometimes the locals stared at him in quiet disbelief at the intensity of his 'rupee pinching'. He said it was due to a super tight travel budget. Although only twenty seven years old, Michael explained how he owned his own small rubber plantation back in Malaysia which was funding his year long 'budget tour of the world'. He had university degrees in both music and finance and had ambitions to be the CEO of a major corporation. He was certainly putting in some invaluable cost cutting training on his travels as a backpacker.

I got a knock on my door the next morning at 6am. Michael had come up with an idea that if we arrived before Sigriya Heritage Park opened we might get in for free and save ourselves a twenty five dollar entrance fee. We hired an accomplice auto-rickshaw driver and set off through the early dawn with a sleepy eyed buzz of adventure. As we drove along deserted red dirt roads through shrub-land forestry, I caught my first glimpse of Sigriya faintly illuminated by the first light of day. It was a truly awe inspiring sight. A towering lump of solid red granite rising majestically almost two hundred metres above the surrounding forest plains. A magnificent palace city was built on its flat summit in the 5th Century while Europe was in the grip of the Dark Ages. Our plans to sneak into Sigriya by means of stealth were thwarted by a massive water-filled mote built around the world heritage site, over one thousand five hundred years ago. It was still effectively keeping out uninvited intruders. "How about we swim across", suggested Michael to our driver. "Not a good idea, snakes and maybe crocodiles in there you see", was the reply from our driver.

In fairness the ticket price proved more than worth it. The path leading to Sigriya passed through a symmetrically planned ancient royal park complete with now empty garden reservoirs which was once fed by an elaborate underground system of aqueducts . Further towards Sigriya, rock gardens and a maze of paths and stone stairways criss-crossed the site. Climbing up a modern metal stairwell, we passed by frescoes depicting beautiful bare-breasted ladies from a millennia and a half ago, who once entertained the king and his courtesans at Sigriya's palace. Shafts of bright golden sunlight climbed along the red granite cliff face above, as we stood in front of the ruins of a guarded staircase. once in the shape of a Lion's mouth and two gigantic paws. The sense of grandeur and wonder that this feature must have created in early visitors to Sigriya can only be imagined. Even today with only its colossal Lion paws remaining it could be easily included as one of the wonders of the world. The Lion was built as the sole gatekeeper to the palace and represented Simha, legendary founder of the Sinhalese race. This lion gives Sigriya its name from *Simha-giri* meaning Lion Mountain.

Only ruins of the palace now remained on the summit of Sigriya but the surrounding views were breathtaking. To the north and west the land stretched off into a seemingly endless horizon. Distant pale blue mountains rose to the south, while to the east, stretched a vast forest park where leopards, wild elephants and even the last bands of aboriginal tribal people called Veddah still hunted. We sat a while with a local tour guide who explained to us the ancient history connected to the site. In the 5th Century AD, a Prince Kasyapa seized power from his Father King Dhatusena and had him executed. Reviled by many for his dastardly deed, he moved the seat of royal power to Sigriya. He then built the impenetrable fortress palace to protect himself from his many enemies. Then after taking all this trouble, he led his army out into open battle in sight of Sigriya. His forces got lost in a swamp and then fled, abandoning Kasyapa to his grizzly fate.

Later in the afternoon I said my farewells to Michael who returned for an afternoon siesta back at the guesthouse. I decided to get some lunch and waited for my bus back to Kandy. Life out in the Sri Lankan countryside still appeared to have a genuinely laid back quality. Outside the café a group of middle aged men took turns playing a board game called Karem using draught like pieces moved with a flick of the fingers. They offered me a chance to play and like most things in life, the game of Karem looked a lot easier as a spectator than as a player. That evening I returned to the Pink House in Kandy and enjoyed a few more evenings of conversation around the dining table and Jimmy's light hearted proposals of marriage to our landlady Eva. On the morning I left for Colombo, I took a final early morning walk around Kandy Lake. Huge trees skirt the lake in a massive leafy crown. Monitor lizards, some seven foot long, basked like miniature dragons along the shore line or on half submerged tree branches. The roof of the Tooth Temple Palace shone a brilliant gold, casting its sun bright refection in the still waters of the lake. For some reason I felt strongly that I would return to Sri Lanka and Kandy before my journey came to an end. For now though, it was time to return to India.

TEMPLE TOURING IN TAMIL NADU

It was a short hour and a half flight back to Trichipalli airport in southern India. Although retracing my footsteps somewhat, the lively culture and big hearted people of Tamil Nadu had drawn me back. Tamil Nadu is the most southerly state in India and home to over sixty-two million people. The Tamil people belong to the older Dravidian culture, the dark skinned original inhabitants of India. The people of Northern India are a mixture of Eurasian and Dravidian ancestry due to successive invasions from Alexander the Great from Macedonia, to Arab Emperors from Iran and the Middle East. I also wanted to visit the Hindu Temples of Tamil Nadu, many of which are listed as World Heritage sites. It seemed a little strange when I stopped to consider that one of the main attractions for visitors to India are its temples. On another level temple touring in India seemed symbolic. There is an indescribable spiritual energy in India. It seems too emanate from the personalised Hindu religion of its people and out of the very earth and landscapes.

Our plane landed in Trichipalli just before midday. The sky was a bright canvass of cotton wool clouds and cheerful indigo blue sky gaps. From the arrivals area I could already feel the heightened atmosphere of India waiting to be experienced. Collecting my luggage, I walked out the front entrance in the hope of finding a bus. Instead I found myself faced by at a gang of taxi and auto rickshaw drivers lined up across the car park. It was like a re-shot scene from the famous Western, 'High Noon'. I had been the only Westerner on the flight. An invisible golden dollar sign must have lit up above my head for suddenly about ten drivers started to run towards me shouting "where you going?" and "I give you good price into city." Suddenly feeling more like an actor in a Monty Python sketch I set off running across the airport car-park with travel bags hanging at the end of each arm. I raced through a a gap in a construction site wire fence followed in hot pursuit by several surprised taxi men shouting, "come back, you are are going the wrong way!"

I got a bus into Trichipalli city centre and began looking for a bus to Thanjavur. With the thought of my stay at the nearby hotel where I had the phantom visitation ordeal, still fresh in my memory, I was prepared to take a bus anywhere before sunset. As luck would have it, I managed to find a bus going to Thanjavur and sat next to a shaven head pilgrim with no English, who insisted on minding one of my travel bags on his lap. After a stressful hour spent accommodation hunting, I found a comfortable hotel room for two hundred rupees or four euros per night.

The following day was spent visiting the Thanjavur Royal Palace and museums. The main museum had a musty smell and colonial old world feeling. Many of the paintings, old books and oddities on display were from Europe. These were presents bought or gifted to the Raja Serfoji. Thousands of ancient books and manuscripts were displayed in an adjoining library once owned by the Raja. Nowadays, scholars and students from all over Tamil Nadu came to read and study here. The local rulers had made Thanjavur an ancient centre of learning, which revealed the cultural depth of India for a millennia or more before Europe's colonial arrival. The Royal Palace dated back to the 16th Century. The Palace Temple was a technicolor wonderland. Huge hexagonal shaped stone pillars were painted in long strips of bright orange, yellow, red and purple. The ornately carved back wall and ceiling was bursting with colours from claret to sky blue and sunshine yellow to lemon green. This ancient culture seemed to understand the positive effect that colours can have on raising our spirits and healing our minds.

As I walked across the central courtyard I was encircled and almost mobbed by a large group of smiling kids on a school tour who implored me to take their group photo. Agreeing to their demand turned out to be an unwise idea as more and more kids seemed to pour out of adjoining galleries and museums. I was saved by a burly walrus-moustached security guard who let me out via a side door exit. On the way back down the street I encountered my first Indian back-packer. It was a strange and awkward cultural experience. He was an Indian guy in his early twenties and wore large dark wrap-around sunglasses. He was also decked out in western outdoor clothing and the essential backpack strapped around his shoulders. As he passed, he asked in perfect English was he going the right way to the Royal Palace. In slight confusion, I simply said "yeah, yeah, straight ahead". It was a reminder that India is in rapid change and a new generation of confident affluent young people feel as much an affinity to Western popular culture as they do to their own.

The next morning I rose before dawn and visited the Bridahishwara Temple complex. I arrived just as the new day sun bathed the sandstone temple walls in soft reddish light. At the entrance, I passed a large temple elephant who patted me on the head with his trunk as a special blessing, after I handed his keeper a few rupees in change. Built by a Chola Raja (king), in 1010AD, a magnificent eighty tonne golden dome had been placed atop a towering seven storey high main temple. In days long before modern cranes, the temple engineers constructed a four kilometre long spiral earthen ramp using the local farming population as labourers. Teams of oxen and elephants then hauled the massive dome up into position before the huge earthen rampart was removed by sheer manpower. Nowadays the Bridahishwara Temple is an important destination for hundreds of thousands of Hindu pilgrims each year.

From Thanjavur I took a train to the temple city of Madurai. Again I travelled by passenger class as the train was almost booked up. No matter what carriage class you travel in India it is compulsory to fill out a lengthy form including your personal details, exact destination, name of train and time of departure. There is nothing luxurious about travelling passenger class, but it's very cheap and it seemed to me a great place to meet people. On this journey I was fortunate to meet a great character called Maharajan. He sat cross legged on his wooden seat and wore a white shirt and *lungee* or traditional wrap around skirt for men. Two bright and age wizened eyes looked at me studiously from a lean face with dark Tamil complexion and a full head of white hair. He shook my hand and introduced himself in perfect English with a Tamil accent. "You know my name is Maharajan which means Great King. I was born before India got her independence from Britain in 1948. My mother could not have known then that it would not be such a popular name in the newly democratic India", he said with a disarming laugh. We shared a juicy orange and hours of conversation which helped greatly to shorten the sweltering five hour train journey. I asked Maharajan his age to which he replied, "I am sixty eight years of age and have been retired now from business for three years. I have a very good yoga guru and practice breathing meditation and yoga stretches every morning. My yoga guru is many years older than me but many times more flexible! It is very good for the body and mind and I now follow a strict diet recommended by my guru. We are very fortunate in India to have such teachers."

He asked me where I was from and if I was married which is a standard conversational question asked by all Indian men. He continued, "I now enjoy reading in my spare time and have read James Joyce 'Ulysses' and 'The Dubliners'. James Joyce was a great Irish writer was he not?"

I then asked Maharajan about where he was from.

"I am from Madurai and now live with my son and his family. I am glad that he has taken over the business which is a car hire company. You see in India it is a custom that one's family takes care of their parents when they get older as there is no pension or retirement plans as you have in the West."

His wise advice to me on my journey was, "be thankful for your blessings and be grateful for what you have," and then wrote on the back of my journal in neat print writing;

3 things which cannot be returned:
A spent arrow shot in anger
A neglected opportunity
Words unwisely spoken.

I promised to send Maharajan the gift of a book by an Irish
writer when I returned home and he gave me his blessings with
the words, "a safe journey and a good wife for you", as we arrived at Madurai station.

My guide-book explained that Madurai is a bustling market town and textile centre as well as a popular destination for
Indian pilgrims and foreign visitors. The main attraction is the
magnificent World Heritage listed Meenaskri Temple complex
built in the heart of the city. While in Madurai I visited the Mahatma Gandhi Museum which is kept open by a trust of community elders who are devoted to keeping Gandhi's spirit alive
in 21st Century India. The museum included information boards
charting Gandhi's life and modern India's rebirth as well. A
large, dusty glass cabinet contained all his worldly possessions
at the time of his assassination which included a blood stained
loin-cloth, walking stick and a pair of glasses. While working
back in Ireland with Community Creations we had chosen as
our unofficial mission statement a quote from Gandhi, "be the
change you wish to create in the world", a simple yet powerful
piece of advice to guide our actions.

Gandhi's peaceful pro-Indian democracy walks were to
eventually force the British Empire to grant India independence
without its people having to resort to a bloody armed rebel-
lion. Unfortunately Hindu and Muslim nationalists then ignited
a bloody religious conflict which cost the lives of hundreds of
thousands of people. It also led to the partition of old India into
the break-away Muslim controlled states of Bangladesh and Pakistan and a new majority Hindu state of India.

After visiting the exhibition I had the good fortune to meet
Mr K.M. Matharajan. He was tall grey haired man of noble
stature and wore a matching bright white shirt and *lungee*. I
guessed that his age as being in his late seventies. The museum
curator had informed me in hushed tones that as a young man
Mr Matharajan had walked alongside Gandhi on one of his famous *Satyagraha* civil disobedience marches. They had walked
through Southern India to the Indian Ocean to make sea salt
in the traditional custom which had been forbidden under Brit-

ish economic law at the time. Many were beaten and arrested along the way, but their hugely symbolic walks were to rock British Imperial rule in India to its very foundations. Mr Matharajan offered me tea and spoke with a thoughtful energy in his voice when I asked him about Gandhi and his legacy and relevance to modern India. Leaning back in his office desk seat, he started by sharing with me a personal story about Gandhi. "When India finally gained independence, Gandhi was invited to New Delhi to meet Prime Minister Nehru. Gandhi hitched a ride from the train station with a farmer driving a bullock cart. They were stopped several times by traffic police along the way and the farmer was verbally hassled each time. When Gandhi finally reached Government buildings he asked Nehru to explain why the bullock driver was stopped and hassled so many times. Nehru tried explaining that due to road developments and an increase in truck and bus traffic, bullock carts were now a danger on the busy streets. Gandhi paused for a few moments and then replied, "surely one should restrict the danger and not it's victims." He paused a moment before adding, "you see, Gandhi did not swallow our modern servile acceptance of all things labelled as progress."

Mr Matharajan paused again while twisting a pen between his hands and then with a growing passion in his voice added, "farmers have been the backbone of India for thousands of years but many are now being driven to desperation. Many farmers were offered loans to modernise their farms, loans that banks knew they could never have hoped to pay back. Some farmers in India have become so poor due to globalisation that they can't even afford to buy rice for their families. In India, rice is subsidised to five rupees a kilo, less than ten pence in your money. More mechanisation and intensive use of fertilisers is using up more precious resources and oil to produce food and is damaging the environment. Oxen could still do the work and the natural fuel crops they consume could be recycled back into the earth as natural fertilisers. Gandhi knew all this. He realised that self sufficiency is the real freedom."

Evening sunlight streamed in through the tall narrow office windows as Mr Matharajan leaned forward on his desk chair before continuing, "the world is changing quite rapidly and India is also changing. There has always been change from one generation to the next but quite frankly I am very sceptical about consumer culture and its impact on society and our natural environment. I do not believe that we should exploit anything from the earth that we cannot renew. As I grow older I now see so much more clearly. We should become trustees for future generations rather than robbing them of precious natural resources such as safe drinking water, clean air and freshly grown wholesome foods."

As I left Mr Matharajan's office and set off through Madurai's busy streets to my hotel room I felt conflicting emotions welling up inside. I felt fortunate and inspired to have met with Mr Matharajan but at the same time saddened at what I had heard and apprehensive, not only for India's future but that of our planet as a whole. Over the next few weeks I began to see that my own ideas needed to change. Connecting back with ancestral wisdom would not benefit society or individuals alone unless we also adapted new ways to connect back to the environment, to the earth and somehow ultimately within ourselves.

My hotel room in Madurai was located on the top floor of a massive budget hotel complex. From my balcony I looked across at a lime green ornamented minaret belonging to a Muslim mosque. In the distance, the wide blocky buildings of Madurai Junction train station stretched out below me. Whatever material the hotel roof was made of, it trapped the daytime heat to an impressive degree. My nights were spent being slowly baked alive in a stifling sweat box. Lying naked on a sheet, I felt like Paul Newman in the movie 'Cool Hand Luke' when he is thrown into the tin-roof oven type punishment cell. This feeling was amplified by the fact that the windows on my hotel room also had iron bars to deter thieves from the outside. The few hours of sleep I snatched before dawn were regularly interrupted by a man singing the praises of Allah from loudspeakers fixed to the nearby minaret. He was calling the Muslim faithful of Madurai to morning prayer. Despite the unwelcome dawn alarm call, the chant to Allah was hauntingly beautiful. The singer carried his voice up with the first part of All-ah and then held the second 'ah' part in a continuous heart seeking note until it slowly faded from his voice like a wave returning to the ocean.

The city of Madurai has been an important centre of trade, culture, learning and poetry, dating back to the 4th Century BC. It was in this ancient city that the modern Tamil language was developed, now regarded as one of the oldest surviving languages in Asia. The famous Sri Meenaskri temples of Madurai were built in the 1600's which is kind of recent as Indian history goes. It is difficult to describe just how visibly 'out of this world' the temples are. Eight tall towers some fifty metres high, reach into the Madurai skyline and are decorated from top to bottom with literally thousands of multi-coloured clay and stone figurines about two feet high. The beautiful figurines depict stunning princesses, dreamlike gods, temple priests, round wasted merchants, haughty Raja kings and hundreds of other real and imaginary characters from Indian life at that time are. All were still awash with bright techni-colours. It looked in ways like some psychedelic architectural experiment an artist from 1960's America had dreamed up after taking a mind-blowing acid trip. This was no personal counter-cultural statement however. Instead it was part of mainstream religious art in 17th Century India. These temples were among the most holiest and most revered in Hindu India. They had been built by the finest artists and craftsmen of the day and sanctioned by the elite class who ruled back then. Now I began to understand why so many Tamil people, regardless of circumstances and background, seemed so ready to smile and be happy. Their culture and places of worship seemed to encourage them to be 'high on life and live daily life in spirit'.

People flocked from all over India on trains and buses to visit the Sri Meenaskri temples and at times it was dizzying to walk the ancient narrow streets heaving with people. On the day before I left I saw a colourful procession of over two hundred Hari Krishna followers mainly from Europe and North America, perform in the main temple in Madurai. One young polish woman who has been learning traditional Indian dancing for fifteen years amazed the crowds of Indian pilgrims who came to watch her. The Hari Krishna's worship one Hindu God called Krishna, while 'Hari' means God. The majority of Hindus on the other hand have around three hundred and thirty million deities and Gods to choose from although there are four or five main Gods that everyone knows. I was informed by a local pilgrim that it is not uncommon for every member of a household to have separate preferences as to which main Hindu God they pray to. If that doesn't sound confusing enough there are also 'specialist' Gods they call on for performing such tasks as mending a roof, bringing in the harvest or even fetching water. Ultimately though, as in most major religions on the planet, Hindus believe in one ultimate God source.

On my final evening in Madurai I found an internet café to check my emails from home. Before I had left for India a few friends had urged me to send group emails back every few weeks so as to share travel stories and experiences. After some initial resistance to this idea I decided to type up an email every fortnight and send it to friends and family on my email address list. I got a big surprise upon reading an email from my sister Donna. She congratulated me and informed me that she read one of my travelogues in the Donegal Democrat the previous week. Someone on my email list had forwarded my travelogue to Michael Daly. From the many positive comments received, I decided to continue writing a regular journal.

Another email had arrived from John Ahern informing me that he and Maria were having a terrific honeymoon, touring the sights and beach resorts of Sri Lanka. He had also sent me a link to the Kopan Meditation Centre website. A few clicks later and a programme of events for visitors came up on the computer screen. A ten day introductory course was starting on the 6th of April and a few places were still available. That gave me just under three weeks to travel three thousand miles from Madurai in the far south of India to Katmandu in Nepal. Taking a credit card from my money belt and with a renewed sense of adventure I booked myself a place on the course and decided to get back on the journey trail.

MALAKAR'S HERBAL WHISKEY

My next destination was the town of Kollam in the state of Kerala, directly west of Tamil Nadu. There was a palpable buzz of excitement on the train platform at Madurai the following afternoon. The entourage of Hari Krishna followers who had been performing over the weekend were evidently waiting for the same train. Some sat around singing and playing hand drums on the platform. Some followers handed out Hari Krishna leaflets, while others kept an eye on piles of luggage and instruments. Indian passengers watched on with pleasant amusement as our train arrived and screeched slowly to a halt. It was going to be passenger class for me yet again, only this time a longer ten hour journey. My fellow Hari Krishna travellers were evidently much better organised and had booked first class carriages, with air conditioning. I consoled myself with the fact that my train ticket cost me only ninety eight rupees or just under two euros. One of the fun things about travelling passenger class is you can get to sit in the open doorways of the carriages with your legs resting on the steps and feeling a fleeting part of the passing countryside. This is how I passed the evening hours, watching the flat dusty thorn shrub countryside of Tamil Nadu go by as the sun set like a Martian red globe on the Western horizon.

Later in the journey we were to receive some unexpected guests on board. As our train rattled through the pitch dark Indian countryside our carriage was suddenly and unexpectedly filled with a blizzard of tiny white moths. People clambered to draw down the train windows but it was too late. The moths soon covered everything including little sari cloaked princesses who shrieked as amused relatives bundled them up under blankets. After the initial commotion our carriage settled down, and both moths and people alike drifted off into slumber.

Hours later I woke up to find not only did everyone in the train look different but they were also speaking a different language, Malayalam. I was now in the South-western Indian state of Kerala. The people were light brown skinned rather than black and in facial appearance looked more European. At the next stop, a squad of late shift construction workers boarded the train, laughing and teasing each other in their language. Two men and a young fellow sat down next to me. Sure enough, it wasn't long before they started singing Keralan folk songs. Their songs sounded sort of Arabic and as if every note was being dragged and squeezed from their hearts. Both men were 'contesting' each other, singing song for song. They also had a strange hand movement dance which they did as they sang. It looked like they were slowly playing an invisible violin and cradling a baby back and forth in their arms at the same time. When I tried copying their singing and hand dance movements the fun really got going. They then asked me to sing. Half way through the first verse of 'The Homes of Donegal' which is a slow Irish ballad I knew I was losing my audience rapidly. Forced to think quickly, I remembered an Irish song we learned in national school called *'Beidh Aonach Amarach i gContae an Clár*. This song had a far faster livelier rhythm which others could clap along to as it was sung. As I performed my theatrical farewells and disembarked at the next station, my newly made Keralan friends were singing the chorus out the window to me.

Kollam was a busy and not so picturesque town. I had chosen the town as a base to explore Kerala's famous 'Backwaters', a large low lying area of inland rivers, lakes and canals. It was late night and I was glad I had booked cheap and cheerful accommodation in advance. My state run hostel was situated on a lake shore opposite the town.

I was wakened suddenly at dawn, this time by Keralan singing that carried across the lake on loudspeakers from a far shore temple. After the fun on last night's train I began wondering whether Kerala was some kind of singing Mecca. The receptionist informed me the singing and music was part of a week long religious and cultural Devi festival.

Kerala has a tropical climate similar to Sri Lanka's. If you were to take a small plane trip over the region you would see an almost continuous cover of lush coconut palm trees and deep blue waterways. The region is also famous for its spicy fish dishes, cashew nuts and fresh fruit. Kerala has had contact with the Arab world and European traders for over a millennium and its rich abundance in natural resources was well known to both the Greek and Roman civilisations.

After a day spent wandering the streets and markets of Kollam, I decided to take a canal tour on the Waterways. I joined a group of German medical students who had spent a month volunteering at a Cancer hospital in upstate Kerala. Being a tourist party of eight people, we were divided up and directed on board two shallow-bottomed canoe like boats. We were to be shown the smaller canal systems which link country neighbourhoods along the Backwaters. A local boatman stood at the bow. He propelled and steered us along with a fifteen foot wooden pole similar to those used by the Gondoliers of Venice, but without any fancy costume. It was a truly magical experience, as our traditional style canoe glided silently through the winding canals beneath the shaded banks of coconut trees. As well as providing shelter from the hot tropical sun, the roots of the coconut trees help keep the narrow mud banks together during the monsoon flood season. Birdsong replaced the drone of cars and other mechanical engines. Around every bend in the waterway, there seemed to be a new enchanting scene waiting to be enjoyed. We passed by a young brother and sister playing on a tied canoe next to a homestead almost camouflaged by trees. Further on, we had to carefully navigate past a bemused looking cow standing in waist-high water and tethered to the bank. Our tour stopped along the way to watch older villagers making rope from the hairy fibres of small brown coconuts. At another site visit, we were shown how the same type of coconuts were used to make oil in the traditional manner for lamps and cooking. Back on a winding stretch of canal, we began hearing the whoops and hollers of men growing closer. The boatmen nudged our canoes towards the left side bank as a group of fishermen paddled swiftly past us on their way to open water. What an excellent way to navigate I thought as the whoops and calls of the fishermen faded slowly out of our hearing range again.

On the way back to our hotel one of the German girls complained to me that the canal tour was not what she expected. She seemed deeply upset and in genuine bad form as if she was somehow cheated by the tour organisers. The conversation got me thinking afterwards as I walked into Kollam town how two people can go on the same journey and one feel miserable while the other joy. I reflected upon times in the past when I felt miserable and wondered what was actually separating me from being happy.

It was now late March and the sub-continent of India was beginning to heat up uncomfortably with daytime temperatures in the mid-thirties Celsius. The humidity was quiet high in Kerala and I felt myself coming down with some kind of sinus and flu type illness. From Kollam I took a five hour bus journey upstate to the town of Allepy. Built along a main canal artery, Allepy is the starting point for many tourists wishing to explore the picturesque Backwaters. Boat vessels lined up for hire along the water front, ranging from half day waterbus tours to luxury cruisers with thatched roofs complete with captain, cook and waiting staff. Local people with bags of shopping cued patiently behind a brown rusty iron bridge for state run water buses, as many outlying villages and country areas are unreachable by road.

After finding guesthouse accommodation for the night I decided to venture out for a late evening walk. As in Sri Lanka, there is no twilight after sun set due to southern India's proximity to the equator. Night and daytime are held in almost equal balance throughout the year. By sheer coincidence I came across a procession of almost two hundred Sari clad women walking gracefully in two lines through a quiet street. In their right hand they each carried a small tea light candle and as they walked, they softly chanted a song in honour of a Hindu Goddess Devi. It was a truly enchanting spectacle. The procession and street was lit by a halogen light and a generator strapped to a bicycle drawn cart. This in turn was wheeled and directed by two Indian boys. I followed the procession at a respectful distance, until it passed over a canal bridge and watched as the candle flames reflected and danced on the calm dark waters flowing beneath.

Later that night I developed a chesty cough and in the growing humidity, felt my sinuses and lungs filling with fluid. Dragging myself out of bed the next morning I walked with into town to find a pharmacy. My legs felt as heavy as lead and every step was an effort. After explaining my symptoms to a serious faced pharmacist he gave his rapid three word prognosis, "climatic variation problem", then dished me out twelve tablets and a bottle of cough mixture. As he seemed quite confident I was going to live, I deciding not to press my own concerns or his clearly limited patience. Instead, I duly paid up for my medicines and returned to my guesthouse bed.

After a full days rest I boarded a bus from Allepy going north to Kochi city and then took a ferry across to Kochi Island. Now a bustling city of over a million people, Kochi was the site for the first European colonial settlement in India founded back in 1503 when the Portuguese sailed in and ruled until 1663. It was then occupied by the Dutch for a short time before coming under control of the British empire. Nowadays Kochi is home to a busy commercial deep-water seaport and a large Indian naval base. It is also a popular year round tourist destination for luxury cruise-ship passengers. Whatever historical character or local sense of charm Kochi once possessed, seemed to be totally sucked dry by the huge daily number of visitors to the island and my overnight stay there was less than memorable.

The following day I managed to get a late afternoon bus from Kochi to Calicut in the northern part of Kerala state. My plan was to book a flight the following day to Mumbai and from there, continue my journey by train and bus. I now had just under two weeks to reach Katmandu and start the meditation course. On the bus to Calicut I met a young Indian movie producer called Charlie. He introduced himself in novel terms as currently married with three girlfriends. Charlie was of small lean build and no more than thirty five years old. Despite the stifling heat, he wore a woollen Chicago Bulls cap over his head and sported a designer beard and moustache. He had an air of likeable mischief about him which he backed up with rapid fire African-American style English. After initial introductions and overly enthusiastic offers for me to direct an Irish-themed Hindi movie, Charlie fell into a temporary coma-like deep sleep. Perhaps he was telling the truth about his exhausting love life. Considering how much our bus shook and jerked about on the crater-laden roads, sleep seemed to me an almost impossible feat. Charlie miraculously came back to life just as our bus arrived at Calicut bus terminal. He offered to help me find a city centre budget hotel for the night which I gladly accepted. "You've got to meet my friend Malakar, man", he said along the way. "He lives up in the hills a few hours from here and a friend will take us tomorrow. Get yourself a good night sleep and I'll collect you at one tomorrow afternoon, right". I didn't even get a chance to explain my plans to book a flight to Mumbai tomorrow. Charlie was already away out the door, talking in soft apologetic tones to one of his girlfriends on the phone.

Charlie arrived back at one the following afternoon but seemed a little troubled about something. Conversation was scarce as we walked to the bus station.. I guessed it was family trouble, but didn't want to pry. All he would say is that we were heading up into the mountains to meet some good friends. It was yet another hot and humid day in Kerala as we stood around waiting on a bus. After about an hour on a packed rickety bus we stopped at a station and waited for Charlie's friend Saif, (pronounced Sayeef), to pick us up in his car. Saif was a tall slim smartly dressed fellow of 23 years and like Charlie a member of the Muslim faith. He drove a brand new compact black Mitsubishi car. It felt like the lap of luxury, especially with the air conditioning on. Saif had got a half day off from the ICC international insurance company in Calicut where he worked as a broker. We soon got into an interesting conversation and I asked him what he saw as some of the positive and negative impacts of globalisation in India. "Me personally, I am the first person in my neighbourhood to be able to afford to buy a car. This is a direct result of the career opportunities which became available to me when the insurance market in India was deregulated. A negative consequence of globalisation is that road repairs and surfacing is now sub-contracted out to private road contractors. They cut costs on road fill and even tar. The roads have got very bad and are wrecking my good car." We drove through an area of lush coconut trees and forest. It became almost impossible to spot the electricity poles or brightly coloured mud brick houses peering out from behind high earthen banks. Soon we were climbing up steep hair-pin mountain bends while deep mountain valleys cloaked in bright green forests began stretching out below us. Saif then turned the car air-conditioning off and automatically wound down the windows. We collectively breathed in the sweet fresh mountain air. It was an indescribable relief from the oppressive heat and humidity of just a few hours ago. After stopping off to buy beers at a Government run off-licence, our next stop was a chicken farm where Charlie and Saif picked out supper. As part of Islamic law people of Muslim faith may only eat meat from animals that has been killed by 'Halal' methods. This entails the throat being swiftly slit with a knife and its blood drained before the meat is considered clean to eat. Born to the supermarket generation and removed from the cruel realities of farming I sat in the backseat of the car rather than watch this ritual slaughter. Moments later the backdoor opened and a limp freshly killed chicken wrapped in plastic, landed in the seat beside me.

Saif and Charlie jumped back into the car and we drove for another few miles before turning off up unto a steeply winding narrow dirt track. We stopped at the front yard of a mountainside farm-house. Malakar our host was standing at the door dressed in a white shirt, orange lungi and sandals with large arms outstretched to us as we pulled up.

"You are very welcome my good friends", he proclaimed and then embraced the air out of my lungs with a bear hug. Malakar was a truly larger than like character with a broad beaming face, large brown moustache and hair combed back and standing slightly upright. Trained as a scientist he had worked abroad in the Gulf States for many years before returning to his native

Kerala. He had bought a farm of land in the mountains and decided to turn his efforts to growing herbs for medicinal healing and his gardens were full of exotic looking plants and flowers. Turning to Charlie he said, "I wish you had been here a few hours ago Charlie, you should have seen it. The newspaper journalists came up from Calicut to photograph a very rare Sunyita lotus flower in my garden that I rang to tell them about. It is the first of its kind to bloom this year. Come quick and I will show you." The sun had set a brilliant crimson red far off to the west and rafts of mist began forming over the forested valleys stretched out below us. Sounds also carried up from a nearby village in the brief dusky light. A small child called out, a dog barked, the high pitched voice of a woman sang from some radio, a motorbike started up with a splutter and rev.

We followed Malakar over to a small garden pond. Rising up from a patch of sea green lotus leafs was a white lotus flower attached to a long tall slender stem. Its petals were closed and bunched up. "It is too late, she is going to sleep now but tomorrow morning she will reveal herself once again," Malakar informed as he cupped the lotus flower gently between his hands and gave it a kiss.

A young boy then suddenly appeared on the street and after receiving instructions from Malakar in Malayalam, ran back down the lane with the plastic bag containing the chicken. We took seats and a table out unto the front street and beer bottles were taken from a bucket of cold water and opened. As darkness fell, Malakar's solar powered porch light came on. From snippets of conversations I gathered that Saif and Charlie were involved with Malakar in a business venture to build a small eco-friendly guest house for tourists. They were also involved in a local charitable trust to gather and preserve local herbal medicinal lore. Charlie did a lot of the talking while Malakar did a lot of laughing. He had a wheezy high pitched laugh which added a general hilarity to most of our conversations. On one occasion he disappeared inside his house and re-appeared with a pottery jug in one hand. "As my guests you must try some of Malakar's finest herbal whiskey. I brew this only for medicinal and social purposes", he added as his body shook with laughter once again. "It is guaranteed not to cause hangovers so please drink up." A local woman in a head scarf then arrived on the street carrying a plate with our chicken supper cooked up in spicy sauces.

As we sat and ate heartily I asked Malakar to explain to me some of the core beliefs and practices of Islam and the Muslim religion. He chewed on a piece of chicken as if collecting his thoughts for a few moments before answering. "The main reason that Muslims pray five times a day is that we believe it brings meaning to our everyday lives. Otherwise we would be falling through life from one day to the next as if in a dream. Our daily call to prayers are our daily call back to reality and the spiritual meaning of our lives. The holy month of Ramadan is a time for us to abstain from food between sunrise and sunset. By fasting it also serves as a means to cleanse and strengthen the body's immune system and encourages our devotion to prayer."

I also got a fascinating insight into the Keralan culture and economy. Saif informed me that his father was working in the Arab Emirates as were millions of other Keralans. It seems that Keralan people have been trading with and working in the Middle East for many centuries. Like Ireland was up until the 1990's, the Keralan economy is still dependant on economic emigration and remittance money sent back to support families. "When I get enough money together and a work visa", Saif said, "I will join my father and uncles there too."

We sat, talked, drank, sang and laughed until after midnight when the solar powered street light went out. I felt my head clearing in the high fresh air and it was a real relief not to worry about mosquitoes biting at this high cool altitude. The rooms were sparsely furnished but as a guest I was given one of the beds. As I settled down to sleep I thought that these people certainly didn't match up to my ideas or perceptions of suspicious 'Western hating' Muslims often portrayed in the Western media. The next morning I put the question to Saif that since the September 11ᵗʰ attacks, most of the reporting on Muslim matters in the Western Media has been to do with Islamic extremism. His reply was surprisingly philosophical. "This might be true but our media in India is also biased to serve its own interests. Every government and organisation has its own particular agenda. People should know that truth is a personal journey. After all you have come here and met us and can now make up your own mind." Saif paused for a moment as if collecting his thoughts into one definitive quote for me. "Knowledge with self respect and understanding is the only true progress, then you can learn to open your ears and listen to what the other person is really expressing."

Before we left the next morning Malakar took us for a short tour of his herbal garden or 'natural laboratory' as he liked to call it. Every plant and flower he showed us seemed to be a cure or treatment for one ailment or another. He had a natural passion and connection to his work. Malakar posed for a photograph by his prized lotus flower before we left. Bathed in the first bright rays of morning sunshine the lotus began unravelling its gift of brilliant white petal radiance to a new day. The return journey with Saif and Charlie back down to the sweltering lowlands was a lot more quiet as last nights revelry began to take its toll. As we said our farewells back in Calicut I thanked both of them for bringing me on such a special trip to see Malakar in the mountains. As they drove off, Charlie shouted out the passenger side window, "hey man, don't forget, we got to make that movie someday."

My immediate mission back in Calicut was to book a flight to Mumbai which cost me less than fifty dollars. On the way back to the hotel I decided to buy a traditional South Indian orange and gold *lungee*. It's difficult to describe the relief in a humid tropical climate of changing out of a pair of western style trousers and boxer shorts into a two metre length wrap around light cotton cloth which is then tied with a double knot at the belly button. Let's just say that it was a truly liberating experience for the lower regions. As I walked down a busy city street in my shirt, *lungee* and sandals, I thought to myself, the Scots had the right idea in holding on to the kilts as a traditional man's dress. It was a sad day indeed when gallant free-thinking

Irishmen were finally consigned to the tight constraints of modern trousers and sweaty shoes.

As well as being a land of coconut trees and religious tolerance, Kerala also has a strong tradition of electing socialist political parties to Government. One of the results of this is that the state of Kerala has the highest percentage of people who are able to read and write in all of India, as well as a comprehensive, free health service. Although free market globalisation is bringing pressure to bear on Kerala to privatise more services there is still a level of principled opposition to profit focused governance. One example is that Kerala continues to ban all Coca Cola drinks from been sold in the state. This is a result of a dispute in which the Government discovered that Coca Cola factories were secretly sucking dry the wells of rural farming communities to manufacture their soft drinks and also sell on bottled water. The Keralan Government ordered Coca Cola to shut down their factories immediately and have continued to ban their drinks until a compensation deal for local farmers is agreed upon. Keralan officials showed backbone in standing up to corporate greed.

Before leaving Calicut and Kerala I paid a visit to a small Catholic chapel in the city centre which Saif and Charlie had recommended to me. As we had driven past it in Saif's car, I was informed that the chapel was not only popular with Christians but Muslims and Hindus as well, especially on a Friday. On this day if you light a candle by the altar and make a wish, it is believed you will find true love. Of course it was my luck that I had to be leaving on a pre-booked Thursday morning flight to Mumbai.

I was developing a great admiration for the religious tolerance and worldly awareness of the people of India who seem relaxed rather than threatened about living in a multi-religious and multi-cultural society. This great diversity of religions and spiritual practices has served only to invigorate and renew Indian culture. To give an example, there three different Catholic traditions alone in Kerala, made up of Syrian, Roman and New Life Catholic churches. My next stop was the mega-city of Mumbai, formerly known as Bombay. From there, I planned to take a train up into the high hot dusty heartland of India known as the Deccan Plateau.

Into the Heart of India

Mumbai is the centre of India's Bollywood's film industry and a booming international financial centre. Despite its reputation as a must-see destination, within two hours of setting foot in the place, I knew I had to take the 'high road' out of it. This in itself proved quite a stressful challenge. With a population of over fourteen million people, every square metre of space in downtown Mumbai seemed crowded with people. A hot midday sun, smothering humidity and a hanging haze of air pollution, only added to my sense of urgency to exit.

I joined a cue of about five hundred people at a branch line station to get a ticket to the main train terminal. Everyone cued in long rows around a roofless courtyard. A steady trickle of sweat began running down my back with the relentless heat. Thankfully there were ten ticket counters open to keep the cue moving along at a bearable pace. The next challenge was to try and actually get on a train. The first few trains were so packed that men literally held unto iron hand rails outside the passenger carriage doorways. Eventually with travel bags securely fastened I plucked up the resolve to try and get on one of the trains that stopped at the platform. I ended up ploughing through a crowded carriage doorway, propelled forward by a surge of commuters behind me.

Upon arriving at Mumbai's main train station, my next mission was to find a toilet to answer the call of nature. This involved once again strapping my backpack and travel bags to myself before navigating my way into the foulest smelling latrine I had ever experienced. Giant black cockroaches skated across a urine soaked floor playing chicken with those who dared enter their diabolical domain. Forcing myself to take a glance into a squat toilet cubicle I thanked my lucky stars I hadn't any more pressing business to attend do.

I managed to get a last minute passenger class ticket to the state of Maharashtra. I sat sweating in a sauna-like carriage waiting for the train to move out of the station and create some fresh air. From my open carriage window I watched in quiet disbelief as our train slowly passed by mile upon mile of Mumbai's sprawling slums. These were vast townships of mud, timber and brick shacks, seemingly piled up on top of each other. Corrugated iron roofs reflected molten bright under a relentless afternoon sun. Herds of goat and water buffalo wandered across broken wasteland, rubbish tips and barren ridges, beneath which stinking streams and rivers flowed like open sewers. Millions of surviving, aspiring, coping people lived and made an existence in these slums. Mortgage interest rates, foreign holidays and the Dow Jones Index of Irish shares, were concerns from another planet.

For hours our train trundled and clattered up into the Deccan Plateau, India's massive central highlands. We began climbing up rain-parched forested valleys. It seemed as if some unseen giant had taken a blow torch to this dusty hill-country and twice daily scorched the already rain starved landscape. Some woodlands were charcoal blackened from past blazes while smoky grass-fires smouldered in places close to the rail tracks. The land would have to endure another three months of intensifying heat before the monsoon rains finally arrived.

As our train reached the Deccan Plateau, the land changed to arid open grass and shrub-land, with mysterious canyon like mountains rising steeply from the high plains. From the steps of my train carriage door I watched the sun set behind a striking table top mountain. For a moment the sun's corona seemed to explode like a ruby red super nova before it sank behind the mountain bringing its sharp timeless contours into shadowed but vivid focus.

Later that night I got off at what I thought was Jalgaon station. I had pre-booked a room in a nearby hotel from a pay phone in Mumbai. As I passed a line of auto-rickshaw drivers, noisily touting for business I turned around and shouted, "I don't need an auto-rickshaw, I am perfectly happy to walk to the Plaza hotel." After a short puzzled silence they collectively broke into near hysterical laughter. It was now my turn to stand in puzzled silence. One of the auto rickshaw driver then piped up, "this is Chalisgaon not Jalgaon, you are more than walking distance from Plaza hotel, I'm afraid". This sent them all in fits of laughter once again. Tired, hungry and bemused I walked off towards the lights of a local pharmacy shop counter to look for directions. The pharmacy owner was a tall broad shouldered Indian man in his early thirties. He introduced himself as Subash and invited to help me get another train but first insisted I have tea. Minutes later I was sitting behind a brightly lit pharmacy counter trying to show interest in a World Cup cricket match played out on the TV set. At this stage, word had spread through the village about the Western backpacker who got off at the wrong station. Groups of teenage boys gathered at the counter with laughs primed and urged their cheekiest spokesperson to pipe up, "hello, hello, how are you? where are you going?... this is Chalisgaon!"

Thankfully, Subash soon closed the pharmacy for the night. I helped him pull down and lock the metal shutters to his shop, before he insisted on bringing me to a local Chinese restaurant for a meal. Subash had a warm generous manner. He talked about how being a successful businessman gave him a responsibility to look after not only his own young family but also to provide for his parents and extended family in whatever way he could. As a Hindu he followed a charismatic guru called Sai Baba. I noticed his picture hanging inside the pharmacy. In it Sai Baba posed like a surreal joker with a massive head of curly hair and beaming smile. As we waited for our meal, I asked him to write a few words of wisdom advice on the back of my journal,

"Do not be selfish in life.
Always help others who are in trouble and try and guide them.
Respect your parents."
Signed: Bajaj 'Subash' Kanhiyalal

After we ate, Subash took me to the train station on the back of his motorbike and showed me the platform to get the midnight train to Jalgaon. My night's drama wasn't over yet, though. The train clerk would not issue me for a ticket until after twelve midnight or my ticket or sharply my explained that my ticket would be invalid. This was an unexpected stress, as my train was due in at midnight or just before it. The large waiting room was almost empty. An old woman lay on the tiled floor under a telephone booth, her head resting on two wrinkled clasped hands. A dog lay stretched out next to her. On the far side of the room, a grey haired man slouched across two waiting room seats, roaring loudly to himself in his sleep. I could almost hear the station clock ticking in my head as I kept my prime position at the clerk's counter. A train horn blew somewhere in the distant night, a signal it was approaching the station. I anxiously watched the thin seconds-hand ticking slowly around the large waiting room clock face before the clerk re-opened the counter with a haughty air of self importance, and issued me a ticket. I arrived at Jalgaon station an hour later, in a sleepy stupor and checked into the fancily named Hotel Plaza for a few nights.

The next morning I walked unto the street outside to be greeted by a hot dry blast of air. I had never before experienced heat like it. It felt like someone was holding a giant invisible hair dryer just inches from my face and body. My eyes squinted and burned in the bright sunny glare, while my lips began to dry up and crack. The temperature was close to forty degrees Celsius. Over breakfast I planned the next part of my trip. I had just over a week before I had to be in Katmandu, Nepal. I had come to Maharashtra state to see the world famous caves of Ajanta, and was still considering making a short stop at Mahatma Gandhi's ashram in a village called Sevagram.

Before continuing my travels, my immediate priorities were to hand wash my laundry and offload some of my travel luggage. I had come to realise that an ongoing struggle when travelling as an independent backpacker, is keeping clothes, books and souvenirs to a minimum so that you don't begin looking like an over-packed mule horse. Deciding to visit a post office and send a clothes and gifts parcel back home. I was soon to discover that posting parcels in India was a whole new experience.

Upon locating a post office I was apprehended by a clerk at the front door who bluntly informed me, "you need a tailor." I was about to take offence when he pointed to the clear plastic bag I was carrying and added, "you need to get parcel stitched." I stood blankly staring for a moment until another man who was leaving the post office, randomly walked over to me when he heard the fuss. He was wearing a tea-towel like scarf around his head to keep off the sun and simply said, "ok, come with me." We jumped on his motorbike and weaved our way through market squares and side streets until we reached a shopping mall. Walking up the main entrance steps, we stopped inside at a small counter where an elderly tailor wearing a long white shirt and jam jar glasses, sat. After a long chat in broken English, he agreed to stitch up my parcel but first said we would need some cloth. Off we went across the mall to the draper shop man and bargained for twenty rupees or forty cents worth of standard white cloth. Back at the tailor shop, a small crowd had gathered and the questions began about where I was from, was I married and did I play cricket. The elderly tailor got busy on his foot pedal sewing machine and soon had a water tight parcel stitched for which he charged me just thirty rupees, the equivalent of sixty cents. Asking my motorbike guide to translate, the tailor then asked would it be possible for me to get him started with a job in Ireland. Everyone laughed and I told him, "I will see what I can do."

My motor-bike guide then left me back outside the entrance of the post office, refusing to accept anything but a thank you and handshake before revving off down the street. Back inside, a clerk handed me a big blue marker and then instructed me to write my home address on the front of the parcel and accommodation address in India on the back. When I mentioned that my father was a postman back in Ireland, I was suddenly ushered in behind the counter to meet the postmaster. One of the other clerks served us tea in his office and he asked me, "do post men in Ireland have trouble with cross dogs?" A commotion then arose to try and find a cheaper levy charge to post my parcel, which they managed after a concentrated discussion in Marathi, their native language. With my parcel stamped with several red wax seals, my post office adventure had come to an epic but happy conclusion.

While getting an early morning bus the following day out to the Ajanta Caves, a truly bizarre encounter happened. As I sat in my seat down the back of the bus waiting to depart, a young smiling Indian boy no older than twelve years old hopped on the bus and walked down the aisle to where I was sitting. He produced a gold coloured key-ring with the Indian flag on it. At first I waved him away thinking he was trying to sell it to me. The young boy simple nodded his head and smiled wider before placing the key-ring in my hand, then walked back off the bus. He stood and waved as the bus left the station. I sat on my seat deeply puzzled until I turned the key-ring over. On the back was a smiling image of Mahatma Gandhi. I had only made the decision to visit Gandhi's ashram in Sevagram the night before, which is not a common destination for tourists. I smiled to myself and got the overwhelming feeling that we are someway guided and re-assured by signs, encounters and events in our everyday lives by some mysterious higher source. Often these forces work through us without our even knowing. Perhaps when we travel and break away from our fixed routines, we become even more open and sensitive to these simple but life confirming events.

After two bone rattling hours, the bus driver dropped me at a turn-off to where another shuttle service took visitors to the Caves of Ajanta. The driver brought our shuttle bus of mainly Indian tourists up through a winding valley of earthen yellow hills and bare sun scorched trees, to the front entrance . Although initially taken aback at the steep twenty dollars entrance fee for non-Indians, the travel budget sting soon faded. The Caves of Ajanta were stretched out along the cliff face of a massive seam of black basalt rock, along a horse-shoe shaped gorge. The cave entrances revealed massive pillars, balconies and strange guardian like creatures carved out of the cliff face.

The Caves of Ajanta were built between 500 BC and 500 AD when Buddhism flourished in Northern, Western and Central India. Most of the caves were man made and in total, contained twenty five large temples, carved out of solid black volcanic rock. The caves are so ancient that they were lost from local memory until the 19th Century. A British army officer by the name of Captain Smith re-discovered one of the temple caves by accident, while hunting a tiger through the then heavily forested valley. No one seemed to know what happened to the pursued tiger. The Japanese Government had donated millions of rupees in recent years towards helping restore and protect the Ajanta Caves as well as financing the unusually smooth tarred roadway leading up to the visitors centre.

Standing inside some of the two story temple caves at Ajanta, felt like being part of some enchanting scene straight from a 'Lord of the Rings' movie set. Some of the massive stone pillars even had stocky dwarf like creatures carved around their base. The ancient temple architects had chosen the mountainside of a south facing river gorge to harnessed the sun's reflection cast on the river below. At a certain time each day, this reflected sunlight illuminated the faces of giant Buddha statues placed at the back of each temple. Along the sides of many of the temples were alcoves where Buddhist monks once sat in silent meditation, contemplating the impermanence of their own existence and the ever changing nature of all things. Some of the temple ceilings and walls still revealed faded but brightly coloured murals depicting celestial beings. Another ceiling mural showed faded traces of an ancient royal procession, giving a tantalising glimpse of just how visually awe-inspiring these temples must have been in their heyday.

While walking up to the furthest caves in the sweltering heat, I acted in a short-tempered manner with a local man who was trying to sell me crystals. I was annoyed afterwards at how sharp I had been and was glad that he was still there when I returned back down the trail. He introduced himself as Zahir and we sat and chatted a while. A gaunt sombre man in his mid forties, he had a quiet reserved manner and speech and wore a white head scarf to keep off the sun. He explained to me that he was a farmer from a nearby Muslim village and sold crystals as a money earner during the dry season. After telling me some history about Ajanta I agreed to buy some crystals from him. He then offered to show me a good place to swim higher up the gorge. We climbed atop a high ridge overlooking Ajanta before carefully climbing down a short but steep cliff face. Ancient waters had carved a large deep pool out of the surrounding solid rock. The water was unbelievably refreshing when I dived in. I was glad I left my tracksuit bottoms on for when I re-surfaced it seemed like half the local village were looking down at me from the cliff edge above. Some of them shouted down in the Marathi language to Zahir. When I asked them what they were saying he smiled and replied, "they say they never saw such a white skinned person before." On the way back up the cliff face we passed a large beehive hanging under a shaded ledge. Zahir informed that this was where he got his honey from.

I bought three crystals of quartz, amethyst and moonstone of Zahir and handed him a fifty rupee note which he was happy with. We parted company as friends, at the main road junction back to Jalgaon before Zahir was hoisted on board the back of a crowded truck heading in the opposite direction. The sunset cast a fiery glow into the fading blue sky and it suddenly seemed like the surrounding golden brown hills were sheltering some great mystery or discovery, somewhere beyond them. I felt further drawn to the ancient arid heart of India, as a large milky full moon rose and took her night-time stage.

My last night in Jalgaon was spent in the company of an Australian woman, Billie Jackson and her daughter Ronnie, who were travelling through India together. We sat under the stars on a rooftop restaurant and swapped travelling stories of our adventures so far. From their stories, I learned that travelling as attractive Western women in India has its drawbacks, as they found many young Indian men in particular to be overbearing nuisances. It seems that many Indian men do not perceive the Western woman with the same code of respect as they do Indian women. Their perception caused mainly by the media, is that women from the Western world are highly sexualised and promiscuous. There was no telling them any different.

The novelty of travelling passenger-class, finally wore off on a packed airless Saturday morning train journey to Sevagram and Gandhi's ashram. I got talking to a young man who worked as an agricultural advisor selling pesticides for a large Indian petro-chemical company. We talked through a forest of arms and he noticed that I was beginning to fade from the cramped conditions and heat. "At the next station ", he began to advise, "you should move up to a 2nd class air conditioned carriage. It is not so difficult, you find a train official and tell him that there was a mix up with your ticket and that you wish to be moved up. Have some money ready, no more than fifty rupees, and he will find you a seat."

I almost took the head off a small dazed grey haired man with my backpack while squeezing out of the passenger class carriage and made a quick dash up the station platform at the next stop. Ten minutes later and a black suit jacketed official was writing me out a new fifty rupee ticket, before he escorted me to an air conditioned leather bench with tinted glass carriage windows. It was a different world up here and with a deep sigh of relief I nodded off into siesta land.

An hour later and I was in an animated discussion with three men sharing the same train compartment about history and modern politics in both India and Ireland. Two of the men were lecturers returning home for the weekend, while another younger man was on his way to meet his prospective wife, and looked understandably nervous. The younger man Chander, explained that nowadays, marriages are not strictly arranged between two sets of parents as was traditionally the case in India. He added, "younger generations of Indians are now exercising more freedoms in searching for potential marriage partners, through online dating agencies, with the rapid growth of the internet. We have already sent each others photos and are both happy to meet, now I shall get a chance to know her as a person."

In the carriage compartment next to us, a group of young Indian women in bright colourful saris of yellow, red, purple, and greens were chatting, giggling and busily applying cream from small blue and white tins to their face and hands. When I enquired off one of the lectures as to what they were doing, he turned his eyes upwards, "they are using 'fair and lovely' face cream to make their complexions appear lighter. When I explained that in Ireland women apply tanning lotion to make their skin appear darker, we shared a good natured laugh at the unfathomable mysteries of the female mind.

Within moments of stepping off the train at Sevagram station my eyes stung with the heat. It must have been close to forty five degrees Celsius. By the time I arrived at Mahatma Gandhi's ashram in the back of an auto-rickshaw, my mouth had dried up and my lips began to sting and chaff. It was frighteningly hot. My sole concern became to find water which I was given from a clay jar in the ashram kitchen. I was then escorted by a small cross looking man to a simple sparsely furnished room. When I enquired about showers he grunted, "no showers, simple facilities here." Sevagram means 'village of service' and this is where Gandhi used to sometimes retreat to rest, write and meditate in between his epic Satyagraha campaign walks to gain India's independence from the British Empire. Ashrams are quite common in India and usually promote India's cultural activity through either music, yoga or religious practices. Sevagram is now run by a small group of volunteers dedicated to keeping Gandhi's spirit alive and running local schools for under-privileged children. In my room was an old wooden bed with a single sheet, while my en suite bathroom comprised of a water tap, bucket and hand held jug for showering. Work began each morning at 6am and everyone helped for two hours before joining morning prayers. We then ate breakfast together. All our food was freshly grown and prepared from fields and gardens surrounding the ashram. Needless to say, our meals although small, tasted amazing.

My first meal at Sevagram was chapatti bread and vegetable curry freshly prepared and cooked over a large clay fire oven in the kitchen. At 6pm everyone gathered under a large leafless tree which Gandhi, known affectionately as 'Babu' had planted many years earlier. A huge silent beehive hung beneath one of it's upper branches. Men sat on one side, women on the other. Everyone sat cross-legged on mats. Prayers were then said from the Hindu, Muslim, Buddhist and Christian holy books including the 'Our Father' in English. A short stout jovial man then began playing the sitar and other residents began singing an uplifting hymn as a yellow sun set behind a grove of trees in the courtyard. As the ceremony proceeded, a young woman dressed in cream white woven cloth, spun a yarn of wool on a hand powered wooden sewing machine to honour Gandhi's belief in self sufficiency. Gandhi had used the manual sewing machine as a powerful symbol representing the dignity and independence of weaving one's own clothes, at a time when India was flooded with Western style garments from the linen mills of Britain. For some reason Sevagram, brought me back to memories of my grandparents farmyard in rural Tipperary. There was the same dry dusty smell of the gravel and hedges during the warm sunny months. There was also the same feeling of life lived at a much more natural pace, free from the relentless pressures and expectations of the modern world we have come to accept as normal.

The following morning I was wakened with a loud rapid tapping on my door at 5-30am. After a simple prayer service I retreated back to my bed for half an hour. Work began at 7-30am and I teamed up with a young American man called Kevin. We were then served a wonderful corn bread baked in a stone oven. I was exhausted and suffering from the heat and constant travel. My symptoms were a chesty cough and congested sinuses. I kept my spirits up by remembering that the climate would gradually change as I travelled further north towards Nepal. After breakfast, Kevin and I were assigned to help a young Indian woman by the name of Lollita. She led us to a small back garden to help harvest a garden of tomatoes and prepare an adjoining plot now choked with weeds for replanting. The morning sun was still low in the sky which made the heat and work bearable. Lollita had a bubbly sense of humour and almost always finished her softly spoken English sentences with an infectious laugh. As we gathered small ripe tomatoes into shallow woven baskets she talked about her life living and working in the Ashram. "When I first came here to stay, my family still had expectations for me to marry. Now that I have been here for over three years, I am coming to realise that a life dedicated to the Ashram is right for me. I will be quite happy without a man I think", she said, before breaking into bright laughter once again.

Kevin then talked a little about himself. Only in his early thirties, he talked about his work back in the U.S., where he runs a successful marketing agency He had decided to take time out to travel to India and had already spent two months volunteering at a local village, teaching English. He regarded himself as a devout Christian with great respect for the teachings of Jesus. He believed that the Christian church in the West was in a deep crisis. As he put it in his soft Oklahoma drawl, "most Christian churches no longer preach what Jesus said, but only about his radical and transformational teachings." He was interested to hear that there was an Irish saint named Kevin from Glendalough in modern day Wicklow. He was even more interested to hear that legend has it that he spent most of his life living alone in the wilderness and had animal disciples, who watched out for him as he lived in and travelled through the danger filled oak forests of Ireland.

My short few days stay at Sevagram allowed me a chance to see just how simple a philosophy Gandhi lived by. Our modern consumer society seemed far removed from the path that he took. I left wondering was there a middle way to be found. Before leaving I took a photo of a notice board which was propped up outside one of the small wooden houses which Gandhi once stayed in. It read;

THE MAD RUSH

The people who are in the mad rush today, increasing their
wants senselessly suppose that they are enhancing their importance and real knowledge. A day will come when they will
exclaim, "what have we been doing?
One after another many civilisations have risen, flourished,
declined and disappeared and in spite of the big boast of
human progress, I am inclined to ask...to what end all this?
What's the purpose?
Darwin's contemporary Wallace has said that despite the
various discoveries of the past 50 years, the moral height of
mankind hasn't increased an inch. Tolstoy said the same thing.
Jesus, Buddha, Prophet Mohamed all have said the same thing.

Mahatma Gandhi.

I waited in sweltering heat at Sevagram train station platform
for the train. It shimmered into view like a watery mirage sail-
ing along the rail tracks. My next destination was the holy city
of Varanasi, a twenty-four hour train journey away. The train
brought us down from the sun baked Deccan Plateau to the
vast forested hill country and fertile valleys of Madhya Pradesh
State, before sunset. As the night lengthened, the carriage I
was in began to crowd with passengers. People began to bed
down for the night wherever they could find a space. This included across overhead luggage racks, under seats, or stretched
out on the passenger aisle. At the next stop I once again took
my chances and decided to try and travel 2nd Class Sleeper for
the night. I walked through countless carriages but every berth
seemed full with countless double bunks, each occupied with
somebody trying to sleep. Just as I was beginning to think that
my 'carriage hopping' luck had finally run out I bumped into a
train official. With forty rupees in hand I explained my situation. He listening without expression, like someone who heard
it all before in as many different languages. He then replied
curtly "yes, come please follow". We walked back to another
carriage where he pulled a middle leather bench from the wall,

between two already occupied bunks. I was never so happy to see a train bunk in my life. Despite the frequent noisy station stops which included train official whistles, intercom announcement and loud food vendor pitches, I still managed to get some sound sleep. In fact, I was beginning to enjoy the constant buzz and stimuli that is India.

At 7am on the second, I was tapped firmly on the shoulder by my lower bunk and upper bunk neighbours. I raised two sleepy eyes to see two Indian men holding their wrists up to my face and tapping in tandem at their watch faces. Moments later and my bunk was secured back against the wall and space was made for me to sit. The train to Varanasi was a fascinating microcosm of Indian life. There were no restaurant carriages for starters never mind desserts. Instead, a small army of independent vendors plied their produce through the trains, serving chai (tea), coffee and snacks. At station stops it was possible to run out and buy veggie pastries called *samosas* or fruit and bottled water. The train aisles were in fact a busy laneway of people passing through from carriage to carriage. These included strange looking *Sadhus* or holy men with painted faces and wild hair, carriage sweepers who swept the rubbish into bundles, musicians who sang or played a flute and beggars who put out their hands. They were all looking for a small donation of rupees from passengers. As the sun rose in the sky, the carriages got hot and the train began stopping more often. On one occasion two enterprising teenage boys appeared in our carriage sliding along a large fish box full of vanilla flavoured ice cream tubs. Few on board refused this surprise treat.

Our train was now passing through the fertile Ganges valley, the cradle of ancient civilisations going back thousands of years. Sun blackened farmers with wrap around head scarves sat watching their buffalo from straying into crops. Other farmers laboured busily, preparing rice paddy fields for the coming monsoon season. Towering chimney kilns rose in places out of the farmland plains with countless stacks of red-brown building bricks built underneath.

As our train clattered over a high steel bridge, I caught my first glimpse of the famous Ghats of Varanasi. Stretched out along the south facing bank of the mighty river Ganges was a seemingly endless line of Hindu temples and human cremation platforms. Behind the Ghats stretched the ancient three thousand year old city of Varanasi. I felt strangely apprehensive as I disembarked at the train station. Just as I was becoming more accustomed to the heightened energy of India, the city of Varanasi seemed to take it to a whole new uncomfortable level. Running the gauntlet of auto-rickshaw and taxi drivers, I found a hotel close to the station. This helped put my mind more at rest in case I needed to make a hasty departure.

The next morning, I rose at 6am and got a cycle rickshaw driver to take me down to the Ganges. I held so much expectation about the Burning Ghats of Varanasi from articles read, documentaries watched and travel stories that it in someway spoilt the experience for me. I had imagined Varanasi in my head, many times. Ancient narrow streets shrouded in shadow with mystery around every corner, mist rising out the sacred Ganges river revealing a flotilla of candle-lit leaf boat offerings, as thousands of Indian pilgrims chanted and bathed by the waters edge.

The reality I encountered was narrow streets shrouded in cow dung, while pushy tour guides lurked around every corner. By 9am the sun was already shining down strongly upon the Ghats which are wide stone steps leading down to the Ganges. By being simply aware of my unmet expectations, they soon dissolved, and I came to realise a new freedom in simply observing and experiencing Varanasi in the present moment. In front of me were over one hundred Ghats, stretching for more than two miles along the north bank of the wide and silently flowing Ganges. Each Ghat is used by a particular caste, as Indian culture is still very much caste structured. People in India belong to a particular caste by birth. If you are fortunate enough to be born into a Brahman caste you will more likely be a teacher or bank manager, while if you are born into a lower caste, you are more likely to be a street sweeper or labourer. This might at first seem hugely unfair, but we in the West with our own class system and subtle segregation, should perhaps be careful before taking the moral high ground. Caste systems in India give people a strong sense of identity and belonging and are a supportive community to fall back on, in times of hardship.

I made my way through stacks of neatly cut timber logs and soon smelt smoke wafting from one of the Ghats up ahead. A part of me wanted to return to my hotel, as I knew recently dead bodies were being cremated. Another part of me though, was compelled to experience it. From the vantage point of a small Hindu temple I sat and watched as the body of an elderly Indian woman, dressed in a beautiful white sari, was laid on top of a firewood pyre. The cremation took place on a small concrete platform above a set of wide steps leading down to the Ganges. The dead woman's three sons were standing around the raised platform along with temple priests and cremation officials. The oldest son now in tears was handed a burning torch and lit the funeral pyre. One of the temple guides kneeled down next to me and explained in hushed tones, "Hindu people believe that being cremated in Varanasi by the sacred river Ganges will set your spirit free from the cycle of re-incarnation. This lady comes from a wealthy family. The proper timber for cremation costs a lot of money, maybe they paid thirty to forty thousand rupees. He pointed to two young boys who were sifting through river mud at the bottom of the steps. "You see when this woman's body is burned her remains will be offered to the Ganges. Her jewellery will be collected and donated to a local hospice. A lot of poor people who are dying or terminally ill make their way to Varanasi. They live out the remainder of their lives in one of the hospices in the hope that charity funds will support their wish to be cremated on the banks of the Ganges when they die."

The woman's body was now being consumed by fire and an acrid smell of burning flesh was carried off in plumes of dark blue smoke. It was an uncomfortable sobering scene to observe, but one I felt compelled to watch, as if to break some kind of spell and to come to my senses by realising that our bodies and what we identify as 'I' is merely skin, flesh, blood and bones.

Further along the Ghats I stepped sprightly out of the way, as a herd of buffalo sauntered down some steps for a late morning dip in the Ganges. Sheds were built for the water buffalo next to a riverside temple where they were foddered, milked and their dung dried out in circular pats for fuel.

Just a short distance upstream a group of pilgrim bathed and said prayers. They then took turns in holding their noses and submerging their heads under the dark blue waters. It is said the waters are heavily polluted, yet pilgrims worship the Ganges as sacred, which somehow prevents most bathers from getting sick. By midday it got too hot to walk about anymore and I took an auto-rickshaw back to my hotel. On our way we drove through a busy intersection where four double lanes of traffic met. There were no traffic lights and no speed restrictions and to add to the general melee, a large bull had decided to take a rest in the centre of the road, where he was chewing his cud, oblivious to the organised anarchy of beeping traffic zipping all around him. Pure organised chaos.

After another day and night spent wandering through the Ghats and exploring the old city, I was relieved to be moving on from Varanasi. The people seemed different to those in Southern Indian, not so open and friendly and generally less fun. I took a late evening train to Gorakhpur, situated close to the border with Nepal. By the light of a full moon I looked out on a farming landscape of open fields, small clustered villages and scattered woodland groves. Taking a pen and some notepad paper from my travel bag I finished a poem I had been working on for a few days.

QUESTIONS ON TIME
When we lose time, surely we lose everything
Clocks become our jailers when haste is all time brings
Missing the meals we eat, loved ones, even conversations
Absence grows stronger without inner contemplations
Always rushing to place one foot in an un-dug grave
Time can rarely be borrowed if possible to save
If time means money, what does it mean to be free
Where is it written, this is the way things should be.

Gorakhpur was not a place to spend much time in. It had the atmosphere and run down appearance of a town people had to visit on their way to somewhere else. I sensed that the people who lived and worked here felt the same, except they wished to make some money first. Rats scampered about the rubbish strewn street verges and my hotel room had the sparse look of a half night stop-over.

I woke to another morning of stuffy heat. I still felt in poor health as I boarded a bus to Sinauli and crossed the border after a quick passport check. I was at large in Nepal with a one month visitors' visa. While eating at a roadside restaurant I was sold a ticket on an express mini-bus by a young charismatic Nepali guy with dark glasses. He introduced himself as Arjun and had a polished convincing sales pitch, which included discount overnight luxury accommodation in Katmandu. He even had a colour brochure of the hotel facade and furnished rooms inside. It seemed too good to be true and indeed it later turned out that way. He had three friends hanging about him and as we bargained one piped up, "his name is Arjun, it means Nepalese royalty." Upon handing over a fistful of Nepali rupees to 'Prince Arjun', I was hurried into the front seat of a white Toyota mini-bus which they kept calling an air-bus.

Our bus was soon driving through forested river valleys and our short stocky Nepali driver accelerated onwards at a steady speed. By evening we began winding more slowly, up steep hair-pin bends for hour upon hour. We seemed to be forever tailing behind heavy goods trucks covered in bright paintings with slogans like, 'Sound Horn Please' across its trailer end. As the mountains began to grow higher I innocently asked the bus driver, "are these the Himalayas?" He glanced over at me, chuckled a little to himself, and in a deep gravelly voice replied, "no my friend... these hills are not the Himalayas."

We arrived in Katmandu near midnight and in fairness, a taxi driver was waiting to collect me as Prince Arjun had foretold. On the way the taxi-man announced, "the hotel you were to stay at is fully booked so you are to stay at another hotel called 'The Five Corners'." Even the name sounded ominously suspect. It wasn't the Ritz but it was a classy joint compared to my recent run on accommodation. What a relief it was to lie in a bed which was cool enough to sleep under a blanket once again. The added bonus was not having to worry about mosquitoes sharpening their teeth and hiding in ambush until I turned the lights out. It's the simple comforts in life that you come to really appreciate when budget backpacking, like a clean bed, three square meals and enough money to get to your next destination. All other pressures and concerns slowly lose their importance and fade into memory after just a few weeks budget travelling. It's as if you exchange a heavy back-pack for a lighter world upon your shoulders.

KATMANDU CALLING

The next day I went exploring the tourist district of Thamel, which I can only describe as Disneyland for Western adventure tourists in their twenties and thirties. There were trekking stores, exotic clothes shops, Tibetan antique shops, music and video stores, bookshops, supermarkets, bakeries, internet cafes and a myriad of restaurants specialising in every kind of Asian and European food under the sun...all for about twenty percent of prices back in Ireland. I even found an Irish bar one night, called Paddy O'Shaughnessy's. U2 were belting out a former hit, 'In the Name of Love', as I walked in. A stout Nepali man wearing a traditional hat called a 'topi' didn't see the funny side when I asked in jest, "whats the craic there, you're not Paddy himself by any chance?"

Just a short walk outside the tourist district of Thamel, Katmandu still seemed to retain a fascinating mix of the ancient and the modern. Katmandu means 'City made of Wood' in the local Newar language and many of the older town houses I passed, were timber framed with elaborate door, window, balcony and roof eave carvings. Long narrow shaded streets seemed to twist and curve and then suddenly open out unto tiny market squares called 'toles'. These social spaces often displayed ancient Hindu statues or phone box size temples. Around these 'toles', local fruit and vegetable traders competed for space with small white taxi's, as well as auto and cycle rickshaws.

Wild mountain leopards have been moving into the city in recent years due to habitat loss and they sometimes prowl the quiet streets late at night. Some wary residents had begun to take their dogs and cats indoors before bedtime, less their beloved pet end up as a wily leopards moonlight supper. One morning over breakfast I read a front page story in the Katmandu Post. It reported the strange story of a city-centre Nepali family who woke one morning to find a leopard sitting in their hallway by the bathroom door. It was reported that they then chased it into the back-garden where it lay under a bush. They promptly called the police who arrived on the scene and chased it away with stones. It seemed a much more sensible and practical course of action that trying to drag the leopard into the back seat of the patrol car.

Situated in a large river valley between two hazy blue mountain ranges, Katmandu is not only Nepal's capital but its only real city. The majority of Nepal's twenty two million people still live in the countryside, or in remote hill and mountain villages. It is a truly culturally diverse country made up of over fifteen main ethnic groups including Newar, Tamang, Rai, Sherpa Gurung and Magar, each with their own distinct languages. The more minority languages tend to be limited to an area spanning about one days walk.

One of my main reasons for travelling to Nepal was to attend a ten day meditation course run every year for Western visitors, at Kopan, a Tibetan Buddhist monastery perched on a high ridge overlooking the sprawling city. After two days of eating, resting and sightseeing around Thamel, I was a little apprehensive yet determined to try it out. I had visions of it being an austere style retreat and stuffed the bottom of my backpack with chocolate, cereal and fruits before I left. A taxi left me up at the front gates where a smiling monk in red robes opened a side door and beckoned me in. I was given a key at reception and was pleasantly surprised to find I was sharing with only one other room-mate in a comfortable double room. There was even a modern shower and flush toilet. "I could get used to this", I thought to myself.

I was wakened the next morning by someone ringing a loud bell outside the window. Crawling out of bed, I pressed the light button on my watch and with a mixture of disbelief and dismay saw it was only 5-30am. Morning meditation began at 6-30 each morning in a large Buddhist temple called a gompa. Buddhists believe that the road to enlightenment lies through the practice and development of morality, wisdom and meditation. Meditation is regarded as the key practice to working with and understanding the mind, which is ultimately the creator of both our suffering and happiness. As the Tibetan Buddhist teacher Sogyal Rinpoche wrote in his spiritual classic, 'The Tibetan Book of Living and Dying', "fortunately we live in a time when many people all over the world are becoming familiar with meditation. It is being increasingly accepted as a practice that cuts through and soars above cultural and religious barriers, and enables those who pursue it to establish a direct contact with the truth of their being. It is a practice that at once transcends the dogma of religions and is the essence of religions."

Reading this same paragraph for the first time almost ten years previously had sent fireworks going off in my mind. I had been compelled to follow his advice and helpful instruction to sit for the first time, in silence and stillness on a chair in my bedroom at home. From that single life changing event, I now find myself in a Tibetan monastery outside Katmandu in far flung Nepal

There were around eighty Westerners on the course, from all different religious faiths and backgrounds, and from diverse parts of the world such as California, Canada, Mexico, South Africa, Japan, Germany and not forgetting Ireland. A big surprise was the fact that the majority of the participants were under twenty-five years of age, which made me a kind of senior. Our days were taken up with short meditation sessions, teachings and lively and engaging group discussions. Although our days technically didn't finish until 8-30pm each evening, there were long breaks in between for meals, reading, visits to the bookshop or library and walks around the peaceful gardens. This may come as a surprise to many, but sitting in stillness, cross-legged on a cushion, is actually quite tiring. I found myself taking afternoon naps and regularly falling into a deep recuperative sleep. Our teacher was a small bespectacled Buddhist nun in her late fifties called Ani Karen. From Sweden, she had originally come to Katmandu as a hippie on a holiday, but visited Kopan one day and that was it for her. She had taken vows as a Buddhist nun shortly after, and Kopan monastery was now her life and home. For the first few days of the course, she sat on a small chair on a low altar in front of everyone and answered every question imaginable about Buddhism for hour upon hour. She never lost her cool or patience and gave everyone a thoughtful or thought provoking answer.

Breakfast, lunch and dinner was served in a large airy cafeteria and again the freshly cooked food was all surprisingly good. After every meal participants took turns to volunteer with the kitchen staff and help with the washing up. It was also a time to meet and chat with other people as we were asked to maintain silence during many of the mornings and afternoons.

We shared the monastery grounds with over two hundred monks from the ages of ten to one hundred, many of whom were originally from Tibet. For the younger monks Kopan was a sort of school and university wrapped into one and they spent their days attending *puja* (prayer chanting services), lessons and work chores. All the monks had their heads tightly shaved and wore saffron red and yellow robes, as the Buddha had wore in India over two thousand, five hundred years ago. After just five days at Kopan monastery and without any medicines or vitamin supplements, I was quickly regaining full health again. I also began to ponder how important a role the mind plays in maintaining and restoring our overall health.

My roommate turned out not to share my enthusiasm for Kopan, however. James was a forty-eight year old motor-cross biker and playboy from Australia, who was on a six month tour of Asia with his long term girlfriend. From what James told me I gathered their relationship had hit a definite rocky patch. Upon arriving in Katmandu his girlfriend had decided to check into Kopan monastery and James reluctantly followed. He had a wry sardonic personality, typical of many Aussies which I find funny and I couldn't help but get some amusement out of his situation. One evening before lights out, he confided in me, "I don't know maite about this whole bladdy Buddhism thing. I mean, if you ask me it's a whole blooming money racket. 1've seen the Buddhist monks down in Thailand roight, with their mobile phones and riding around in fancy motorbikes. I'd like to be down in Thailand now doing some bike trails and chilling on the beach, but what can I do. My girlfriend has been in a roight bladdy strange mood recently. One minute we're in Katmandu, looking at buying a statue of the Buddha, the next minute she's telling me she'd like to be a blooming nun. I mean, what would you make of it. I'd be out of here like a shot, I can tell you if I didn't think it might be a phase she's going through."

For the next three days I found myself reluctantly filling the role of a voice message carrier between James and his girlfriend. One evening James triumphantly informed me that they had patched things up. They had decided to take a week's break from each other before travelling on to Thailand together. My reward was even more peace as my snoring roommate left for the bright lights of Katmandu.

During my final few days at Kopan I got talking with a twenty-five year old rather reluctant Tibetan monk called Lobsang Gyaltsen. When I told him I was from Ireland his face lit up and he asked me, " ah, do you know the movie Braveheart?" Replying that I did, I then asked him where he had seen it. "Oh you know, sometimes I escape for a while and watch DVDs' with my friends. Morgan Freeman is my favourite actor. Have you seen him in Shawshank Redemption? That was a very good movie. I don't like movies which are violent though, as they usually have a very poor story-line." He paused to send a younger monk on an errand before continuing, "I was in Scotland once. We were playing Tibetan music. It was very cloudy and it rained a lot. We were playing at a festival in the Highlands. All the locals seemed to spend the evenings in the pub, drinking beer and whiskey, although we were not allowed to go in."

I then asked Lobsang about Tibet and how did he come to be in Nepal. A sadness came into his voice as he explained how he had fled from Tibet as a young child with his family to escape persecution by the Chinese. "We lived in a remote part of west Tibet near the holy mountain of Kailash. We still have cousins living there. It is difficult to get information anymore. The Chinese have stopped killing the Tibetan people like they used to. Instead they now make hard laws on Tibetans with tough punishments. My uncle bought a second hand car a few years back and the Chinese took it from him. Everything the kids learn in school now is through Chinese and you can be sent to jail and tortured just for having a photo of the Dalai Lama." Lobsang began to look far older than his years as he recounted stories that family members brought out with them after escaping from Tibet. It sounded like the Chinese were trying to slowly break the Tibetan peoples' culture and spirit. It seemed all the more tragic considering that before the Chinese invasion, Tibet was one of the most spiritual and peace loving nations in the world.

On one of my last nights on the course at Kopan, all seventy participants were invited to the main gompa to experience a special puja ceremony. The gompa serves as a temple for monks and lay people to congregate and meditate. We sat on two long rows of cushions to the side of the gompa. Two hundred Tibetan and Nepali monks chanted in unison while a small group of monk musicians played huge drums, long horns and large metal cymbals which they crashed together at certain times of the chanting songs. A wise old Lama sat in half light on a high throne overlooking the gompa. He wore a tall yellow curved hat on his head and seemed to be deep in meditation with his eyes only slightly open. There was an indescribable energy in the gompa with the rising and falling throat chanting of so many monks sitting in long rows facing each other. In an unexpected moment I felt my mind settle of itself into a deep calm peace. It was as if my thoughts were like shower clouds cleared in a fresh summer breeze, leaving a big spacious clear blue sky to relax into. I glanced up at the Lama once again and this time, felt a great natural affinity and respect for him. He was performing a slow hand movement ritual called *mudra*. The position of his palms and fingers would change slowly as if in some secret harmonious sign language dance with the chanting monks. Behind him towered a large gold leaf painted statue of the Buddha which gazed down serenely on the proceedings. Below the Lama and to his side, sat a very old and revered grey bearded monk, in sitting posture. During the second half of the ceremony some of the younger monks rushed around serving plastic cups and small Madeira cakes from shallow cardboard boxes.

Other older monks walked more carefully behind them, serving warm milk tea which made me feel right at home.

On my last night at Kopan, I walked up the steps to a small steep circular hill where two huge pine trees grew. There was no one else about as the course had finished days before. Although hesitant in coming to Kopan I was now reluctant to leave. The roof of the sky was lit up with stars. I gazed up in awe, considering for a momen,t how seemingly infinite and vast the universe is and how fragile and small our own living planet is in the overall scheme of things. Kopan Hill was where the personal astrologers to the former kings of Nepal studied the cosmos and predicted future events. I imagined an old wizened man with arms folded behind his back, watching the night time heavens revolve around him. Probing for signs. Forming meaning from a celestial tapestry.

Looking South down into the Katmnadu valley I gazed out at a newly created galaxy of electrical lights. Dogs barked and car horns sounded off in the distance. Kopan monastery was winding down to sleep around me, yet the faint chanting of Buddhist monks once again rose up from a nearby gompa. I closed my eyes and imagined what it would have been like when Tibet was a land of monasteries on the roof of the World. I said a silent prayer wishing that centres like Kopan monastery, whether they be Christian, Buddhist, Hindu, Muslim, Jewish or other, serve as a beacon of light for people through the times ahead. I walked back out through the gates of Kopan the next day, deeply at peace in myself and up for a trek.

I had always been drawn to mountains from an early age and in particular my native Bluestack Mountains back home in County Donegal. Now in Katmandu I was just a day's bus ride away from gazing up at some of the highest snow capped peaks on Earth. Buying a back-pack, trekking maps, permits and all the mountain climate weather gear I needed, I set off on my Himalayan adventure.

Katmandu bus station was sheer chaos the following morning and it was only through the kindness of a local Nepali that I found my bus. The bus was over-packed due to a national strike the day before. My backpack was thrown up on the roof-rack and moments later that's where I found myself, perched on a blue plastic chemical drum, surrounded by smiling Nepali passengers. It was 7am and I was on my way to the village of Jeeri in East Nepal to start a three week trek through the Solu-Khumbu Himalayan region.

The first few hours on the bus roof were a daring novelty, like being allowed to sit on a high trailer load of hay-bales as a kid. As we climbed slowly up and out of the Katmandu Valley, the views became more and more stunning. I made friends with two young Nepali lads who taught me to say in Nepali, *"Mor Jeeri Chave Chu"*, which they told me meant, "I am going to Jeeri". As we passed through mountainside villages, they would ask me to shout it down to unsuspecting locals and then burst into fits of laughter. We had great fun with the other passengers, teasing and singing songs. We stopped for lunch and generous helpings of Dhal-Bat at a village called Malay. Dhal-Bat is the staple meal for most Nepali's and consists of curried vegetables, lentils, chopped potatoes and rice. This turned out to be a super-energy food that would sustain me on my treks ahead. For many Nepali's, its their staple diet, year in, year out.

Our bus continued to snake its way up narrow dusty hair-pin bends, past old farm hamlets with rosy cheek children and scuttling hens. Along the crest of one mountain summit, we passed through a huge chalk quarry. One of the lads pointed excitedly and shouted, "dolly mixture quarry, dolly mixture", while rubbing his hands theatrically around his face. So this was the raw ingredients for 'fair and lovely' face cream.

The last few hours of our journey was nothing short of an endurance test, as our bus swayed from side to side and a relentless sun beamed down upon our heads. One of my fellow travelling companions to Jeeri was called Ram, who told me he lived with his Mother in Katmandu. There was a sadness in his eyes behind all the smiles. Although only thirteen years old he was travelling to Jeeri to work at a guesthouse. It would be three months before he would get holidays to go home again. We had been travelling for ten hours and I wrapped a trekking jumper around my head to try and keep the sun off my already sun burnt face. At our final roadside stop before Jeeri a young mother and child ran towards the bus in the height of excitement. A Nepali Dad wearing a traditional topi hat, was arriving back from Katmandu with a large cardboard box containing a new TV set. Other family members appeared to help him as he lowered it from the bus roof.

Ram then suddenly grabbed me by the arm and started shouting, "look, look Keith, Himal Gourishankar. He was pointing half way up the northern skyline, high above a forest cloaking the valley side. From a swirling cauldron of angry black and greyish clouds rose the sharp edges of a giant snow capped mountain. My heart missed a beat. My first glimpse of a mighty Himalayan peak.

If These are the Foothills...

Booking into a small guesthouse without electricity I was given a hot bucket of water to shower in, a meal of Dhal Bat and a small wooden loft bedroom to sleep in. There were no more roads from Jeeri, just a main footpath highway. By 10pm the village street outside was silent. Just as I was falling asleep I began hearing the distant rumblings of thunder over invisible Himalayan peaks while occasional bright flashes of thunder lit up the room. I wondered was it an ominous or good sign for my own twenty-one day trek. It was approaching the end of the dry season when the monsoons carry up cloud and moisture from the Indian sub-continent to cloak the Himalayas. A voice within seemed to say, things will be okay if I have faith in the unknown journey ahead.

The guesthouse rooster woke me up at 6am and the friendly owner made me a breakfast of porridge and scrambled eggs before I set off. I had carried my trekking boots in the bottom of my back-pack the whole way through Sri Lanka and India. At times it had seemed a crazy extra weight to carry. That was until I slipped my feet into them and realised how important it was to have comfortable footwear. The first hour felt like a veritable walk in the park as I walked across the village bridge and along the start of the trail. Then as if out of nowhere, the worn clay brown path suddenly veered its way almost straight up the side of a steep hill. Minutes later I was sitting with my head between my knees on an old tree trunk. Slowly getting my breath back, I could hear my own heart pounding in my ears. I looked over at my blue back-pack in growing frustration as if I was handcuffed to a fellow overweight hamstrung fugitive. Instead of the sound of barking hound dogs in hot pursuit, I heard dark thunder clouds gathering off in the near distance. "How can I turn back now?" I said to myself. "What will I write in my next travelogue to the newspapers back home, after giving a big build up to my Himalayan trek?" The thought of a ten hour deflated bus journey back to Katmandu was enough to stir some adrenaline into my tired limbs. Not even half way though the first round it was quite simply too soon to throw in the trekking towel, so to speak. Hoisting my back-pack back over my sun burnt shoulders, I puffed my way on up the trail. Moments later an elderly mountain man skipped past me towing a kid goat in his wake and greeted me with 'Namaste' which came out as Namasteeeeey.

A few ominous rumbles of thunder later and the skies opened in an unmerciful deluge of rain. Luckily, I spotted a mountain-side hamlet up ahead and took shelter inside a small tea shop. A man, his wife and two small girls and a boy greeted me with smiles. It was darkly lit but dry. To the left as I walked in the door, was a small wooden shop counter and wall press which displayed a few fading groceries. Behind this was gas powered kitchen stove. To the right was a long wooden table and bench seats where I sat down. Next to this were three beds side by side. The kids played near the door as the woman made me tea. The man sat cross-legged on one of the beds looking out at the rain. My cousin Patrick Gallagher had told me of an old shop that once existed beside his cottage up in the Donegal hills, dating back to the late 1800's. I wondered how much different this shop and family scene was to that old small shop. It too had been built beside an ancient *boreen* or cow path that led across the high moorlands to the small town of Pettigo. I sensed something timeless and special about this small tea shop and its family owners as I sheltered from the thunderstorm. A small kid goat suddenly scuttled in the doorway and was bundled up into the arms of one of the older girls. A red hen then poked its head inside for an informal visit. It began self contentedly pecking the floorboards for a few tiny scraps before departing again with a flutter of wings. The man rolled up a cigarette and blue wisps of sweet smoke soon swirled through the air on its way to the day-lit doorway. The tea was the best I tasted in ages. As claps of thunder exploded overhead and the rain sounded even heavier off the roof, I asked the girls in broken Nepali to sing a song. The older sister needed no more prompts and started into a Nepali folk song which she sang in a sweet free voice. Realising she was next to sing, her shy younger sister ran over to one of the beds in a comical attempt to hide. With a sheet over her head, she started into a song. Then forgetting the words, she began shaking with giggles. Soon we were all laughing along with her. They then pointed to me to sing. Clearing my throat I sang 'The Homes of Donegal', changing Donegal to Nepal with the second verse going;

"I long to see your happy faces smiling at the door
The kettle swinging on the crook as I step up the floor
And then to see prepared for me a cup that's far from small
For your hearts are like your mountains in the homes of Nepal."

The day soon brightened again outside as the rain began to clear. While putting on my backpack, I pretended to almost fall backwards with the weight which sent the kids into bursts of laughter. With a final wave goodbye I was back on the trail with my heart and backpack feeling much lighter. Not knowing where I was going, but knowing my two feet would have to take me there, I felt a growing joy in simply being where I was.

I soon reached the top of a small mountain pass and for the next few hours descended down into a narrow rocky sided river valley. On the way I passed stone walled fields of flowering potatoes and an elderly shepherd who drove on a herd of goats. He had placed straw muzzles over their mouths to prevent them munching on neighbours crops. By early evening I had reached the village of Shivalaya which nestled on a old flood plain where four river valleys meet. The layout of the village was like something from a Hans Christian Anderson fairytale, with two storey neatly dressed stone houses, built compactly around a long narrow cobbled main street. I stayed with a Sherpa man by the name of Nima and his Tibetan wife who owned a small shop and guesthouse.

Shortly after arriving I heard a commotion further up the street and decided to investigate. I managed to catch the final act of a strange and unsettling Maoist Party concert. Four young Nepali teenagers, two boys and two girls, were performing a kind of dance routine to the beat of some Hindi Pop music playing on a generator powered sound system. The dance routine looked like a bizarre blend of Nepali folk and Hip Hop. Sitting behind a long table and presiding over the concert were a row of shifty looking Maoist committee members all wearing dark glasses. A crowd of villagers gathered round and watched on in amusement. As the song came to an end, the committee members threw out four toy machine guns to the teenage dancers who then pretended to spray everyone with bullets. Some of the villagers ducked dramatically and laughed, but it seemed a little unsettling all the same. Thankfully the Maoist rebels in Nepal are very much a watered down version of their Chinese Maoist comrades.

As I sat eating a hearty breakfast the next morning, Nima taught me some basic Sherpa phrases such as the standard greeting 'Tashi Delek' and thank you 'Touche Che'. Before leaving, I watched in quiet delight as a pair of swallows swooped busily in and out feeding their newly hatched clutch of chicks through the open front grocery shop.

The trail wound steeply out of Shivalaya and I was soon finding the going tough in a surprisingly strong afternoon sun. I had set myself the target of reaching the Deorali Pass by late afternoon, but my legs and lungs now struggled to deliver me there on schedule. Climbing and descending back down the equivalent of Ben Nevis in Scotland each day, might not be everybody's idea of fun. This is what I was about to attempt for a full week, as I walked across the Solu foothill range of the Himalayas. A well worn foot path was the one and only roadway. Up and down this trail went caravans of pack horses and their drivers, porters carrying super-human loads of goods on their back, goat herders, trekkers and locals carrying fodder, firewood, sacks of rice or simply visiting friends and relations living in the next valley.

At an altitude of three thousand metres, Deorali Pass is just about high enough to cause altitude sickness. Although there were two guesthouses next to the pass, I decided to stop only for lunch and descend down to the lower altitude hamlet of Bandar. Clouds swept like sweeping mist down Deorali street as I sat and ate my Sherpa stew and a sugary glass of hot orange cordial for extra energy. The cloud began to clear again as I descended down into the next valley at a brisk pace. Stopping for a short water break, I became aware of just how peaceful this valley was. Without roads, there were no sounds of any motor engines. All I could hear were birds singing and the wind rustling through the trees that lined the trail. Further down the valley I passed a few two storey houses made of bright cut stone. Tall flag poles stood in the front yard upon which fluttered large multi-coloured Buddhist prayer flags, indicated that the people living here were Sherpa. Reaching Bandar by early evening I booked into an empty guesthouse and felt a sickness coming on me. I went to bed early, hoping a good night's sleep would see me right by morning. Instead, I woke at midnight with a pounding headache, gurgling stomach and in a massive hurry to use the nearest toilet. Two hours later, it felt as if my insides had been flushed down the toilet from both ends. I slumped back into bed in a slight fever. I was puzzled as to what was wrong with me. It was either altitude sickness or giardia, (an intestinal parasite infection), or possibly an unpleasant combination of both.

I woke the next morning to sharp rays of sunlight piercing through gaps in the curtains. I could hear Buddhist monks chanting while playing drums and a cymbal outside. They were probably looking for alms of the guesthouse owner. Too weak to sit up in bed I wondered for a moment had they been called to give me the last rites. Falling back into an uncomfortable sleep, I woke again during the late evening. This time I could hear the Sherpa owner and a gang of younger sounding men filling sacks with either grain or cement at the side of the house. They laughed and joked as they worked steadily, talking in short bursts of Sherpa. Drifting back in and out of sleep, the next thing I heard was a strange concert of alpine bells ringing out and moving gradually closer to the guesthouse. With great effort I lifted my head to see a long line of lean strong looking ponies being led into the courtyard. Each pony had an alpine bell tied around it's neck and every bell had a slightly different note which together sounded like a loud otherworldly wind chime. The bells lolled me back into a deeper restful sleep. The next time I woke, the silvery light of a full moon was pouring in through the curtains. It was 3am on my watch. I looked out the window and saw that one of the young Sherpa men was down in the front yard loading the ponies up with sacks. As he worked, he communicated with the ponies in a series of "sssshhh sssshhhh hiy hiy" sounds. A short time later his boots came thudding up the wooden stairs into the room next to mine where his friends lay sleeping. He then said something in Sherpa which I imagined translated as.. "Get the heck up you lazy layabouts, I've my ponies saddled up and I'm hitting the trail now!" I heard one fellow get up and follow him down the stairs. The others roused sluggishly. Moments later, the head fellow was back down in the front yard, leading his ponies out the front gates and down the path, bells chiming magically, then fading into the quiet moonlit night.

All the next day I lay in bed slowly realising that no mountain toughened Sherpa woman was going to 'molly cuddle' me back to health. Struggling down to the kitchen, I was given a bowl of hot porridge and some water before retreating back to bed. The following morning I awoke feeling much better, despite meeting a gaunt unshaven dark eyed reflection of myself in the toilet mirror. After breakfast I went for a short walk down through Bandar. Upon getting sick, I had reconciled myself to the fact there would be no pharmacy in such a remote area. Sure enough, less than fifty yards from my bedroom window had been a chemist shop. A woman doctor with perfect English took my blood pressure, before prescribing me a box of vitamins, rehydration salts and a course of tablets for giardia.

The next morning I felt strong enough to continue and set off with a group of four trekkers who had arrived the night before as some welcome company. One of the group, Marc from Germany, had just spent two weeks hitch-hiking through Ireland with his girlfriend before coming to Nepal. I was interested to hear what he had to say of his experiences. "You know our German guidebook said that the southern part of Ireland is much friendlier than the northern part, but this was not our experience. We were so glad we ignored the guidebook and went north. Donegal was one of the friendliest places we visited. We went to a pub in Donegal Town and drank some Guinness there. The barman Cillian, then put us up in his house for the night. This would never happen in Germany. The next day it was amazing. We were hitch-hiking to the Cliffs of Slieve League and an elderly man from Kilcar gave us a lift. He stopped off in Killybegs to let us take photos of the fishing boats and then drove past his own turn-off to leave us to the village of Carrick. Donegal was truly an amazing place."

After stopping for lunch, I decided to let my trekking buddies go on ahead so I could walk at an easier pace. The foot paths in Nepal often take the shortest straightest line up a mountain, which can be punishing walking. Some of the trail is so steep that locals build wide stone steps to make travel a little easier. All afternoon and evening, I walked higher and higher along a huge mountain ridge, past sleepy farming villages and gazed down from a dizzying vantage point at a deep river valley far below. "If these are the Himalayan foothills" I said to myself, "how the heck am I going to trek up the high mountains?" As I passed through a lightly wooded landscape I heard music up ahead. A small Nepali porter in a black woolly hat was sitting cross-legged in the middle of the path playing some sad Nepali folk tune on a wooden flute. I sat down next to another porter as the day dissolved into a dusky half-light and we listened to his friend play a few more tunes. It felt as if the craggy trees which swaying gently in a breeze with outstretched branches were listening intently to the music being played. Even the mountain itself seemed in some way, to be listening in the background stillness.

Further along the trail, I was glad to be reunited with my new trekking friends Marc, Tim, Emily and Kelly at the village of Dagcha where they had found a guesthouse. We all looked like misplaced miners with our head torch beams shining out in front of us. Getting up for a late visit to the outdoor wooden latrine that night, I stopped on the way back to look up at the stars. With no light pollution to dim the cosmos overhead, the clear night sky revealed a breathtaking vivid canvass of brightly shining stars. Then, from behind a distant rocky peak, one of the largest full moons I ever saw, rose majestically, illuminating the high valley in a soft milky glow. I stood fixed to the spot, my very being filled with awe.

While we ate our porridge breakfast the next morning on an outside wooden bench, a huge eagle swooshed over our heads gliding on the early morning breeze. We then set off for the high pass of Lamjura La which at 3,353 metres was to be the highest altitude I would climb so far in my trek. As a comparison Ireland's highest peak, Carrantuohill is 1,038 metres high while Ben Nevis in Scotland stands at 1,344 metres above sea level. We set off at a brisk pace along worn paths through rhododendron forests shrouded in cloud mist. As the weather cleared we came to a large mound of stones and two poles from which lines of multi-coloured prayer flags flapped in the wind. We shook hands in joyful exhilaration at reaching the pass and then took turns to snap photos for each other. The trail ahead then took us back down into the next valley for a four hour punishing hike to the town of Jumbesi. That evening at our guesthouse, I ate freshly baked apple pie and custard which tasted beyond words. Our guesthouse owner's wife explained in broken English that they were the last apples left over from the previous autumn's apple harvest. The prospect of eating apple pie for a second evening was as good an excuse as any I could think off to rest an extra day in Jumbesi and to wash and dry laundry before continuing the trek at my own pace.

I was now four days away from the Sherpa market town of Namche Bazzar which had begun to take on near mythical status in my mind. Even the name Namche Bazaar sounded suitably mysterious. It is also the place where most expeditions to Mount Everest stop to acclimatise and where altitude starts becoming a big issue.

One of the main advantages of walking to Namche Bazzar as opposed to flying directly from Katmandu to the mountain airport of Lukla was it helped to build up a level of stamina before tackling the higher Himalayan treks.

By early afternoon the next day, I had my journals updated while the laundry was washed and hanging out on the guesthouse clothes line. Beyond the clothes line was a large front kitchen garden full of potato plants and some side ridges of carrots and onions. With a few hours to spare before sunset, I decided on taking a short walk around the town. Jumbesi was quiet and subdued as if caught in a permanent lazy Sunday afternoon time warp. The paved streets were nearly deserted, shops closed but not run down.

A thunderstorm swept up from the south as night fell. A young Danish fellow and his Nepali climbing guide joined me for dinner. He introduced himself as Rasmussen and although only twenty two years old, seemed uncommonly mature and grounded for his age. He had just returned from a mountain climbing expedition up the Khumbu region, after spending three months inspecting schools around the Jumbesi area, which had been allocated funding by a Danish NGO, (Non Government Organisation).

His Nepali climbing guide, Shree Maharajan spoke perfect English in a measured deliberate manner. Although no more than thirty years old, he had a world weary look in his eyes. As an intense thunderstorm rumbled and flashed outside and the guesthouse lights dimmed, Maharajan told us how he has noticed the effects of Global Warming while working as a trekking and climbing guide in the Nepali Himalayas. "Each year the weather patterns become more and more unpredictable. Other guides have told me that since 1980 some of the smaller glaciers have completely disappeared. I have only been a guide for ten years and I've seen glaciers disappear with my own eyes. Some of the major glaciers up in the Khumbu near Everest have been retreating up to ten metres each year. It is very clear to see when you re-visit a certain area year after year. I have also noticed in recent years, while climbing up familiar glaciers how much my pick axe sparks while striking the snow field. You can see blue sparks coming from the pick axe. This means the glacier snows have partially melted and re-frozen into block ice."

He paused for a moment looking at the flames flickering up around the lid of the pot bellied stove and continued, "Global Warming is not good news my friends for us Nepali people. Annual melt-water from the Himalayas feeds the rivers which provide not only Nepal but much of Northern India with water for drinking and crop irrigation during the pre-monsoon dry season. If the glaciers continue melting, then much of Nepal and India could be facing drastic water shortages within our lifetime."

The next morning I hoisted up my backpack and set off once again to follow the brown clay road to Namche Bazaar. It was a bright May morning and the trees and hillsides were bursting with new growth while small birds seemed to brim over with high spirited song. The small town of Jumbesi slowly shrank to the size of a matchbox in the valley below. I then turned a bend and the trail levelled off and hugged the waist of a high mountain for an hour or two. Settling into a rhythmic walking pace, I began to feel a sense of bliss in simply being on the trail as two snow-white curvy cumulus clouds peeked their heads above a high grassy alpine ridge ahead.

Close to midday, the trail began dipping down into a thickly forested valley floor. Shortly after passing an elderly man who was stooped down weeding his vegetable garden I came across, 'my walking stick'. It was literally dangling loosely from a tree leaning over the trail. Someone had been cutting back the hedge with a machete and had partially hacked it. It was a thin straight offshoot branch of hazel-like timber and came away with one sharp two handed tug. At first, it looked too long and had an untidy frayed end where it came away from a main branch. Placing the thinner side under my hiking boot, I snapped about a foot in length off its end. Upon studying it a while longer and taking a few trial strides forward, it was fully adopted as my walking stick for the journey ahead.

Outside the hamlet of Ringmu I noticed large orchards surrounded by high stone walls but alas the guesthouse owner informed me that the village apple stores were all gone. With apple pie was off the menu, I consoled myself with a mars bar which are a trekkers delicacy out these parts. From Ringmu I began a long gruelling four hour ascent to Taksindu La Pass. Dark rain clouds once again closed in as I neared the summit. It then began to spit rain as I quickly descending the steep trail down the far side. It seemed as if the rain was teasing and playing with me. I raced down the valley while swirls of mist moved down the mountainside around me. Random rogue raindrops continued to fall behind me and splash on my head while the trail ahead was dusty dry. Although my legs muscles began to ache, it felt like I would be a spoil sport to stop and let the rain get the better of me. When the hamlet of Nuantala appeared far below through a window of cloud it gave me an extra boost to stay in the race. I now carried my walking stick to my side, as the rain gave chase. Hens clucked nervously and skipped out of my way while children called out after me. It seemed as if spots of rain were tapping me cheekily on the shoulders as I reached the outskirts of Nuantala and booked into the first guesthouse I came to. Within two minutes of walking through the doorway, the heavens opened with a white flash and almighty crack of thunder. The next morning I woke after dawn to find the torrential rain had cleared. My trekking adventure was entering a new stage. I had spent a week on the trail going up, over and back down the high Himalayan foothills. From now on, however, the trail would only get higher and higher as I began to trek towards some of the highest mountains on Earth.

The homesteads around Nuantala seemed a lot more run down and the people much poorer than the Sherpa villages I had passed the previous days. For a time the trail descended down into a huge rhododendron forest. Unlike Ireland the rhododendrons had not grown into dense thickets, but instead the bushes grow into a high tree canopy which lets in light and space for other plants to grow on the forest floor. Bundles of sawed timber lay in scattered heaps beside the trail in places.

The air was mild and humid inside the forest. I saw my first snake slither silently across the trail in front of me, its skin a warning fluorescent green. The faint roar of a river grew then louder up ahead and soon I was standing at the near bank of a large metal suspension bridge. I checked my trekking map. I was about to cross the Dudh Kosi river for the first time, its volume greatly swollen with early summer glacial melt water from the upper Himalayan valleys. It flowed downstream in a loud milky green torrent, churning up water, rocks and clay in its path.

By early afternoon the trail came to the small village of Jubhing. It had a totally different feel to the Nepali and Sherpa villages I had passed through previously along the trail. The stone houses and farm sheds were thatched with large tightly woven reed mats, which flopped over the roof making natural eaves for rain water to flow off. The landscape was strewn with boulders of all shapes and sizes, between which small gardens of recently planted maize poked through. Many of the small sheds for livestock or storing timber were built against the side of large boulders as ready made wall or roof supports. The valley seemed to have its own milder micro-climate which encouraged lush vegetation. Even the people looked and dressed differently. I was now in the land of the Rai.

A short distance up the trail, I was overtaken by a group of women and children. They were walking up the valley to work in the terraced mountainside fields. One of the younger women carried a woven basket on her back, from which a young infant peeped out at me. They were followed by a teenage boy who had a long kukhuri knife and sickle strapped to his waist. The Rai People are among a minority of ethnic tribal people in Nepal who were never colonised by European or other Asian powers. Even the armies of the British Empire at the height of its military power in India, failed to defeat these people. I wondered how many young Irishmen or Scots had met their death in the mountains of Nepal, fighting past ancestors of these people, and how ludicrous a mission it had been in the first place. These ethnic warriors were so highly respected for their toughness and resilience that to this day the British Army hire young men from the region to form elite combat regiments known as Ghurkas, with their distinctively shaped kukhuri knives.

All afternoon I trekked through the Rai homeland, stopping in the village of Kharikola for lunch. An hour later I had begun the short but punishing climb up to Bupsa. I really felt for the porters I passed along the way who carried super-human pack loads, often over eighty kilos on their back. They had to carry a t-shaped walking stick with a smooth flat top which they sat on to take the immense weight off their feet after every few steps on the steeper sections. With no roads in or out of East Nepal, these poor people supplied guesthouses and villagers with luxury items further along the trail, such as cases of beer, boxes of mars bars, toilet rolls etc. When I finally reached the hamlet of Bupsa, it was early evening. As the weather had continued to clear, I decided to push on for the hamlet of Poiya, about a two hour walk further up the mountain. The lower valleys began to open up in a magnificent panoramic view. I could see sections of the trail I had trekked over the previous two days, stretched out far below. The late evening May sunshine bathed the straw-brown terraced hills and deep green forested slopes in a fresh, vivid light.

I stopped to take my backpack off and was soon enjoying a short nap under a trailside tree. Then after a time, I heard the sound of people approaching. When I lifted my sun hat and opened my eyes two Nepali men were standing a few yards in front of me. One of the men introduced himself as Dhana Rai. He had very good English. His brother who wore a base ball caP remained silent, but nodded his head in recognition. Dhana explained that his brother was ill and needed medical treatment. As the nearest hospital was in Katmandu they had to walk a day and a half from their village up to Lukla where there was a small airstrip. From there, they would take a thirty seater plane to Katmandu. Both men were of medium height. Dhana was about forty years old with neat black hair, a round open friendly face and kind inquisitive eyes. "Where are you from", he asked. When I said Ireland, his face lit up and he insisted that I walk along with them. He waited patiently as I hoisted my backpack over my shoulders again, while his brother walked on ahead of us. We immediately struck up a friendly rapport and chatted away as we walked up along the high rocky trail. Dhana stopped at a vantage point and pointed back down the valley to where his village was, now just a collection of brown specks on a distant terraced mountainside. He told me that he lived there with his young family and was schoolmaster of the local school. He showed me a photo of a newly refurbished classroom for junior infants and hanging up one of the walls was a green, white and gold tri-colour. "That's the Irish flag", I blurted out in surprise. "Yes, I have Irish friends who raised money for our new school" Dhana replied.

It turned out that Dhana Rai had been a cook for the Team Ireland Expedition to Mount Everest back in 1993. The team of Irish climbers that had stepped up to the challenge had included Dawson Stelfox and Dermot Somers. Stelfox had became the first Irishman to summit Mount Everest. The Irish climbing team had struck up a lasting friendship with Dhana and upon returning to Dublin, had established a charity to raise money for his local village back in Nepal. Dermot Somers had been unfortunate not to make the final push to the summit of Everest on that expedition. He had since gone on to make a number of popular adventure trekking TV series which have been screened on the Irish channels RTE and TG4. This included following and recording some of the great surviving human migrations on foot from the cold snowy tundra of the Arctic circle to the baking hot desserts of the Sahara.

As Dhana and I walked up towards a forested mountain pass, we discovered an amazing co-incidence that connected us through Dermot Somers. While on my travels through North America the previous year I had sent an e-mail to Dermot Somers, who I had met and become friends with on an historic walk from West Cork to Leitrim. He had replied to a previous email saying that he was preparing to do a new documentary, following an epic migration of people and animals in West Nepal. I had enquired about the possibility of joining him, but Dermot had explained to me that it would be too expensive and difficult to obtain permits. This was the very same trek that Dhana Rai had been part of and had helped organise from Katmandu, on behalf of Dermot Somers and his film crew!

As we rounded the trail and walked up through a natural pass between two giant boulders, Dhana pointed out the sacred Sherpa mountain of Kumbhila, far off in the distance. It rose up from a bank of grey cloud like a jagged pre-historic dinosaur tooth on the northern horizon. This was the direction I was heading. As the last rays of golden sunshine retreated down the valley floor hundreds of metres below, my heart soared with the sheer wonder of where I was and my chance meeting with Dhana. I felt compelled to sing a song for the moment and chose an old Irish song *"Mo Shean Dún na nGall"* which translated means 'My Old Donegal'. Dhana smiled and watched me while I sang. If I felt somewhat a visitor here, then the song I sang felt deeply at home. It was like my ancestors were singing through me. Place, memory and time all dancing in a swirling spiral of lyrical air. I rested in the song and felt it flowing through my very heart. I sensed Dhana new all this as he listened. When I finished he said quietly with a smile, "you know the accent you sing in is quite close to that of the Rai people!" He then took a measured look at my walking staff, produced a small knife from his pocket and started to carve the frayed top end which had come away when I tugged it free of the tree. A few moments later he handed it back to me. "Now, this is your *latee surpa*, your snake staff!", he exclaimed in a giggling laugh. Sure enough the top of my walking stick did now look like a snake's head. I was delighted with it.

As the sky began to cloud over, night began to fall and Dhana informed me that we were still more than an hour's walk from the hamlet of Poiya. We set off again at a brisker pace across streams and over ridges, while the forest seem to close in around us in the quickly fading twilight. "Have you heard of the Ban Jakhri?", asked Dhana Rai, knowing what my answer would be. "Some people say that it still lives in the high forests around here and is active at night. Some people think it is a shape shifting creature that can change from human to animal form, while others think it is a forest spirit". Suddenly the forest took on a more mysterious aspect and I found myself looking around more carefully. "Have you see the Ban Jakhri?", I asked Dhana. He laughed for a moment and then replied, "I have not seen it, but I will share with you a strange experience. One time I was travelling through these same forests a few years ago with a group of friends. We lit a fire and camped out under the trees for the night. At one point, we woke up as something was violently shaking the branches far above our heads. We had no lamp to see what it was and when we shouted at it, the noise in the trees stopped." I then asked Dhana about the Yeti, the mythical wild man of the Himalayas. "It is said they live higher up in the snow mountains, but these high forests are said to be home to the Ban Jakhri". Dhana could clearly sense my interest on the matter. While many people consider such stories and beliefs as superstitious nonsense, I believe they have a deeper significance and psychological importance to older cultures. Since the Industrial Revolution the trend has been for society to use only the functional left side of the brain. This was important if people were to be controlled, persuaded to work long hours in unhealthy conditions and be disconnected from the natural world, so that it could be plundered and destroyed for profit and greed. Our own ancestors may well have seen the world through very different eyes. With access to both sides of the brain they had far greater personal intuition and could possibly sense spirits and read omens which helped them avoid certain areas, predict future events and most importantly, remain connected to the natural world. I often pondered what significance the lone fairy bush in Ireland had to our ancestors and how people avoided building houses or livestock sheds on certain paths or lay-lines, said to be the domain of the "fairy folk", our very own nature spirits.

As we walked on through the tall forest path, Dhana told me another light hearted story about the Ban Jakhri. "The older people in our village tell stories of how the Ban Jakhri is attracted to fire and would sometimes sneak into a camp where woodcutters were sleeping in the forest. There is one story where a wood-cutter woke up and opened his eyes to see the outline of a Ban Jakhri warming himself by the camp fire. He was too shocked to move but when one of the other men turned over and farted in his sleep, the Ban Jakhri let a grunt and vanished back into the forest!"

I laughed at Dhana's story out of nervous relief more than anything else, and was glad to see the flickering house lights of Poiya hamlet through the dense gloom of a darkening evening. Dhana had recommended we all stay with friends of his that owned a small guesthouse. His brother was already warming himself by a solid fuel stove when a tall Sherpa woman and her daughter, both with bright rosy cheeks, ushered us inside. Although exhausted I needed a wash and after a short while was handed a hot bucket of water in a metal pale along with a plastic jug to rinse myself and a candle to light the way.

By the time I returned to the guesthouse a dinner of dhal bat was ready to be served up for us. Dhana and I sat up for hours and by the light of an oil lamp exchanged ghost stories. I told him about the ancient Irish belief in the 'wee folk' or fairies. I related tales I had heard about the Banshee, how she followed certain native Irish families and how her blood curdling cries were taken as an omen that someone in that household was about to die. In exchange, Dhana told me more tales of the Ban Jakhri and how to hear it playing a drum close to a village in the depth of night, was a harbinger of a death to follow. We had ourselves well and truly spooked. A sudden flash of lightning and rattle of thunder outside only added atmosphere to our frightened conditions, even though neither of us were prepared to admit it. Finishing our hot cocoa, we then retired to our rooms which were located across a yard. The dark looming forest behind the hamlet lit up momentarily in another flash of lightning, as we bid each other good night. As I shuffled into my sleeping bag and lay my head on a pillow, two deafening claps of thunder exploded overhead. I tried to reassure myself that no Ban Jakhri would venture out on such a bad night.

The next morning began wet and cold and we warmed ourselves by the kitchen stove as our Sherpa landlady cooked us up breakfast. The three of us then set off for Lukla airport, about a four hour trek further up the mountain valley. As we walked we spotted an early morning plane flying down the valley, hundreds of feet below us. It appeared the size of a bee and made a similar noise relative to its size. Dhana talked more about his own community and his plans to improve their lives. He explained that poverty and alcohol were growing problems. Many of the goods porters were uneducated Rai people, while the Sherpa people who lived mainly in the higher Himalayan reaches now sent their children to universities in America to become doctors, pilots and scientists. The Sherpa communities had benefited greatly from tourism, especially by providing mountain guides, porters and hotel style lodgings for the well funded Himalayan expedition teams who arrive each Summer from around the world. Many people pay huge sums of money for the challenge to reach the summit of Mount Everest and to be able to say, "I climbed the highest peak in the world", at dinner parties. Many end up paying the ultimate price for their adventure. Frozen corpses lie scattered across the ravines and ledges of Everest, a sobering testament to its hostile environment. Dhana shared with me his idea to develop hydro and solar power in his Rai homeland as well as eco-tourism projects to counter-act an emerging environmental crisis in East Nepal. In measured, concerned tones he explained, "as the population continues to grow, more and more forests are being cut down to make land available for cultivation. Rare animals like the red panda and Himalayan bear are under increasing threat. Without tree cover, many steeper valleys under cultivation are experiencing landslides and severe soil erosion in the wet season." Dhana also shared with me some of the religious and spiritual traditions of the Rai. "We practice a religion called Kirat, this is a mixture of Buddhism combined with older shamanic elements. We believe that when someone dies, their spirit can be in state of confusion and they may feel lost. A certain amount of time after a person is cremated, an appointed person in the village will go to a quiet area of the mountain along with relatives and friends of the deceased. A small feast will be held in memory of the person who died. The Kirat priest will then contact the deceased and take them from the lower reaches of the Rai homeland and guide their spirit to this ancestral place, speaking the names of familiar features and landmarks along the way. This way the deceased person's spirit is said to find peace and recognise loved ones gathered in their honour. They can stay in this area until they wish to pass on to a heavenly realm or be reborn again." I found this Rai belief fascinating. It was somehow re-assuring to think that a community should carry out such an intimate ceremony in reverence for someone who had died. I liked the thought of being taken on one final tour when I too pass on, past all the familiar townlands, loughs, fields and hills of my child and adulthood. To be guided by a close friend, relative or spirit healer and then, be invited to rest a while by a quiet mountain stream and hear for a final time, the song of the skylark above the high heathery moor land.

By late afternoon, the rain had cleared and we reached a fork in the trail. One path led to Lukla airport perched on the summit of a mountain, the other path which I was taking, led to Namche Bazzar, gateway to the high Himalayas. I shook hands with Dhana and wished him and his ill-brother well. "Perhaps you will return some day Keith and visit our village, maybe we can do a documentary on the Ban jakhri!". These were Dhana's parting words delivered with a kind smile and bright clear eyes.

A short way up the trail, I passed once again high over the mighty Dudh Kosi via a long metal suspension bridge. Suddenly the landscape began to change yet again. I had been traversing a trail along the steep waist of a high Himalayan mountain for two days. Now I was entering a narrow glacial valley, strewn with giant boulders and steep pine forested sides. Large stone walls stretched off in every direction, intersected by narrow paths with rock hewn steps. Some of the smaller fields had potatoes, carrots and onions growing in them. It felt like strangely being back on the Aran Islands except many of the boulders had the Tibetan blessing '*Om Mani Padme Hum*' carved many times into their rock faces. I was now in the high Kumbu region, home to the Sherpa people. These hardy mountain tribes settled in East Nepal many centuries ago after migrating across the high Himalayas from Tibet. They took with them a devotion to Buddhism and Padma Sambhava, a Tibetan equivalent to St. Patrick. He is revered for taking the teachings of the Buddha across the Himalayas during the 8th Century AD. The Sanskrit words *Om Mani Padme Hum* are repeated like a sacred mantra by devotees which translated mean, "may compassion and wisdom be united within me."

As the sun began to sink in the late evening sky, my immediate concern became to find a guesthouse for the night. I continued walking through a land of bright stone walls and kitchen gardens until I arrived at the sleepy village of Nurning. As I walked over a bridge, a group of young children coming the other way, ran over to their mother and began pointing excitedly at the walking staff I was carrying. I pointed and swerved the head of the stick in their direction making a SSsss snake sound and said in dramatic jest "latee surpa". Their mother smiled and the kids looked up in silent wonder then started repeating in a playful chorus, "latee surpa, latee surpa, latee surpa."

Nurning also had the appearance of a village from a medieval children's story book with narrow cobblestone streets and two storey stone built houses huddled around dimly lit courtyards. I knocked on the door of a guesthouse and was soon standing face to face with a cross looking Sherpa woman, who backed up her severe countenance with a half hearted invite to view a spare room. Being too tired to take offence I took the room and asked for a meal of vegetable '*mo mo*'. Pronounced 'mow mows', they are a tasty Tibetan dish containing diced potato and vegetables mixed with spices and wrapped in flour to make delicious bite size nuggets. The stern guesthouse woman's two small daughters were doing their homework as I sat down to eat my dinner. A short time later, I was helping them with their English spellings in a general move to thaw relations.

Later that evening while reading, I could hear strange noises from downstairs, punctuated by the sound of women chatting occasionally among themselves. I decided to go down to place my early morning breakfast order, but also to satisfy my curiosity as to what exactly was going on. The landlady together with three friends and her two daughters were sitting around a large black and white TV set in the dining room. All eyes were transfixed on some Nepali drama. They barely noticed me as I passed and the landlady took my breakfast order with one eye still on the flickering screen. The television age had arrived in Nurning too, for better or for worse.

My Sherpa landlady sent me off on a full stomach and even managed a smile as I gathered my staff and back-pack. With a spring in my step I took off up the one and only high road to Namche Bazaar like a mountain goat. Many organised trekking expeditions to Everest Base Camp and beyond land in the tiny mountain top airport of Lukla. If they are rich and time poor, some hire a helicopter from Katmandu to fly directly up to Namche Bazaar. Many get terribly sick as they haven't taken time to acclimatise to the high altitude and some have to hire another helicopter to take them back down the mountain.

By the time I reached Nurning I had been walking for well over a week and had gradually acclimatised to the thinner air. On my way up to Namche Bazaar I was full-time overtaking sluggish trekking groups that landed in Lukla. I felt like Sean Kelly, Ireland's famous cycling star of the 1980's, as he used to power up the hairpin alpine bends leaving a string of perplexed and exhausted cyclists in his wake. On the trail past Mojo village, I paid one thousand Nepali rupees (just over 7 euro), for my trekking permit into Sagarmatha National Park. While cueing, I got talking to a young German fellow called Tim and his Nepali trekking guide and we walked together for an hour or so. A short time later, I got a horrible and unmistakeable rumbling sensation in the lower regions. Luckily, I was directed to an outdoor latrine by a kindly farmer, just in the nick of time. It was the onset of giardia, more serious than diarrhoea but not as severe as dysentery. I was glad to be in an outdoor latrine and said a wee prayer that the wind was not blowing towards any major population centres such as Katmandu.

From my previous experience earlier in the week, I knew I had to get to a pharmacy in Namche Bazaar by evening and begin a course of tablets. First, I had a punishing three hour trek to contend with but mercifully had no more emergency stops to deal with. I kept up a steady pace by reminding myself that the poor porters I passed were hauling over six times more than what my back-pack weighed. The trail snaked its way up through high pine forests until at last, Namche Bazaar appeared bathed in late evening sunshine. *Tashi Delek* was now the standard Sherpa greeting, as I passed some smiling locals. Although Namche is the main market town for the entire Khumbu region, it had the appearance from a distance of a Swiss Alpine Resort without the large woolly yaks, Tibetan traders and Sherpa townsfolk. Although just three days walk from the Rai homeland, Namche Bazaar felt like a different world with bureau exchanges, hotels, plush trekking gear shops, bookshops and bakeries all geared towards affluent trekkers from Asia, Europe and North America.

Within moments of arriving, the low evening sun was engulfed by a thick fog that raced up from the deep valleys below and threw a steely grey cloak over the town. I made it to a pharmacy just in time, and was given a prescription and some re-hydrating minerals to dissolve in water. I would have to stay two nights in Namche Bazaar to acclimatise to the higher altitude and so let my intuition choose a good guesthouse. I found the Lama Guesthouse high on a hill overlooking the main town and I instantly struck up a friendly rapport with the young Sherpa manager called Ramesh. He cooked me up a dinner of chips and steak with pepper sauce. It was such a welcome change from dhal bat that it nearly brought tears to my eyes. As the temperature began to drop outside, he plugged in a heater and offered me a glass of whiskey. We sat up until late in the night talking about Buddhism, girls, work, politics and the Himalayan mountains. Ramesh had worked as a mountain guide before taking over the guesthouse and had some hair-raising stories of near fatal accidents while on expeditions. His main advice to me was if altitude sickness strikes, find every means possible to descend fast. Even two hundred metres down the mountain may make all the difference to a quick recovery. He recounted a story of a trekker who became dangerously ill from high altitude and lack of oxygen to the brain. With time running out he was strapped to a yak herders horse which was then sent galloping down the trail to the next village. This quick action saved the man's life.

Despite been physically exhausted that night, I found it difficult to sleep and put it down to the high altitude. All I could see from my bedroom window the next morning was a thick fog which hung over Namche Bazaar and wet everything in a cold drizzle. I used my rest day to buy some more essential trekking gear, get more Nepali rupees from the bank and check up on emails. An email had come in from my friend Ian Wasson back in Ireland to say he and my cousin Dermot had booked their flights to New Delhi and Katmandu to meet up with me. I took a quick glance at the date they were arriving and gave a sigh of relief, as it gave me ample time to explore the Khumbu region and spend a night or two at a remote hermitage as I had planned. My giardia had also stopped and I felt strong enough to continue on the trail to the smaller Himalayan peak of Gokyo Ri which was a four day walk from Namche.

Just as the day was nearly over the fog retreated down the valley and two brilliant white snow capped peaks appeared strikingly on each side of the town. Towering to the right was the jagged snow laden peak of Khumbila, meaning "God of Khumbu". Ramesh informed me that the mountain is considered too sacred by the Sherpa to climb. I decided to keep my fitness levels up with a short thirty minute walk and followed s steep trail leading out of Namche to get a panoramic view of the two giant Himalayan mountains before sunset. Near the top of the trail I met the young German guy Tim once again. He was taking photos and told me that he and his Nepali guide had fallen out and parted company. As we sat on boulders enjoying the view, two more Western trekkers passed us and stopped to chat a while. One of the guys was from the U.S. but had a Nepali passport. They then set off down the trail. Myself and Tim began talking about altitude sickness when suddenly he collapsed right in front of me. I held his arm and watched the blood literally drain from his face. When he regained consciousness he began to panic slightly and staring wildly around him started shouting, "I can't see anymore, I cannot see". There was no way I could possibly carry Tim as he was over six foot three inches in height and I quickly realised I needed help to carry him down the mountain as quickly as possible. I ran for all I was worth down the trail until I caught up with the two trekkers we had met a few minutes previously. Together the three of us managed to carry him down the trail without falling. All the while, Tim was lapsing in and out of consciousness and sometimes attempting to talk to us but all his sentences were jumbled up. We had descended about one hundred and fifty metres in altitude, when all of a sudden Tim began talking coherently again and insisted that we let him down as he wanted to walk. Two of us walked either side of him until he became visibly more steady on his legs. Soon we reached the outskirts of Namche Bazaar again. We were all quite shook up, but naturally relieved at the same time. I walked Tim back to his guesthouse and sat with him until he ate a dinner and drank a litre of water. He said he had been experiencing headaches for a few days and had stopped eating. We talked over what had happened and he promised to rest a few days in Namche Bazaar and go see a local doctor.

THE SKY TRAIL TO GOKYO RI

The following morning I set off on the next stage of my adventure, to climb Gokyo Ri, which I hoped to make in four days. I was now at over 3,440 metres or 11,286 feet above sea level. From now on it was important not to attempt ascending any more than 400 metres per day to reduce the chances of getting altitude sickness. My destination was Tengboche hamlet and its famous Buddhist monastery. I reached the high Himalayan settlement of Tengboche just as thick cloud began to race up the valley behind me. The hamlet was little more than a few guesthouses and an interpretive centre scattered over a small high grassy plain. Overlooking the whole scene was the visually stunning Tibetan-style monastery of Tengboche complete with red robed Buddhist monks attending to their daily chores and responsibilities. Although the sun had not yet set, temperatures were already dropping close to freezing. I booked into a cosy guesthouse and enjoyed a dhal bat dinner. Later that night as I sat around the stove, the guesthouse owner told me about a shepherds path that would take me to the hamlet of Dole, which he claimed was just over a half day's walk from Tengboche. From there he told me I would be just two days trek along a high trail to Gokyo.

I was woken by my alarm at 6am as I had planned to attend the early morning *puja* in the monastery. When I put on my layers of clothing and went outside, it took me a while for my mind to comprehend what my eyes were trying to take in. To the north, were the twin giant snow peaks of Lhotse and Mount Everest gleaming brilliantly white in the dawn sunshine. Arching over the eastern skyline was the awe inspiring large summit of Ama Dablan with its flanking lesser peaks. I felt like I was looking up from underneath at a gigantic eagle with its wings not fully stretched but poised for flight. As I gazed up more intently at Ama Dablan, I noticed streams of fine snow crystals were being blown by high altitude winds of its summit into the light blue sky. These magical snow streams were illuminated silver by the sun which had not yet risen above mighty Ama Dablan. Looking west across from our guesthouse, Tengboche monastery nestled beneath a background of jagged snow capped peaks. Its split level building style reflected the mountain landscape, as did the tall white temple gompa and smaller terra cotta red gate houses and buildings. It was clearly a time honoured example of human architecture seeking to reflect this special Himalayan environment.

Upon making my way up the main steps of the gompa, I left my boots in a corner and entered a dimly lit room where about twelve monks sat upright with legs crossed on cushions. We were offered a mat at the side of the gompa to observe the monks perform puja which entailed a mixture of prayers, chanting and ceremonial rituals. Early morning rays of sunshine began streaming in the window revealing ornate gompa pillars painted in wildly bright yellows, oranges, greens and blues. I couldn't help but think of the natural setting for Tengboche monastery, as this puja was taking place on the roof of the world. "As long as there are places like this in the world", I thought to myself, "then surely there is hope for humanity." The puja lasted an hour and as I was leaving I shared a side splitting laugh with a young monk. When I asked him what the giant jar of incense by the temple door was for he replied in a softly spoken voice, "that would be for the trekkers smelly sock feet!"

I then paid a short visit to the interpretative centre and found out about a project started by the lama and monks of Tengboche monastery to help sustain and protect for future generations, the rare and special wild medicinal herbs that grow in this region. After breakfast, I double-checked my own route with another local villager before setting off.

The path I took led around the back of Tengboche monastery and soon I was walking through old growth forest. The air was cold and still around me. It was after mid morning and yet the whole north facing mountain side was still in the sun's shadow. The trail began to descend steeply and at times I had to hold unto branches or crouch down to avoid slipping. At the same time, the sound of a fast flowing river began coming into hearing range. A short time later and I had emerged from the forest and was now standing on the bank of a roaring white-water glacial river. In front of me looming large, was a high mountain drenched in bright sunlight and at its base, the trail I was to follow. There was only one considerable hitch to my further progress which I studied with growing trepidation. A solitary rickety wooden bridge.

I stood motionless for at least five minutes studying the situation and in particular the bridge. It spanned about twenty metes of churning white water so in truth, was no Indiana Jones style rope bridge. At the same time it had no railings and was missing several wooden walk-way panels. I reminded myself for extra caution that a plunge into this river could spell personal disaster. I looked around again in the hope of spotting some local people. There were none as this was high mountain wilderness. I then spotted several fresh footprints leading up to the bridge and weighed up my options. Mustering up some extra courage and employing the concentration of a bomb disposal expert I took a few tentative steps unto the unsteady bridge. A few nervous moments later and I had made it to the other side.

My reward was to be bathed and warmed up by bright sunshine. Taking a few swigs from my water bottle, I set off up the side of the mountain following the trail which was little more than a dusty goat path. It soon became a gruelling test of resolve and I could feel my lungs working overtime to compensate for the thin high altitude air. Every fifteen minutes or so I stopped for a few minutes break to take on water and employed a simple breathing meditation technique to keep both my body and mind calm and focused. Onwards I ascended while the mountain seemed to grow ever more immense and steep with each laboured footstep. I was greatly relieved when a side pass began to open up ahead and a short while later I caught a glimpse of Phortse village in a valley far below. The wind blew a lonesome dusty swirling song around me as I picked my way down along the rocky trail. Passing by a long mani stone wall, something compelled me to do three clockwise circuits in thanks for getting this far safely. By now I had a tried and tested lunch routine worked out. Dhal bat took about thirty minutes to prepare and cook the vegetables and steam the rice. Rather than getting myself into a hungry impatient state, I developed a routine of seeking out a comfortable bench to stretch across I would then place a hat over my eyes and drift off into siesta slumber.

Re-fuelled on dhal bat and with the sun still high in the sky I made a decision to push on up the valley to Dole which would still keep me within a safe altitude height gain for the day. I was now back on a main trail used by locals and trekkers and could relax a little. I crossed the Dudh Kosi river once again, this time over a new long metal suspension foot bridge. As I left the twin hamlet of Phortse Tenga I realised from my maps that every step from now on really was a step steadily upwards. I was on the sky trail to Gokyo and my entire being was buzzing with a renewed sense of adventure.

Due to the steepness of the trail out of Phortse Tenga the local villagers had at some point in history built stone steps up the side of the mountain, usually wide enough for two yaks to pass. Similarly In Ireland, ancient trails called *bothair* were always built wide enough for two cows to pass. I traversed up flight upon flight of mountain stone stairways until the trail took on a more gentle gradient and resorted back to a gently meandering path. I passed through tall rhododendron forests and dark blue waterfalls tumbling down from unknown heights. I was now too high to hear the Dudi Kosh river far below but could see its waters shimmering in the last golden rays of evening sunlight, as it carried its gift of life giving water from the highest mountains on Earth. Rarely have I enjoyed an evening trek as much. The only person I met was a young Sherpa boy, who was driving two large snow white yaks down to Phortse Tenga.

Stopping by a waterfall pool to wash my face and fill my water bottle, I thought to look at my reflection in the settling water and then hesitated. It was as if a voice within said, "what do you want to do that for?" I chuckled to myself, it was a good question. Did I need to see my own physical refection to know how I was or should I just check inside. I felt very much at peace within myself and happy to be experiencing such a wonderful walk in such spectacular surroundings. In thirty years from this moment I would look different and certainly older but on the inside perhaps I could recognise a timeless familiar friend with no need for mirrors.

Twilight was surrendering its last light when I arrived in the hamlet of Dole, which was no more than a few scattered guest lodges and farmhouses. It was a choice between the Yeti Inn and Himalayan Lodge. I was glad I chose the latter as it was both a friendly and warm place to spend the evening. Over a delicious dinner of vegetable and cheese pasta I got talking to a Swiss fellow around my own age by the name of Bastien and an Indian couple in their late sixties. This Indian couple initially came across as quite short tempered and aloof, but they seemed to relax as the evening went on and we shared many funny travel anecdotes. They were from a Brahman or higher caste in India and the gentleman informed me that he was an architect. He had handed over the firm to his eldest son. Now he and his wife were going to the places they had always dreamed of and talked about as newly weds. We were all travelling along the 'Sky Trail to Gokyo', now just a two days walk away.

After a steaming bowl of porridge the next morning I felt like a recharged Celtic warrior. The cartoon character Popeye may have derived his extra-ordinary strength from spinach but I'm sure the mythical Ulster warrior Cú Chulainn never want off to battle without his fill of porridge, heated over a fire. Bastien waited for me to pack up and we set off together. He turned out to be an easy going and funny trekking companion which was just as well as it was to be a tough foot slog. Our destination was the hamlet of Tenga at an altitude of over 4,400 metres above sea level. The path rose steeply out of Dole. As the morning sun rose into the deep blue Himalayan sky, I looked back from the crest of a ridge high above the hamlet. The sight literally took my breath away. Dole was perched on a ten acre plateau of deep green grassland intersected with neatly kept stone walls and a cluster of two storey buildings. The hamlet and enclosed green fields stood out like a lucid vision, in contrast to the surrounding mountain and scrub woodland, all deep and light shades of brown. Sherpa farmers had created this high altitude oasis through sheer will-power, hard graft and patient determination.

On the far side of the ridge the trail to Gokyo snaked its way ever northwards up the side of the Dudh Kosi valley, now only a stream, choked by scree and glacial rock. The landscape began to turn harsher. At this altitude neither trees or bushes grew. As the oxygen in the air became thinner every step began to require twice as much effort. Another less serious side effect of altitude we experienced was giddiness. A stray yak seemed to take a shine to Bastien and started to follow us, stopping every time we did to catch a breath. Now this may have been mildly funny at sea level, but up where we were, the thought of an amorous yak had us both doubled over in stitches of laughter. I even knick-named our yak Yannick after the late 1980's dread-locked French tennis star Yannick Noah. Bastien stopped to look closer at our yak and swore they could have been separated at birth. This sent us both off on an another extended bout of laughter. The high altitude merriment of it all.

We stopped for lunch in the tiny village of Machermo, where houses were set among a maze of high stone walls. A small smiling man waved and beckoned at us from the front door of a guesthouse as if signalling, "the party is on over here lads". Yannick the Yak seemed equally convinced, but disappeared around the back of the guesthouse upon our arrival.

Our cook for lunch introduced himself as Ang Zampa. After a hearty meal of dhal bat he brewed up some tea and sat down to chat with us. I asked him about the Yeti as it was in the village of Machermo that a child was allegedly abducted by an unidentified creature for several days before being released. As recently as 1998 a Sherpa woman had been mysteriously murdered on the Gokyo trail. After a police investigation the official report cited, "Yeti attack", as the cause of death. He answered me straight faced which suggested to me that he took my question seriously. "There have been no sightings of Yeti here now for many years, only in winter time do they come close to villages and many people that live here then move away." He paused then looked up at a mountain which rose to the west of the village and pointed up at a ridge. "One winter's evening I saw a line of creatures crossing over the high mountains up there. I do not think they were yaks", he added quite soberly. One of us then lightened the conversation and we both warmly shook Ang Zampa's hand before we went on our way. There was still no sign of 'Yannick the Yak' as we set off. Perhaps she had led us there and was working a tourist percentage scheme with Ang Zampa. I pictured her lying in the backyard contently chewing the cud after a large meal of sweet hay for her efforts. Maybe 'Yannick the Yak' had the last laugh.

We reached Tenga and our guesthouse for the night after a further tough three hours trekking. A stiff southerly wind had picked up and swirls of misty cloud raced up the high mountain valley past us. The land had become even more barren and was similar in appearance to photos I had seen of the highlands of Tibet from a feature in National Geographic magazine. In fact from our map, Tibet was less than twenty miles away, due north behind an immense wall of mountains. Tenga consisted of a single newly-built guesthouse and small sheds surrounded by more stone walls. An immense land slide had destroyed the previous guesthouse and surrounding farmsteads only a few years earlier. Tenga was very atmospheric in an eerie way and I suddenly wondered had people died when the old hamlet had been destroyed by a sudden cascade of earth and rock. The weakening yellow evening sun was swallowed up by a thickening stream of mist and low cloud which flowed against gravity, up the immense river valley of the Dudh Kosi towards Gokyo.

The guesthouse owner was a pretty young Sherpa woman with bright red cheeks called Dickie. After we were showed our rooms down a concrete hallway we immediately made our way back to the dining room which had a warm solid fuel stove. There we were greeted by a young American guy named Dan. He was taking a break from volunteering with an English language school in India to trek in Nepal. He seemed very mature and wise for his nineteen years. We huddled around the stove as darkness and bitter cold descended outside. Our hostess Dickie, regularly lifted the lid of the stove and let an armful of dried yak pats tumble into the rising flames. At this altitude yak are an essential part of survival. Not only are these strange looking hairy ox-like creatures used as pack animals but also as a source of meat and milk. Their dung is left to dry out on stone ditches and shed walls and provides an essential fuel source for cooking and eating. After Dickie cooked us dinner, we all sat around the stove by the light of a dim oil lamp and shared travel stories. I attempted to ask Dickie about what had happened during the landslide but my own intuition told me to drop it.

As I went to bed I felt a little spooked and was actually glad to hear Bastien coughing and clearing his throat in the room next to me. A lonely draught whistled up the guesthouse hallway outside. Sinking my head inside the warm sleeping bag I said two extra prayers before nodding off to sleep, one for any poor souls who lost their lives in that landslide and the second that I would not have to get up in the middle of the night and use the toilet at the bottom of the hall.

The wind and sweeping cloud had vanished by the next morning. Bright sunshine shone upon us as Bastien, Dan and myself set off like the three 'treketeers' for the village of Gokyo. The landscape was now elemental with pre-historic looking immense boulders fields and no signs of vegetation. It felt like walking through the beginning of time, yet these mountains are relatively young in geological terms. In fact the Himalayas are still growing in height, pushed upwards in a pressure squeeze between two immense tectonic plates. We walked slowly with carefully measured breaths and took plenty of rest breaks as our bodies tried to adjust to the decreasing oxygen in the air.

The threat of altitude sickness looms over all trekkers at these heights and it can strike without much warning or regard for a person's level of physical fitness or even mountaineering experience. Back down in Namche Bazaar, my guesthouse host Ramesh had recounted a story relating to the legendary climber Edmund Hillary. He became the first man to conquer Mount Everest, the highest mountain in the world back in 1951, along with the Sherpa climber Norgay Tenzing. The word "conquer" feels boastful and arrogant though, considering the amount of people who have perished in the fifty years since their successful ascent of Mount Everest, which soars an incredible 8,872 metres into the sky. Norgay Tenzing had left sweets on the top to appease the mountain gods. It certainly didn't do any harm as they also both managed to make there way back down Mount Everest safely. The story Ramesh told me, however, happened years later when Edmund Hillary was preparing to climb a minor peak in the Solu-Khumbu region. He became so unexpectedly ill due to altitude sickness, that a mountain rescue helicopter had to be hurriedly arranged through the New Zealand embassy in Katmandu to air lift him down to a safer altitude in the foothills.

Onwards and upwards we trekked, on our own unique adventure up to Gokyo and a chance to summit a lesser peak without requiring climbing equipment or oxygen masks. By late afternoon, the trail took us around a scree strewn ridge and there stretching out in front of us was Gokyo lake. It was an impressive size and circular in shape, at least a half mile in diameter. From the shoreline it looked very deep and equally cold. It had been formed over the past few thousand years when an immense glacier carved it out of the mountain floor, before it either moved down the valley or melted. As the tiny village of Gokyo appeared on the southern shore of the lake, I turned around in a full circle and fell an awe inspiring silence. It was the middle of May and yet huge snow capped mountains surrounded Gokyo lake. It was one of the most desolate yet wildly beautiful scenes I have ever witnessed.

As we approached the village the lads seemed happy enough to let me choose our guesthouse. We passed by the most popular trekking haunts and took a steep winding path to a guesthouse tucked back behind the main village. A friendly Sherpa woman in a bright head scarf came to the door and welcomed us warmly inside, which made us feel instantly at home.

Her name was Pema and she quickly busied herself making three hungry 'treketeers' a lunch of dhal bat. We waited contently while staring out the large windows at the immense vista. The air felt so thin that to laugh or exert oneself physically would mean literally running out of air, so I just sat there and waited for my body and lungs to adjust. Food seemed to help although I noticed Bastien going pale in the face after dinner. He was coming down with a bout of altitude sickness and soon after, took to his bed in between emergency trips to the toilet.

When my own strength recovered I decided to go for a short hike to the back of our guesthouse before nightfall. Once again, huge banks of low cloud began racing up the valley and across Gokyo lake, giving the high tundra landscape a mythical otherworldly quality. These were clouds that had pushed up from the hot plains of India, now in full monsoon season, hundreds of miles to the south. Clouds that had once rained the dual gifts of water and new life upon parched Mother India were now reaching their journey's end. They would not pass beyond the giant wall of high Himalayan mountains guarding the mystical land of Tibet to the north. Instead they were destined to dissolve back into infinity once day turned to frosty night. As I reached the crest of the hill behind Gokyo it began to dawn on me what I was looking out at. Stretching eastwards for perhaps five miles snaked a gigantic glacier. Its surface was coated with millions of rocks from the size of huge boulders to tiny pebbles, all gathered by the glacier as it moved like 'Father Time' down the mountain. As I sat next to it I could hear it fizzling and cracking like a large living rock and ice entity. It was a glacier similar to this one that had crafted and sculpted the mountains back home in Donegal perhaps 20,000 years ago and punched a hole through super hard granite to form *An Bearnas Mór* or 'The Big Gap' mountain pass. I felt like a privileged time traveller who had been allowed to pass through a different sort of gap. I acknowledged the glacier respectfully before turning my heels on the loose gravely ridge and clambered back down to my guesthouse.

Curtain-like showers of hail and sleet soon drew a wintry grey twilight across Gokyo lake. I checked in on Bastien before asking Pema to make some dinner for us. Dan kindly offered to wake me at 6.30am the next day. If the weather was clear we would attempt the steep ascent up Gokyo Ri. It was so cold that night that I slept in my bed with my clothes on in a thermal sleeping bag under two duvets and a thick woollen blanket.

Dan woke me the next morning with a few rapid knocks on my bedroom door and a favourable weather report, "the skies clear for now man and the sun's coming up." By the time I got dressed and reached the dining room, Dan had already gone. Our host informed me that he had just taken a cup of tea before leaving. I was going nowhere, particularly up a high altitude mountain, without a substantial breakfast and preferably porridge which Pema obliged me by making. I called in to check on Bastien again before leaving. He said he was feeling a little better but would wait until tomorrow before attempting another trek. Gathering my water bottle and 'latee surpa' staff I explained to Pema where I was going and set off in the over optimistic hope of catching up with Dan. I passed by a hamlet of farmsteads before crossing a wide shallow stream via stepping stones. The trail then skirted along the eastern shore-line of Gokyo lake before zig zaging directly up the southern slope of the mountain. After an initial energetic start I began to slow down rapidly. I was stumped and surprised at how difficult it became as it looked such a short distance on my trekking map from the village up to the peak. I deciding to rest a few minutes on a small boulder and took a swig from my water canteen. A southerly wind began to pick up and a steady stream of white clouds began yet again flooding the lower valleys. Soon Gokyo Ri would be enveloped in cloud for the day and the opportunity to enjoy its magnificent views would be lost. My mind became crowded with conflicting thoughts of expectation and possible disappointment. I thought of turning back but something deep inside urged me to continue on. I began to find it difficult to catch my breath due to the relentless steepness of the trail. "If only I could see the peak", I told myself in a gush of self pity. "I would then at least have a finishing point to struggle towards". To break this self defeating inner dialogue I began repeating a motivation mantra to myself, "just a little further, you can do it, just a little further." Becoming elated on my own biological cocktail of euphoria and adrenaline, it slowly occurred to me that I might actually make it in time. The first wispy clouds brushed off Gokyo Ri and descended as a local mist around me. A few anxious minutes later and the mist lifted, allowing me to catch my first glimpse of Gokyo Ri, adorned in a web of multi-colour prayer flags. I felt like crying with joy as I edged my way step by breathless step towards the summit. It was just myself, Dan and a tall thin Japanese fellow in his twenties on the summit that morning. I had met him a week earlier on the trail, wearing only a pair of flip flops. He had been clearly determined to continue on and someone must have gifted him a pair of trekking boots. We all shook hands and congratulated one other before Dan and I took a few photos for each other. The Japanese guy didn't have a camera and possibly didn't even want one. He was definitely on some major personal journey, unique to him.

The view from atop Gokyo Ri was simply stunning. We were surrounded by a three hundred and sixty degree vista of seven of the highest mountains on Earth. I felt my spirit soar despite my physical exhaustion of trekking to a height of 5,500 metres. The upward drifting cloud cover unexpectedly dispersed revealing a magnificent view of Mount Everest and its twin companion peak, Lhotse. To the north was magnificent Choyu Peak and the towering snow wall mountains of Tibet. They seemed close enough to reach out and touch in the thin crystal clear air. To the west rose the jagged razor sharp peaks around the Renzo Pass and to the far south another glacier capped giant in the form of Mera mountain. The scene was truly awe inspiring.

I then thought of what the mountaineering guide Shree Maharajan had said back down in Jumbesi, as a thunder storm rumbled outside our guesthouse. He had witnessed firsthand evidence of retreating glaciers in his short time bringing people on mountain climbing trips into the Himalayas. If the scientists ominous climate change predictions come to pass, then many of the Himalayan glaciers will have disappeared by the end of the 21st Century, along with most of its melt waters that are the source of nineteen major rivers than include the Indus, Ganges and Brahmaputra. These vital rivers help irrigate the crops of millions of Indian farmers and their families.

I said a quiet prayer in such magnificent surroundings that we will wake up to the understanding that we should all be careful guardians of this precious life-giving planet of ours for future generations, not short term wasteful consumers of its dwindling resources. Spotting a flat shaped rock close to the summit, I instinctively sat down in a half lotus position facing north to Tibet and meditated quietly for a few minutes. Again, I sent out a thought wish that the people of Tibet may one day be free again from Chinese oppression.

For a long time then myself and Dan just sat in silence, taking in the views and sharing a few light snacks. I gazed back over in the direction of our planet's highest mountain. It was as if the mysterious power in nature had decided to place a magical crown of snow capped mountains here on the roof of the world. Mount Everest, known locally as *Sagarmatha*, (the jewel in the crown,) towered majestically into the blue morning sky.

It was time to descend as once again, cloud began rising up from the lower valleys. Dan went on ahead as I still felt tired and wanted to take my time going back down. Gokyo lake looked like a giant mirror, perfectly reflecting the surrounding mountains and sky on its still sea green surface.

On the way back into Gokyo village I stopped by the wide shallow stream to re-fill my water canteen. An elderly Sherpa man slowly made his way over stepping stones a short distance downstream from me. He suddenly stopped in mid gait and turned to greet me. He was carrying a heavy creel shaped basket on his back, strapped over one shoulder. He saw me filling up my water bottle and shouted over, "water here, good to drink, water down in Namche Bazaar, not good". At the same time as he gave his opinion on the water in Namche he squatted down while balancing on two stepping stones in a comical and fully understood body gesture for diarrhoea. I let out a hearty laugh and he laughed hoarsely at me laughing! "Aye, you're right", I added, before we both went on our respective ways.

Dan was already packing up when I returned and was ready to set off for the Chola Pass with a group of trekkers after lunch. I put some Nepali money in his hand as we shook our farewells, figuring he was on a very tight budget. Thankfully Bastien began to recover from altitude sickness and got up in the early evening to eat. Pema lit a fire for us and I joked that we were going to have a party tonight in the guesthouse. As a yellow watery sun sank behind the mountains, I went down and watched the local herders driving their yaks into high stone wall enclosures for the night. They had had been out grazing the slopes of Gokyo Ri since early morning and I recognised the old man I met by the stream earlier. The air was full of herders whoops and hollers while the chilly evening air made misty breaths of yaks and people alike. Pema told us that hungry wolves and snow leopards sometimes cross over from Tibet in the hope of catching a stray yak with food so scarce in the high mountains. She also said that some local villagers still believe that Yeti still live in the high mountain valleys to the north of Gokyo lake. This renewed my fascination with the Abominable Snowman or Yeti, especially due to the fact that tomorrow I planned to cross the Renzo Pass and travel a remote trail down to Thame village. From there it was my intention to visit and stay a few days at the remote Lawudo Lama hermitage and cave. Belief in the Yeti is still clearly widespread among many natives people of the Himalayas, including the Sherpa. Although most of the peoples of the Himalayas had adopted Buddhism as their religion, these Yeti seemed to belong to a much older folk belief system.

As in Ireland it seemed that often a thin veneer of Christianity was applied to fairy folk religion and other ancient beliefs that clearly had roots in an earlier more nature-based faith. Like the medicine man story I was once told on Vancouver Island, the shamans, druids, medicine holders or seers who went out into wilderness to contact these wild men often received special powers that benefited their respective tribes. These wild humanlike beings exist in a world between myth and reality which still fascinates us in today's modern world as it connects with some primal mystery. In Himalayan folk belief there seemed to be two types of Yeti. Both appeared to be covered in thick red or grey fur like hair. The smaller Ban Jakhri or forest/river dweller also known as the Chu-Te in Tibetan and Sherpa language is much more placid and shy while the Ri-Mi or Mountain man, also known as the "abominable snowman" is believed to grow up to eight feet tall in height and can rip a fully grown yak in two pieces. This was not the creature I wished to meet tomorrow on the Renzo pass, especially in a foul, hungry mood. I shuddered to think that my latee surpa staff might well end up as a useful skewer to barbeque me upon!

Pema was clearly a devout Buddhist. Before making our dinner she recited her mantras holding mala beads between her clasped palms while facing north towards Tibet. Pema then made us free popcorn for our party after dinner. As the sun-set painted violet and gold coloured bands across the high mountain skyline I sang "Destination Donegal" in a slow sean-nós style. Pema then sang a Tibetan folk song for us before recounting for us in excited tones how she had once gone on a pilgrimage to Bodh Gaya in Northern India. It is said that the Buddha attained enlightenment there while sitting in meditation under a Bodhi tree. We enjoyed a truly wonderful evening, sitting around the warm stove sharing stories, songs and laughing. By 9pm it was bed-time. As I extinguished my bedside candle I looked out my bedroom window which faced Gokyo lake and beyond to the dark silhouette of mountains which loomed large on the northern horizon. Somewhere up there among those wild peaks was the Renzo Pass. The stars sparkled so brightly in the frosty night sky, that they seemed to cast a soft otherworldly glow over the village rooftops and Gokyo lake itself.

After breakfast the next morning I said my farewells to Bastien and Pema and paid up for my lodgings and meals. I was feeling strong and the morning was clear and sunny, so I decided to take on the Renzo Pass myself. Using the stepping stones to cross the wide stream, I skirted my way once again along the eastern shoreline of Gokyo Lake. I tried to judge my way using my map and tracking visible signs of the trail. After a frustrating hour of back-tracking and growing confusion, it was time to admit to myself I was well and truly lost. It was then that I spotted a small herd of yaks being watched over by a herdsman on the far side of a valley. As I got closer I recognised the herdsman. It was the same old man I had met by the stream yesterday. Of small but wiry tough build he wore a navy blue wool cap pulled right over his head. His face was dark and weather hardened like tough crinkled leather, yet his eyes were wise and shone brightly. I decided on saying hello in Sherpa "Tashi Delek". "Tashi Delek", he replied back in a sing song voice and added directly with an inquisitive smile, "Where are you going?"

Now that was a good question.

"I wish to cross the Renzo Pass", I replied, "but can't seem to find the trail to get there."

He studied me up and down for a few moments before speaking again. "Where are you from?" he asked.

"From Ireland, you know near England, way back west in Europe", was my best effort.

"Ah Ireland", he exclaimed, but I don't think he really knew where Ireland was and what did it really matter. He put two hardy mountain hands to his hips as if to give his back a good stretch and then looked up to the sky and back down at me again before asking, "how long did it take from Ireland to Nepal by plane?".

I really didn't know the answer to question number three so made a stab at, "eh...about ten hours I'd say".

"Ten hours by plane, it is a long way to travel", he declared which was right enough.

He didn't seem to have any more questions. I didn't want to seem too direct in demanding directions for my own self created tight walking schedule for the day so I decided to engage in a little more friendly chat. His name was Nima (pronounced nee-ma) Tenzing. When I asked his age he informed me he was eighty-three years old.

I smiled and told him, "I wish if I get to your age, that I'm as fit as you."

He laughed heartily at that. "Now my eyesight is not so good but one time a young German man who visited Gokyo sent me field glasses. Then I could see a long way when the yaks were way up on the mountain," he said, breaking into a new laugh.

Pointing up to where I thought the Renzo Pass was I decided on asking the big question, "Do you think it is safe for me to walk over the Renzo Pass today?"

He looked me over for a few moments, "yes you can make it", and then answered his own silent question, "you want to know the way".

With that, he took off on legs that appeared at first to be shaky but appearances can be deceiving as I was soon to learn. To this day I find it hard to fathom how quickly Nima Tenzing took off across a small stream and up a steep hill to the crest of a ridge. I tried to follow him as best I could. At one stage Nima turned and asked me another question as he powered on up the hill. I literally hadn't enough breath to answer him. When we got to the top he pointed out the trail for me to take up the face of a ravine and then rose his finger higher to indicate the direction of the Renzo Pass. It was no Satellite Navigation co-ordinates but as good as I could ask for. Reaching down athletically to the ground, Nima then pulled two big clumps of dry heather, roots and all, with his bare hands before stuffing them under an arm. Kindling for a fire is what I guessed it would be used for. When I asked could I take a photo of him before leaving he waved his hand downwards signalling a polite refusal.

"The old Sherpa people still don't like their photos taken", was his quiet reply. This was once a cultural taboo shared by many Native American tribes people also

We shook hands and smiled our farewells. Nima then disappeared back down the ridge, while I started sizing up the wall of mountains ahead of me.

By the time I made my way up the first ridge I was nearly spent out. I looked at my watch and couldn't believe it was still only 11.30am. Finding a stream to fill my canteen and a smooth rock to sit on, I contemplated whether to go on or not. I then remembered that there was a mars bar somewhere in my backpack. I rummaged around with my hand for a few moments until I felt the prize. The mars bar was like a massive energy boost. I could feel some strange sugar level transformation going on inside which eventually reached my brain like a generator light flickering back on. I walked over to the stream and cupping water in my hand, drank a single mouthful. It was ice cold but sweet to the taste. I then splashed a second palm full of water over my face which was mightily refreshing. Hoisting my back-pack over my shoulders again, I set off in search of the Renzo Pass.

As I walked up through a huge high rocky plateau I began thinking back to my encounter with Nima Tenzing and wondered why he had made such an impression upon me. It was weird but I felt a transfer of something ancient from this elderly Sherpa man, something wildly light hearted and yet deeply rooted in the natural world.

I first had to make my way carefully up a steep ravine until I found myself walking on a huge plateau surrounded on three sides by tall snow capped peaks. One hour passed and then two but still there was no sign of a gap in the mountains to signify the Renzo Pass. All I could see ahead was a gigantic mountain wall with jagged teeth like peaks. The sun now began beating down on my head. Then there was an unexpected crunch under my boots as I trekked across a patch of snow. I heard a bird of prey high above me which let a piercing cry. My heartbeat began increasing and my senses felt like they were starting to work overtime. Suddenly the worn path I was following vanished. Seeing a high ridge to my right I tried to clamber up it to get a better view. It was like climbing up a hill of loose gravel and I had to give up. I started to curse with frustration as I sat down to empty my boots of small sharp stones.

I continued on my way. The midday sun began to reflect off the growing patches of snow and flash in my eyes, further irritating me. It was then I began to make out signs of a trail ahead again. Trekkers and climbers had carefully placed three to four stones on top of one other at intervals to mark the way. This gave me renewed hope for a while. That was until I turned the corner of a rocky ridge and found myself trudging through deep snow, which covered any possible markers ahead. My breath now began to get more and more hollow and I started to hear a strange wheezing metallic sound from the back of my throat. I was clearly approaching or quickly passing an altitude of 5,500 metres again. I was now as exhausted as I felt on the previous days hike up Gokyo Ri except this time I was much deeper into the mountains.

As if becoming physically exhausted wasn't enough to contend with, my mind began to turn on me. It started churning up unhelpful statements like, "you know your not going to make this", and ,"there's no way out of this one you know." I squinted my eyes upwards desperately seeking a gap in the mountain wall, now towering high above me. Still I could see no way ahead. Instead, what I saw were wispy clouds brushing off the jagged peaks above, ominous signs of an approaching weather front. I though about ditching my backpack and making a race back down the mountain to Gokyo village but this would have meant finding the path down a series of steep ravines, possibly in heavy snow and zero visibility.

The sun was still shining though and the first thing to do was calm my mind which I realised was becoming a panicked liability. I spotted a flat topped boulder and dragged myself up upon and out of the snow for a while. I then rummaged with manic haste for some dried fruit in my back-pack and was mightily relieved to still have a mouthful of water left in my canteen. Curling up in the foetal position I decided to rest both body and mind for a short nap. "The situation is serious but far from hopeless", I began re-assuring myself.

Nima Tenzing's image then flashed in my mind as if to remind me that he wouldn't have given me the 'go ahead' if he didn't think I could make the Renzo Pass. I could feel goose pimples on the back of my neck and energy returning to my body. I opened my eyes and lifted my head to look around. It was as if someone had put a pair of dark shades over my eyes while I was dozing with my eyes closed. This was a clear sign not to take another nap. For the first time I became truly aware of where I actually was…in the middle of a Himalayan snow capped mountain range searching for a high pass to cross over. Dark clouds began closing in on the southern horizon.

"Your some boy", I said to myself with a wry smile to lift my spirits, "coming the whole way out here." I had made a firm decision. I would keep on walking through the snow in the direction of the mountain wall for twenty more minutes and double checked the time on my watch. If I couldn't found the pass by then I would ditch my heavy backpack and retrace the way I came, taking my chances in getting back to the settlement at Gokyo.

I began trudging through the snow and set my course slightly left for a promontory of rock about two hundred metres ahead of me along a low ridge. Upon reaching this natural landmark I spotted fresh footprints in the snow leading on up to the mountains now towering high above me. I could scarcely believe my luck. A group of at least three trekkers must have passed the same way earlier in the week. I could even make out where their metal boot crampons had spiked through the now muddy snow. It was much easier and quicker following their trail but there still there was no sign of the Renzo Pass. Then, upon reaching the crest of another low lying ridge I spotted prayer flags fluttering high above on one of the lower peaks. I blinked and looked a second time to make sure I wasn't hallucinating from the high altitude. Thankfully the prayer flags were still there. But where was the Renzo Pass? As I turned another corner my question and prayers were answered. There was no pass as such but a huge flight of rock stairs cut straight up into the face of a sheer mountain cliff face. Dark gathering snow clouds loomed closer as the bright sun overhead suddenly passed into dark shadow. Step by wheezing step I began ascending the high mountain stairwell. I was relieved beyond words to have found this strange yet wonderful route over the mountains. I encouraged myself to keep going by imagining what a relief it was going to be to descend the far side of the pass. To feel my lungs recovering and legs strengthening with every metre of altitude I would lose.

The final few steps led me up to a jagged mountain peak with prayer flags draped, tied and wedged into every available contour and crevice in its solid rock surface. Clouds were now racing in over the high valley I had traversed. A freshening wind began chilling me to the bone. Within minutes I had my thermal trousers, jumper, gloves, jacket and hood on. Looking to my right to survey the scene around me I was taken aback with what I saw. To my right I could see a line of peaks stepped slightly back from one another. As a snow shower slowly engulfed the sun it cast one last golden glow across the mountains. Each peak appeared like a clearly distinguishable head and side face profile of strange ancient looking mountain gods and deities. I reached into my back-pack to take my digital camera out for a quick photo but a voice from inside said, "you are lucky to leave here this day, now go with respect and humility."

Instead I remembered I had a small roll of prayer flags in one of my coat pockets and tied them to a larger string of flags. This was a surprisingly difficult task as my hands were now numb with the cold. With all the air I could muster in my lungs I then shouted out "La Gye Lo!" which in Tibetan means 'The Gods will prevail'. This is an ancient protection custom for travellers in the Himalayas upon reaching a high pass safely.

It was now time to get off the mountain as quickly as possible but the day's challenge was not over yet. To my sudden surprise the steps on the north facing shaded side of the Renzo Pass lay under a foot of snow and ice with snowdrifts banked up in places. As if that wasn't enough to contend with, freezing fog now descended on the mountains. I had to move frustratingly slowly, probing and searching out the winding steps with the sharp tip of my staff. One awkward slip now and a twisted or broken ankle could have spelled disaster at this high altitude with night quickly approaching. I managed to keep my mind from useless worry by concentrating on what direction the solid stone steps were curving down the mountainside. Some of the exposed steps looked newly cut and I realised my good fortune. With each step downwards I could feel my breathing growing deeper and strength returning to my limbs. After a time I came down below the cloud bank and snow line. The steps then gave way to a rough path. Again, small piles of thoughtfully placed rocks kept me from straying off the trail. For a solid hour and a half I descended through a lunar like landscape until I reached the top of a v-shaped valley floor. The mountain range I passed over was so high that the weather front did not affect this glacial valley. The silence was total. I felt insignificant to the point of being invisible in such a vast Himalayan wilderness. The air became milder and the early evening sun poked its head out from behind some clouds. I wondered for a moment had my ordeal been a dream but my body and mind knew otherwise, for it was still reeling from the Renzo Pass ascent. After filling my canteen by a small stream, I lay across a large slab of sun warmed rock and fell fast sleep.

I woke up all of a sudden and looked around me with the unsettling sensation of being watched from afar. My eyes scanned the huge mountains looming skywards on either side of the valley but saw and heard nothing, just overwhelming silence. I looked at my watch. I had slept soundly for well over an hour. I could see from my map that there was a small hamlet further down the valley but how far away I could not estimate. All I could do was in to quote the lyric from a Bob Dylan song, "keep on keeping on." For what seemed like an age, I followed a sandy path as it slowly descended down the valley past small glacial lakes and deserted shepherds huts and yak enclosures. It was exhilarating to be moving on easy terrain and I knew that every mile gained brought me further out of potential danger. It was a great relief to finally see a tiny hamlet appear far below me through a window in the gathering dusky mist. With the possibility of a meal and bed now close to reality, tiredness and hunger was replaced by the raw adrenaline reserve of recognising safety close at hand.

Half drunk on my feet from the day's ordeal I knocked on the door of the first guesthouse I came to. A kind faced lean Sherpa man opened the door and welcomed me inside. I felt like one of those survivors from a Hollywood adventure drama that makes their way back to civilisation and who now begins to tell their story to some open mouthed villagers. In earnest, I began recounting my ordeal to my Sherpa host and his wife. After delivering a few dramatic sentences, however, I came to the realisation that they had very little English as they just nodded their heads and smiled at everything I was saying. At least they could tell how hungry I was and soon I was served up a huge plate of dhal bat followed by a garlic egg omelette and a mug of hot milk tea with a mars bar as requested, for dessert. I thanked my hosts for dinner then feeling rejuvenated and happy to be alive, went for a short walk out among the fields.

The hamlet of Lumdun, enclosed within a cauldron of mist, was a mythical place, especially in the late evening half light. Giant boulders lay strewn across sandy dry fields of cropped grass. Here and there, stone wall field boundaries demarcated fields and adjacent farms. My hosts kept sturdy ponies who peered curiously from behind one such wall to see this stranger in their midst. I had spent time in Katmandu reading up on the history of this remote Sherpa area. As I gazed up along a steep river valley to the northwest, I knew this was an ancient high pass into Tibet, used for centuries as a trade route back and forth. It was now patrolled by units of Chinese border guards operating a shoot to kill policy. The grating bellowing calls of yaks echoed from across some distant cloud cloaked mountain side. I reflected a little on what I had gone through earlier in the day. It had been unwise and inexperienced to attempt the Renzo Pass on my own, no matter what the weather. I had learned that lesson for sure. Another part of me, however, felt the experience was an unexplainable right of passage, something that had been already mapped out for me. I sensed the old Sherpa man Nina Tenzing was in some way part of it all.

By 8pm that evening, I was tucked up in my sleeping bag under a heap of blankets. The following day, I planned to walk to the Lawudo Hermitage and stay a few days with Lama Zopa Rinpoche' sister Ani Samten who was looking after the refuge. I also had prayer flags to deliver to her from a man I had met at my guesthouse in Katmandu. Although I can't recall falling asleep, I distinctly remember waking up a few hours later. I was woken by the unmistakable voice of my friend Ian Wasson calling out my name in an earnest tone as if wanting my attention immediately, "KEITH!" My back sprang up in the sleeping bag in a sort of shock reflex and I uttered the word "Jesus", as a spontaneous shocked response to being woken up in such a manner. I lay back down on the bed pondering what I heard in my sleep but within moments deep slumber overtook me once again.

The next day I followed a barren stony river valley down past the village of Marlung and towards Thame where I planned to stop for lunch and visit the nearby monastery before setting course for Lawudo hermitage. I felt moody and frustrated for some reason which manifested itself by being highly irritable and losing the trail on several occasions. On the way into Thame I got lost twice. On one occasion I ended up at the front door of someone's house and on the other occasion, ended up tangled up in a thicket of bushes. Thorns ripped my trekking trousers and left angry scratches on my hands as I slowly untangled myself. At one stage I took off my heavy back-pack and gave it a few frustrated kicks before hauling it up on my back again and retracing my footsteps.

Then, as I walked into Thame, I glanced for a moment up at the midday sun. What I saw was a perfect vivid circular rainbow around the sun, yet there were no rain clouds in the clear blue sky. I had never seen a weather phenomenon like it. Stopping for a moment to collect my thoughts I pondered was I slipping into some sort of alternative mystical reality, in the light of my Renzo Pass experience. The other possibility was, that I was going slowly mad. My mind jumped back to last night and waking up hearing the voice of my close friend Ian calling out my name.

I began thinking, "am I destined to stay up here in the Himalayas?, put a down payment on a cave with a view? Grow long hair and a beard? Would I write home every few years with matter of fact tales of hanging out with hairy Yetis and half crazy Buddhist Yogis?"

My trail musings were suddenly distracted by pronounced gurgling noises emanating from my stomach region. It was time for a fuel stop of dhal bat. I soon discovered that there was no village centre to Thame. Instead it sort of sprawled out haphazardly across a wide arid windswept valley with a two storey dwelling house here, a guesthouse there and a school off to another side. Against my better judgement I decided after lunch to make the short hike up to Thame Monastery which was perched beneath a sheer cliff face overlooking the village. Although still not feeling myself, I was glad I came to see the library of ancient Tibetan Buddhist manuscripts. The ancient Buddhist texts at Thame were stored on one side of a small gompa temple. My senses became filled with chanting monks, the smell of incense and the light of burning candles. Each book leaf had been threaded together by mindful hands, then placed one on top of another, before being hand bound and protected in the most beautiful cloth and silken binds of white, maroon and sunshine yellows.

These precious scripts had been smuggled across high Himalayan passes and into Nepal for safe keeping. Most of the monasteries In Tibet where these texts were once stored no longer existed. Over two thousand monasteries had been ransacked, looted, vandalised and then raised to the ground by Chinese troops.

In my native Donegal, the Franciscan monks who provided hospice care, spiritual welfare and education for the local population, had been chased into the mountains and high forests by an invading English army. Between 1632 and 1636, four fugitive men of learning, led by chief compiler, Michael O'Cleary, were responsible for collecting, writing and recording 4,500 years of Irish history into a collection of twelve hand-bound manuscripts. These books had to be then smuggled out of the country for safe keeping. Not unlike the Chinese invasion of Tibet, the annals would probably have been destroyed if they had been captured. One of these 'Four Masters' Christian name was *Fearfeasa* (pronounced Far-fasa), which means man of wisdom and learning.

This destruction of the monastic system right across Europe, freed up thousands of men inclined to a contemplative and communitarian existence, so they could fight in huge colonial armies of conquest around the world. Western societies are now paying the price for unplugging the seer, then the contemplatives, then dismantling the more natural village structure. One of the most obvious modern reactions is a growing mental health epidemic and a mushrooming pharmaceutical industry coming up with more and more drugs to patch up our feelings of disconnection, isolation and spiritual emptiness.

I was still puzzled as to what was making me so anxious, as I waved farewell to the monks in the courtyard and descended the trail back into Thame. It was now late afternoon. I was at least a three hour walk to the turn off to Lawudu hermitage where I planned to stay the night. The blue sky overhead quickly shrank and a blustery wind blew expectations of rain to come. The trail descended steeply from Thame down through a narrow valley gorge cloaked in wild thickets of stunted trees and bushes. I felt a surge of energy in my body which is common to trekkers returning back down from high altitude. I was soon cruising and at considerable pace along the trail. While taking a short break for water, a young Sherpa girl of no more than sixteen years old caught up with me. She was carrying a peck of freshly cut grass for animal fodder which was tied together with ropes and balanced across her head and shoulders. She stopped for a moment, then pointed with her finger to me and the trail ahead. Hoisting my back pack over my shoulders I started off down the trail with the young sherpa girl hot on my heels. If I thought I was conducting the pace, she was making sure I didn't slack. For what seemed like an hour we raced through sleepy hamlets past bemused chin-on-paw dogs and wide eyed toddlers. This Sherpa farm girl was literally driving me down the mountain for her own amusement. On the outskirts of another village she disappeared up a side lane at full pace without as much as a 'by your leave'. Stopping to catch my breath, I took out my map and realised that I had missed the turn off for the Lawudo hermitage. The light was quickly fading and I didn't want to arrive at Ani Samten's door unannounced in the dark. Staring forlornly up at the now mist shrouded mountain in the direction of Lawudo, I made a quick decision to return to Namche Bazzar, which was less than a two hour walk away.

The trail back into Namche was carpeted with pine needles which provided a spongy walking surface for my tired legs and weary feet. On the way, I spotted a shaven headed monk of about forty years old sitting in meditation position on an outcrop of rock overhanging an impossibly deep river valley. His maroon cloak stood out in bright contrast to the greying twilight but it was his visible stillness and inner peace that radiated some special quality from him. His grounded presence made him appear a natural part of the landscape.

It was dark by the time I arrived back at the Lama Guesthouse. Ramesh was both visibly surprised and pleased to see me again. Over dinner I told him about my trip across the Renzo Pass. Ramesh informed that I was lucky as it was only last year that the Nepali Government had funded work on the trail and the construction of new steps as seasonal employment for people in the region who stayed in camp sites. When I went downstairs to check the internet I opened my inbox to find three emails from my friend Ian. The last one simply read, "Where are you Keith?"

I read on to discover that Ian and Dermot had landed in New Delhi and were awaiting word from me before they bought tickets to Katmandu. I sent Ian an immediate reply explaining where I was and that I would get a flight back from Lukla airport and meet them both in Katmandu in two days time. I was so relieved that I had checked my emails. I had made a big mistake and thought Ian and Dermot were travelling out to meet me ten days later than they had planned. I could have been up at the Lawudo hermitage totally unaware that Ian and Dermot's holiday plans to meet me in Katamandu were spoiled. Hearing Ian's voice and the strange day I experienced now made more sense to me. This journey was teaching me that there is an underlying 'God intelligence' operating beyond the surface of our perceived reality which manifests in so called coincidences and synchronised events in our lives. I was also learning that everyone has the potential to consciously tap into it.

When I explained to Ramesh that I had to leave tomorrow, he kindly offered to deliver the prayer flags I was carrying up to

Lawudo in person. That night in my bedroom I wrote a short letter to Ani Samten explaining how I felt I knew her a little through the book, "The Lawudo Lama" and expressed my wish to return to the Lawudo hermitage someday and meet her in person.

The next morning was 'Day 20' of my trek on the Solu Khumbu trail. I had unintentionally lost half a stone in weight and was as lean and mean as a mountain goat. I set off from Namche Bazzar at dawn, after a hearty breakfast prepared by Ramesh. I had just over nine hours to walk back down the Dudh Kosi river valley and up to Lukla to book my flight to Katmandu for the following morning. Once again luck was on my side as I hobbled into Lukla eight and a half hours later, sunburnt and jaded but on time to buy a plane ticket. Visibility had been so good that day that a total of five flights had left from Lukla, thus flying scores of trekkers back down to Katmandu who had been delayed for days due to poor visibility and bad weather. This meant I was able to book a seat with my pre-paid ticket on the first flight the following morning. After an hour's recovery sleep and a dhal bat dinner in my Lukla town guesthouse, I decided to walk up to see the famous Lukla airport. At a lofty 9,380 feet above sea level, Lukla is the highest commercial airport in the world. Through a meshed fence I gazed down with gob-smacked disbelief at the size of the main and only runway which was small even by small private airport standards. The runway is just over 1,000 feet long for commercial plane to land and take off from. To put this into context, planes have slightly under the length of three compact soccer pitches, end to end, to land and take off from. At the bottom of the runway I could just make out a ramp where the planes literally take off into thin air, off a gigantic cliff face. From my vantage point it looked like a giant ski jump for mad test pilots.

I was in for a sleepless night back at my guesthouse, as a dog barked out on the street until the break of dawn, while a woman coughed incessantly through the night from an upstairs room. Over breakfast, another American trekker swore that the dog and the lady were barking and coughing in sequence as when one stopped the other went into high audio action. I was delighted to get my *latee surpa* staff on board the plane and past the very laid back Nepali airport security guards. I was duly ushered on board with around twenty other passengers. It felt like we were going on a covert military mission rather than a commercial airline flight. Some of the Nepali passengers produced lumps of cotton wool and proceeded to stuff them hurriedly in their ears. A tray of boiled sweets was passed around and the co-pilot slid the door closed with a loud bang. Everyone then grappled to find their seat belts. I tried not to think about the fact that our plane was about to take off over the edge of a towering Himalayan canyon. When the pilot began to rev up the twin engines for a fair run at the abyss I suddenly regretted not tapping someone on the shoulder for a lump of cotton wool instead of savouring my first boiled sweet in weeks.

The pilot began to really work up the engines and a loud deafening roar filled the plane, mercifully dulling the senses. Our plane first taxied around and faced out into the great blue yonder. Then with a sudden jerk the plane began moving forward at full throttle and mercifully we had enough thrust behind us to clear the ramp. We were airborne and flying through a gigantic canyon like glacial valley. It was strange to be on a flight where the plane was literally dropping altitude from take off. It took just twenty five minutes for our flight to land at Katmandu airport. On the way I recognised some of the mountain passes I had taken days of breathless effort to cross over. The aerial view did my personal trek no justice, for my experiences had logged it as sheer magical adventure.

A bus was waiting for us when our plane landed safely. We were then taken to a back car-park to the side of Katmandu airport, where taxi men were already waiting to tout a fare from us. It was 25 degrees Celsius and rising in the strong mid-morning sunshine. As we waited for the baggage cart to arrive, everyone began to slowly bake and steam in their thermal trekking jackets, chill proof trousers and insulated boots. It was also quite a culture shock being re-introduced to the city's heavy traffic and pollution after spending three weeks trekking in an area of Nepal with no roads. Rush hour traffic on the Solu-Khumbu trail was standing aside to let a line of pack ponies or yaks pass by. I returned to my old guesthouse in the heart of Thamel, drew the curtains against the midday sun and collapsed with tiredness on the bed with dreamy expectations of pizza and pastries later. Resurrected by a cold shower I went in search of Ian and Dermot after checking my emails. By what seemed like the aid of some mysterious intervention the three of us were now in Katmandu and I was looking forward very much to seeing two good friends from back home.

Ian had been a friend for many years. Originally from County Antrim, he had moved to Donegal to work as an environmental advisor for farmers. He was two years older than me, of medium build with short brown hair and designer beard which framed an ever ready mischievous smile. As long as I had known him, he was always the centre of a good party or night out on the town. He and my sister Donna had gone out for a while but myself and Ian had really become friends through a funny coincidence. The day after an outdoor summer party held near a local beach, I had cycled down with bin liners to clean up any litter, beer cans and bottles left scattered around the forest floor. Ian had driven down to Murvagh at exactly the same time with exactly the same intention. Finding a squirrel's nest of two unopened cans of larger for our efforts, we had toasted our 'Wombles-like' forest clean-up.

Dermot was not only a close friend but a close neighbour and first cousin as his Father and my Mother are Brother and Sister. Of average height, Dermot was thin but wiry and strong. He had short light red hair and glasses and a thoughtful, quiet nature. I found Ian and Dermot at the Hotel Ganesh Himal in Downtown Thamel, sitting out relaxing on a balcony and sipping two cold beers. The banter, laughs, jibes and jokes began almost at once between us as happens between familiar friends. I was then served up my first beer in almost a month. I felt like John Mills in the 'Ice Cold in Alex' Carlsberg movie-adapted advertisement who after spending months out in the hot dessert, slakes his thirst with a frosty glass of lager in one satisfyingly, refreshing gulp. We then went out together for a meal and decided on doing a seven day trek up the Langtang Valley. Rather than following popular Irish custom and going 'on the beer' for the night we took the wiser Continental option. We sipped another bottle of beer each before agreeing to meet up again tomorrow afternoon to organise trekking passes and bus timetables. After purchasing our trekking permits for the Lantang the following day, we went in search of some trekking gear. Prices for high street trekking gear in the many Thamel hiking shops is sometimes as little as ten percent of the retail price in the West. In many cases the trekking gear that is sold at phenomenally different prices is made by the same labour at separate factories, usually in China or South Korea. A factory employee may be asked to work a ten hour day on an order for a top U.S. trekking brand like North Face and then cycle across town to another factory and do another few hours over-time for a trekking gear order to be sent to Nepal or Thailand. In one store I bought a bright orange trekking t-shirt. I showed it to Ian joking that I got it to mark the historic new Power Sharing Assembly set up in Northern Ireland. He shook his head in theatrical disbelief and with a rye smile quipped back, "suppose I will have to buy an auld' Donegal Gaelic football jersey when I get back home now!"

Our main shopping trip was to the Rai owned trekking and camping shop opposite the Seven Corners Hotel in Thamel. The owner looked like Mr Mowagai from the 1980's Karate Kid movies, complete with tidy grey chin beard and the same aura of coolness and composure. There were no sales pitches with him and no haggling. Every item of gear was at a bargain price, take it or leave it. He exuded a Zen like presence that automatically commanded respect, sitting up as he did on a stool in the corner of his compact trekking store. I observed with growing admiration, that all his answers to questions about trekking gear requirements from customers never passed the five word mark. "Do you think we will need wind and weather proof trousers on the Langtang trek?", one of us asked anxiously. After what seemed an eternal pause he nodded his head slightly forward and replied, "High up you will need." I felt like bowing as we left but thankfully controlled myself. Instead I shuffled backwards out the door while tilting my head forward and offering an admiring sort of chin scrunched smile.

TEAM DONEGAL'S LANGTANG EXPEDITION

By 7am the next day we had successfully boarded the bus to the Langtang which our guidebooks explained would take around ten hours to reach. The journey was long and arduous and the roads became rougher and windier the farther we travelled. The springs were broken under my seat which gave it a bucking bronco effect whenever a bus wheel landed in a pothole crater, which was all too often. At one stage I thought I was going to gush forth the contents of my stomach on the bus aisle, while suffering some deranged form of motion sickness. Mercifully, I managed to keep a lid on things until we stopped for a rest break.

We arrived at the frontier town of Dunche just before 5pm and Ian scouted out a fine guesthouse called the Annapurna for us to stay the night. This was not Ian's first time to Nepal for he had once done a three week trek along the Annapurna Trail as part of a year travelling around Asia. In fact it was Ian's travel stories that planted the idea firmly in my own mind to some day go on a backpacking trip to Asia. That evening, we sat down to a veritable feast of dhal bat and potato mo mo's and devoured second helpings like men who were enjoying their last supper, before a forced one week march on half rations. Seeing apple pie on the menu, we decided to try that out also for gluttony's sake. When our hosts arrived out with three full apple pies we realised our order had been lost in translation. With considerable determination and gasps of disbelief from Ian and Dermot, I ate a whole pie bar a few pastry crusts but was left feeling like a beached whale. We had great fun around the dinner table as we chatted and laughed freely. Even our hosts gathered around to share in the merriment, as mellowed rays of golden evening sunshine flooded the dining room through a large bay window. That night we looked over our trekking maps with a sense of growing excitement. We made a plan to walk up the Langtang valley as far as Kinjan Gompa in four days, thus giving us an additional four days to walk back out of the National Park.

Bright sunshine greeted us the next morning and before breakfast, I led a short yoga session on the rooftop terrace, basically showing Ian and Dermot the Sun Salutation practice. Before we set off, a son of the guesthouse owner called Som disappeared down into the cellar. He re-appeared a few moments later with walking sticks for the two lads. My *latee surpa*, (snake head staff), and I were now practically inseparable and it continued to attract some curious side glances from locals and trekkers alike. Som took a photo of the three of us outside the Anapurna Guesthouse and Ian joked that I looked like a Californian pumpkin farmer in my newly acquired lime green and yellow sun hat. I quickly quipped back that he looked like a lost renegade member of the French Foreign Legion in his dark blue sun cap with ear and neck flaps. Before leaving Dhunche, Dermot and Ian stocked up on cigarettes for the trek which was not standard behaviour for most modern trekking expeditions. It was a hot sunny morning as we trekked along the bus track to the village of Thulu Barku, before veering of along a forest trail towards the hamlet of Brabal. The trees offered refreshing shade from the searing sun and we stopped past a wooden bridge by a stream to cool our feet and take a cigarette break. A short distance further up we came across a troop of large langur monkeys who moved with loud rustling noises through the trees overhead. While approaching the village of Brabal we heard the unmistakable man-made sound of an axe striking a tree which echoed through the forest. We strained our ears to determine what direction it was coming from and soon realised the echo was coming from further up the trail. A short time later we could hear the sounds of men talking and shouting orders to each other. A large felled tree had created a forest clearing and a man was cutting planks of wood from the huge trunk with skilful measured blows of his hatchet. Another man had a freshly cut plank balanced across his shoulders which gave him the impression of being fitted out with a pair of light aircraft wings.

He began trundling forward on bended knees that seemed close to buckling under the huge weight bearing down on his shoulders. We then watched as he took off up the trail and led us into the tiny village of Brabal. It felt like life here had not changed much in centuries. The people still wore their traditional costumes. The women wore a long tailored chuba or heavy dress over a shirt and a wool belt round their waists, hand woven with the most extraordinary colourful patterns. The men wore trousers and a waist coat and tunic shirt with a kukhuri knife in a cloth belt and *topi* hat. Any children we met seemed well nourished with bright smiling faces. The houses were all built solidly of stone with roofs made of long wooden boards laden down with rocks and stones. Decoratively carved ridge boards ran along the front of the house while wooden shutters were opened to let daylight in the windows. As we ate, men passed by with planks strapped to their backs and we were informed that the local community were building a new Buddhist gompa or temple. The Langtang area was designated as Nepal's first Himalayan National Park back in 1970 and is home to several ethnic groups including Sherpa and Tibetans, higher up the valley. We were now in the land of the Tamang people. This ancient tribe crossed the Himalayas from Tibet hundreds of years ago and have since occupied large areas of land to the North of Katmandu. The name Tamang is said to derive from the Tibetan *ta-mang* which means 'horse-trader'.

After we ate our meals, the lodge owner insisted we visit the new gompa and brought us there personally along a path leading a short distance below the hamlet. The two storey Buddhist temple was situated on a breath-taking site overlooking the lower Langtang valley. Below us stretched lush terraced fields of golden wheat, maize and millet. Inside the gompa, two specialised monks were working at applying gold leaf paint to a huge statue of the Buddha. It seemed like the entire village was there from small children to grandparents, all helping out in one way or another. There was a buoyant excitable energy of a community all pulling together. We left a small donation which was graciously received and a small crowd waved us goodbye as we went on our way. From Brabal the trail meandered upwards through high forest, mainly of fir, pines and spruce. It felt like we had the trail to ourselves as the busy trekking season is from October until early March, when the skies are much clearer and the views of the snow-capped Himalayas much more spectacular. To have the pick of guesthouse accommodation and quiet trails more than compensated.

After a few more hours walking we crested a forest ridge and spied the distant rooftops of Syabru. It was quite an unusual experience to enter the outskirts of a small Himalayan town and be greeted by silence save for the sound of birds singing. From the terrace of our guesthouse lodge we could see further up the Langtang valley. Distant snow capped peaks appeared like a dreamy mirage in the quiet evening gloom.

The next morning we spent another half an hour doing some yoga on the roof terrace. Over breakfast we gazed out at Syabru, perched as it was along a high ridge. Huge alpine pastures and pine forests stretched high above, while below Syabru cultivated terrace fields swept down into a deep forested valley. We had a half day's trek ahead of us descending down the southern valley side until we reached the Langtang river. From there we had to find a bridge to cross over to the northern valley side and begin a punishing two day trek up to Langtang Village. As we walked down through older part of Syabru we passed a middle aged Tamang woman winnowing millet grain. She gathered grain in a shallow basket which she held and shook at head height.

We left Syabru by way of a large steel foot bridge which spanned high over the glacial river. The trail became arduous and energy sapping and we began taking our breaks in tree shaded glades and out of the glare of the hot midday sun. I felt physically drained and wondered was it a good idea to go on another trek so soon. Ian meanwhile passed around dried apricots and fruit sweets to keep us going. We reached the Langtang river by early afternoon and the incessant sound of its wild white-water roars filled our heads. After a lunch break in the hamlet of Bamboo I urged Dermot and Ian to push on for the Lama Hotel to leave us an easier route the following day. Ian was quite content to stay put, as the guest lodge owners seemed friendly. In hindsight it would have been a better decision to stay where we were for the trail up to the Lama Hotel proved to be long and physically exhausting.

It was almost dark when we finally crossed the Langtang River across another steel foot bridge. We trudged half heartedly up a steep trail through gloomy glades of maple and oak forest. We were led into the Lama Hotel hamlet by a white horse which looked straight out of a Celtic fairy legend. It was an atmospheric setting for a hamlet, tucked into a narrow neck of river valley and flanked by two towering forested ridges which seemed close enough for a hard pressed deer to spring across. Just as we were ready to drop on the spot, a tall wiry dark haired man called Pasang beckoned us over to the Sherpa Lodge. As it was off-season, he offered us free accommodation as long as we ordered our meals in his guesthouse. We all recognised a good deal when we heard one, and were soon being led by Pasang up a flight of exterior wooden stairs to our rooms. It had the feel of one of those frontier motels so often depicted in Western movies. All the buildings were made of timber and seemed to have been built recently and in a hurry. I had images of wild Tibetan cowboys riding down from the mountains into town and later, juiced up on rice liquor, spoiling for a fight with the greenhorn trekkers. I would later find out from our lodge owner Pasang that the only bandits who occasionally strolled into town were of the furry rather than hairy kind. During the winter months when locals vacate the village, bears and red pandas often take up residence in the guest rooms and raid any food stores they can get their expert claws and paws upon.

After only two days trekking in each others company, myself, Ian and Dermot chose to sit apart from each other in the dining room as we waited for our late evening meals. We were joined by a French man who looked like a younger version of the Hollywood actor William Dafoe, and his Nepali guide who sat close to the stove. After some greetings in English, the French man remarked, "you are definitely not Israeli trekkers or you would be sitting bunched together like so", and then made an expressive Gallic gesture of two hands coming together. He followed up with, "you must be Irish ,I am thinking, as you guys always seem to fall out and argue with each other while trekking together!". Dermot, Ian and myself looked at each other, as if wondering for a split moment should we take offence. Instead we burst into spontaneous laughter as he had just delivered a pretty accurate assessment of tensions in the Team Donegal Langtang Expedition 2007.

Over dinner we found out from the Nepali guide why the hamlet had such a makeshift feel about it. Just a few years ago after unusually heavy rains a huge landslide of earth and boulders had come crashing down from the side of the valley, a short distance up river. The Langtang River with its massive volumes of glacier fed melt water was suddenly plugged and damned in mid flow. Luckily, any locals in the immediate area had time to flee for their lives before the landslide damn burst with an incredibly pressured release of water. Thankfully, it was off season and no one was killed.

Ian's eyes looked bloodshot the next morning and he explained over breakfast how a mouse had hassled him all night for a packet of trail mix. He had been wakened initially by the sound of a determined mouse rustling in his back pack. Falling back to sleep, he woke again more suddenly, with the sensation of a mouse scampering over his sleeping bag. Desperate to make peace, Ian got up, unzipped his back-pack and flung a handful of trail mix into a corner to appease the persistent wee rodent. Dermot and I greeted the story with howls and fits of laughter tinged with relief, that we hadn't been the ones targeted by the Sherpa Lodge mouse bandit.

Pasang sat down and smoked cigarettes with the lads over breakfast. It was near 11am when we finally set off for Langtang Village, a day's walk up the valley. Pasang sent his seventeen year old son and namesake along with us so we would stay at his cousin's lodge, but we didn't mind as he turned out a to be a great help later in the day. After about an hour on the trail Dermot complained of being weak with the hunger so we stopped at a small lodge to eat again and smoke a few more cigarettes.

As we were leaving, a group of three Nepali men from the local Maoist Party told us they were fundraising for a nearby school and suggested we give a five hundred rupee or three euro donation each. It was an unlikely story and I explained with impassioned tones that we were budget trekkers relying on off-season prices to get by so they were happy with one hundred rupees each. They even wrote us out a receipt, which I gave to Ian and jokingly suggested he add to his end of year tax returns. They were very polite for Maoist insurgents belonging to an organisation branded by the U.S. Government, as terrorists.

Our maps indicated that we had to gain 1,000 metres in altitude before the day was out and that meant some tough uphill foot slogging. We were richly compensated however, with a trail that passed through old growth forests of giant ancient hardwoods. The constant roar of the Langtang River accompanied us on our right hand side. By the time we sat down for lunch, we changed from t-shirts into trekking jackets, as a chilly wind began to blow down the Langtang valley.

The landscape began to change as the valley widened out into immense steep rocky sides and the river faded from earshot. We now passed through low shrub woodlands and temporary camps where Tamang herders and some members of the family move up each year for the summer months. Smoke from a camp fire billowed lazily up into the air, while clothes hung drying on a nearby bush. A small child peered out shyly from behind a darkened doorway. Stone and timber built huts called *Goth* were scattered around the woodland clearing, roofed hastily with bamboo mats and rough thatch. I had always been fascinated by the practice of seasonal migration of people and livestock, which had been a practiced and celebrated part of Gaelic culture also. In bygone days, from mid-May each year across my home county of Donegal and the Western Seaboard of Ireland, teenagers and older folk would have moved along ancient foot trails up into higher mountain pastures with herds of cattle and flocks of sheep and goats. There they built temporary huts or *Boithís* and set up a milking area. Cheese and butter was made over the summer months and stored in bog holes.

Turf was cut and dried and taken down on horse drawn carts for winter fuel. It surely must have been a welcome working holiday for young and old alike, a respite from the monotony and drudgery of daily farm chores down in the lower valleys. I had personally always sensed a feeling of unbounded freedom up on higher ground.

We pushed on to Langtang and the trail now became much steeper. Altitude was now also becoming a factor and neither Dermot or Ian were acclimatised yet. Our pace slowed considerably and I got an opportunity to talk with Pasang. He told me about how he liked school and wished to become a doctor and go to university in Katmandu, but his father could not afford the fees or expenses. He said that as Nepal was still a developing country and the Government did not provide support for students at higher level education. I took Pasang's email and told him I would speak to Dhana Rai to see if he knew of any work available in Katmandu that could help pay his way to continue his studies. As the valley widened out, a high cliff wall began to rise several thousand feet up to our left. Pasang pointed out that Tibet was behind those mountains.

We pushed on up towards Langtang village and as the sun sank in the sky the temperatures dropped quickly. We were all struggling at this stage and Ian looked like he was coming down with altitude sickness. Pasang offered to take one of our backpacks and at one stage began literally pushing some of us up the trail. On the outskirts of Langtang a tiny elderly couple came out to us with a smoke encrusted jar and offered us a drink of home made butter curd. Everyone politely declined except myself, as I wanted to honour their generous offer. It was the most flavoursome curd milk I had ever tasted and knew instinctively it was as good as any pharmacy tonic. I thanked them with the Tibetan words for thank you, *thu-chi-che*, before we moved on. Langtang was a collection of guesthouse lodges and traditional farm houses scattered over a wide area with the old village situated at the top of a ridge further up the trail. The first stars were starting to twinkle in the sky and frost was forming on the ground. Pasang brought us to the Buddha Lodge where we were given free rooms and brought to a dining room where a warm stove was being filled with dried yak pats. We were all exhausted and ate a light meal without much conversation before turning in for the night. Our rooms had no heating but Pasang made sure we all had extra blankets and duvets.

I woke up at 6am and stared out my frost encrusted window. The northern horizon was filled with a sheer solid rock cliff face and above that towered the great pyramid like peak of Langtang Lirung at an incredible 7,248 metres above sea level. Its glaciers shone a brilliant white in the early morning sun and gave it a majestic heavenly beauty, difficult to convey into words. Grabbing my camera, I went outside to try and capture the scene in a photo, but it was impossible due to its immense scale. Instead I walked upstairs and sat in by the kitchen stove, while I waited for some porridge to be boiled over a stove oven. Across from me sat a small ancient looking Tibetan man with skin crinkled from age. He got up beside the fire and melted a daub of butter in his hands before rubbing it on his head and face. He then sat back on a bench and began reciting Buddhist mantras which he counted on his prayer beads, which looked for all the world like rosary beads. After breakfast I walked across boulder strewn fields and stone ditches until I found a quiet private place close to the more gently flowing Langtang river. Sitting cross legged upon the short grass I began to consciously follow my breath entering and leaving my stomach area. After a few minutes the stream of emotions, thoughts and images going through my mind began to naturally slow and a feeling of deep peace and spaciousness pervaded my body and mind. With eyes resting half open, I looked out with fresh sight at the high Himalayan landscape around me bathed in early sunshine and felt a soft breeze upon my face. I was in someway drawing from the special energy emanating from these high Himalayan valleys, like a type of subtle electricity. I felt a strange tingling sensation in my forehead once again, as when Charlie Gallagher showed me the disc I was to take to Montana. I took it as some kind of good sign.

Back at the guesthouse Dermot was having a cup of tea and Ian got up to speak to us for a few moments. He looked as pale as a sheet and his eyes were badly bloodshot. He told us that he was up last night with diarrhoea and felt too sick to trek on today. Both Dermot and myself were quite relieved not to be going any further after two tough days trekking and were content to take a rest day in Langtang. Ian returned to bed. We checked in on him every so often with water and soft drinks, as he felt too unwell to eat. During the early afternoon, elderly couples began to arrive at the guesthouse. One elderly Tibetan couple arrived with the man walking ahead in a cowboy hat, holding a tether of a sturdy pony upon which a woman sat side-saddle. Upon enquiring, Pasang explained that a highly respected Rinpoche was due to call into the Buddha Lodge on his way down from his visit to Kinjan Gompa. As elderly folk continued to gather, I wondered did younger people in the area feel such a strong connection to their Buddhist faith as their elders. It seemed that their culture was experiencing a similar trend to the Western World, where increasing numbers of young people no longer feel their traditional Christian faith is as relevant or important in their lives. In the Buddhist tradition, a Rinpoche literally means 'precious one', a title usually reserved for certain teachers and meditation masters in Tibet who are thought to have become enlightened in a previous life. Through a lifetime of mind training and self discipline, they are able to preserve a deep level of awareness after dying and thus, choose their own rebirth and re-incarnate, over a number of generations, for the benefit of all beings.

As the sun continued to shine outside, I decided to go for a short walk up to the next village of Mundu, while Dermot was content to rest and recuperate at the guesthouse. As I followed the trail that led up past Langtang village, I began to feel the altitude and my breath began to labour once again. Instead of walking onwards to Mundu village my attention was drawn to a waterfall spilling down a steep wall of mountain. I decided to leave the trail and hike up to it instead. When the people of these remote high Himalayan valleys converted to Buddhism, they did not give up their older religion of shamanism with its ancient belief in earth spirits and benign forces. Likewise in Ireland, the people accepted the central teachings of Christ but continued to connect to the older faith practiced by the seers that came before the priests. This is why Ireland, like Tibet, became such a centre for spiritual contemplation and learning during the Dark Ages in Europe. The people had freely supported and encouraged a religion that did not force them to give up their ancient faith which connected them with the hidden forces of life, spirits and the natural world.

I stopped by the side of a large boulder at the foot of the waterfall to catch my breath and then, using a smaller boulder as a leg boost managed to pull and drag myself up unto it. Sitting in lotus position with my *latee surpa* staff by my side I looked out over much of the Langtang Valley. A tall column of dark silver lined cloud rose high into a bright blue sky, from behind which the sun cast a translucent curtain of flowing beams across the steep emerald green valley sides and brown roofed hamlet of Langtang far below me. I felt I was witness to a landscape dreamed by some supreme artist. My eyes then scanned up the valley to see if the Rinpoche and his entourage were on the move, but there were no signs or shapes of people that I could make out on the trail.

Behind me the waterfall flowed like a wispy white horse's tail down the mountain side and filled the air with a steady re-assuring sound of itself. In places, it tumbled behind an outcrop of rock or between crevices, before re-appearing again in a gathered swathe of water, sometimes whipped sideways unexpectedly by a sudden gust of wind. Climbing back down off the boulder, I decided to approach a shallow crystal clear pool at the foot of the waterfall. As I drew closer it came to me to ask permission to take a photo following my previous experience at the Renzo Pass. Immediately my mind questioned this irrational behaviour, "you are asking permission from a waterfall to take a photo?...do you know how fecking crazy that sounds?" Crazy or not I said my few respectful words and though I didn't hear anything back, it felt the right thing to do, before taking out my camera. Before I left I bent down on one knee and drank a few palm-cupped fills of ice cold water from the pool and mindfully splashed some over my face and head.

Upon returning to our guesthouse Dermot informed me that the Rinpoche had came and gone. It was strange that I hadn't seen the large entourage passing by from my vantage point. Ian was thankfully feeling a little better and I questioned him jokingly, did the Rinpoche call in and give him 'the last rites'. The next morning Ian felt good enough to start the trek back down the valley, but first wanted me to walk with him back up the trail a short way. Dermot was once again content to hang out with Pasang and our Tibetan hosts. We stopped by a long row of ancient mani stone tablets, where we could see snow capped Cherko Ri in the distance and the upper Langtang valley. I thought to myself about the mystery of friendship and how it had taken Ian and I from a chance encounter by a beach-side forest, to high up a Himalayan valley in Nepal. After a few photo snaps to show family and friends back home, we shook on our adventure and returned to the Buddha lodge to pack our things. On our way back down to the lodge, a small stout woman in a head scarf stopped us in our tracks and gestured Ian to take a photo of her. Then with a cheeky grin held out her hand in the universal sign for 'backsheesh' (a small amount of money for services rendered!) We bid farewell to Pasang and Dordje our cook who Dermot had humorously nicknamed 'Joe 90', because of his resemblance to the compact action man figure and set off back down the valley for the Lama Hotel at a steady re-energised pace.

It was nightfall before we arrived at Pasang's lodge again, after a full day's walk. Avoiding the room haunt of the now legendary mouse bandit, we checked in before relaxing by the stove. A group of villagers were gathered in Pasang's kitchen, all drinking *racksi*, a sort of Nepali home brew made with rice. Every so often a loud roar of laughter would erupt from the next room, so after dinner we asked Pasang for some *racksi*. With a wide smile he went back into the kitchen and returned with three mugs full of *racksi*, on the house. It had the kick of liquor alright and was soon working its warm way around the body from head to toes. As we chatted I took out my camera to show Ian and Dermot a few photos of the Langtang Valley and waterfall I had trekked up to. As I flicked through the view finder I stopped suddenly at one photo image. I must have looked like I had seen a ghost. There was a strange outline of a long wizard like face in one on the photos taken of the waterfall. Ian asked me what was up and I silently passed him the camera. Taking a few moments to get the image back up on the digital view finder, Ian's eyes lit up too and he uttered, "wow, holy shit Keith, I can see it too, that's unbelievable!" Dermot had a look next and a laugh came to his face when he saw the image too. I then told them the whole story about how I had asked for permission out of respect for visiting the special place before taking the photo. Ian then added, "that's amazing, when we were going around shops in Katmandu I saw a carved Nepali folk mask in a gift shop which looked just like that image.". He then added excitedly "don't delete that photo whatever you do man!" We sat up and chatted a while longer around the stove by the light of a dimming oil lamp. That night I must have wakened suddenly from a nightmare, as the next morning over breakfast Dermot and Ian both informed me that I had woken them from their sleep, shouting "who...who's there?" This had understandably spooked them both out.

We spent a lazy morning and afternoon relaxing and eating on a sun table and chairs outside the Sherpa Lodge. Pasang proved to be a comical character and was clearly popular with the local people also. There always seemed to be people calling by. He walked around the place in a pair of chequered boxers which he wore as casual shorts. He also wore an old trekking t-shirt and long white sweat bands on his arms and seemed to always have a cigarette on the go. After cooking us breakfast, he sat down at the table with us and told his stories about the yeti.

"There had been problems with the yeti many years ago", he explained in slow but understandable English, "Many years ago the old people said that a fierce family, (of yeti), killed and ate some villagers way up the valley."

Pasang either clearly believed in the existence of the yeti or was happy to go along with the old legends as a way of playing up to tourists. I then asked him did people believe there were still yeti living in the mountains of the upper Langtang. "No yeti there anymore", he replied and added flatly, "after the yeti killed people, the villagers hunted and poisoned them out of the valley. People say the rest of them went over the high mountains and into Tibet."

I began to wonder if the yeti had got mixed up in natural mythology and legend with the Himalayan blue bear. These huge bears are known to sometimes stand on their hind legs when startled, can be fierce when defending their cubs and are capable of eating a person if hungry enough.

The morning's storytelling and my questions seemed all too much for Pasang and perhaps still recovering from too much racksi the night before, he lay his head on a sweatband cushioned arm at our table and fell fast asleep. When Pasang woke from his midday siesta we got him to cook us up a delicious Sherpa stew. We then watched as about twelve pack ponies tied to each other were led into the village by three men who looked for all the world like Tibetan cowboys. They started to strap up and tie sacks of grain, rice and other goods unto the ponies which Pasang told us were for villages further up the valley.

It was after 3pm when we finally left the Lama Hotel, which surely must be some sort of record for setting out on a day's trekking with just over three hours daylight remaining. Half and hour later, tempers finally flared up in the Donegal Langtang Expedition Team between myself and Ian. At a fork between two trails, in front of a large extended Nepali family who were sitting outside to witness the strange spectacle, two red faced, cross looking, young Irishmen in western trekking gear, one with a pumpkin farmers hat, the other in a foreign legion cap, began waving their walking sticks wildly and arguing back and forth in a fast sing song nasal drawl, which onlookers may have gathered as being a kind of English. The hens picked up the bad vibes and began clucking and scattering in flustered tones. The third member of the Langtang expedition, wearing spectacles and a sun hat pulled tight over his head, leaned slightly over his walking stick to draw breath and seemed to quietly await the outcome of this simmering heated exchange.

Ian then adopted a deeply irritating new approach in our argument over which trail to take, by speaking very slowly and in broken English, as if to make me better understand what he was saying to me. I responded with a sharp retort telling him not to speak to me, "like a wee child", which we all then spontaneously laughed at, as if to break the mounting tension. In the end I relented, and we took the high road back to Syabru Benzi in the hope of getting a bus back to Katmandu from there. It turned out to be the right choice in many ways although it can be difficult at times to accept when you are in the wrong. We trekked high up the side of a steep valley which gave us spectacular evening views of Thulu Syabru and the far valley side that we had trekked on our way up the Langtang.

We stopped at a tiny remote village called Sherpa Goan, which had just one available guesthouse still open for trekkers. We were greeted by a stooped elderly Sherpa woman in a bright headscarf, who seemed very surprised to see us. She handed us a tattered menu and in broken English asked us what we wanted to eat. It was then that we discovered we had a choice of two dishes, one being an omelette and the other noodles. As we sat around a bench and thawed out from our earlier argument, we spotted our elderly Sherpa host rushing back up towards the kitchen clutching a hand-full of eggs. We were going to eat fresh tonight.

We ate in the kitchen with the elderly woman and her husband, who sat as steady and still as the high mountains themselves. We were glad to pay this elderly couple whatever they wanted for our food and lodgings, as they looked like they were living hand to mouth themselves. I wondered to myself, had they any other family to take care of them. That night a full moon rose large as a saucer from behind the dark silhouette of a huge mountain across the valley from us. Its cool silvery light bathed our faces and the mountain side and hamlet around us in a soft bright glow. The moon felt closer and more powerful up here, as if the Himalayas were her domain and tonight she was sharing her full glory with us.

We got up before dawn, and set off for Syabru Benzi in the hope of making the early afternoon bus. Ian had regained his health and we were all getting on much better. Further up the trail, Dermot spotted a mountain lion sprinting down the mountain side far below us and was somehow able to point out to Ian and I where it was hiding perfectly camouflaged in a tussock of long hay-coloured grass. It was a special moment for us all. Dermot seemed to have an inbuilt hunters instinct and connection with the natural world. While we had been out working turf on the moor-land near home the summer before, he had stopped me and pointed to a forest clearing in the distance where three red deer were drinking at the edge of a mountain lake. It took me a full minute that evening, following the line of his finger, to finally see them.

It was late morning by the time we reached the Tamang village of Kunjung and despite the fact we had set a strong pace, we accepted that we were not going to make the bus to Katmandu that day. It meant we could relax and enjoy the remainder of our trek at a more natural pace. A bubbly Tibetan woman served us porridge for breakfast and joked with us that she might be able to arrange wives for us though we would have to prove our worth as prospective husbands. Dermot was starting to scratch himself and thought he might have picked up a few bed bugs at our last stay, which didn't come as a shock to any of us.

With porridge in our bellies we were ready for the final tough descent down into Syabru Bensi. The steep descent led us down into terraced fields, past teams of local men and women harvesting golden crops of wheat with curved hand sickles while others tied sheaths and stacked them in tidy bundles. Like three trail hardened amigos, we walked across one final long suspension bridge together with sun hats pulled firmly over our eyes. Syabru Bensi was a grimy dusty place with a shifty Mexican border town feel about it. Myself and Dermot were exhausted and sought a shaded alleyway to sit and rest out of the sun and swirling dust wind. Ian set off in search of accommodation and scouted out a nice cheap and cheerful hotel to spend our last night in the Langtang. After a long siesta we met downstairs for dinner and drank a beer toast to our adventure. The Langtang trek had already become legendary, at least in our own minds.

We boarded our bus to Katmandu the next morning at 7am and even before the journey began, I had a feeling it was going to be a long trying day. For the first few hours, the bus laboured up and free wheeled down roads no better than rough mountain tracks. The springs on the bus seats had given up many moons ago and were not definitely designed for tall people. Worse was to come after our lunch stop though. Our bus had a TV and DVD player and soon we were subjected to a dreadfully bad cheap Nepali Hindi movie with awful sound quality. The hero of the movie wore a pair of blue jeans, dark glasses and black leather jacket with the collar turned up and an Elvis style hair do for good measure. He spent much of the movie chasing a sari clad Nepali damsel in distress and beating up bad boys and criminals with the same theatrical action gusto as an old Saturday morning Batman series re-run. The Nepali hero's trademark acting signature was to twitch his large bushy moustache, while looking straight into the camera with glaring eyes. My high regard for Nepali culture was shattered before my very own eyes. Sometimes the damsel in distress would sing of her woes, her voice sounding like a hundred tortured cats screaming in agony, made infinitely worse by the dodgy sound mixing. When the movie credits eventually began rolling, I thought my ordeal was over.

Even worse was yet to follow. The bus driver rummaged around his DVD collection for a few moments as I watched on helplessly. He then held up a DVD to the light to check for scratches or perhaps out of some respectful homage. He then slid it in the player, increased the volume and revved up the bus. It was the 'Vengaboys' Greatest Hits on music video....all eleven tracks. I thought about asking to get off, but my backpack was up on the bus roof, tied fast to a railing. I was a sonic prisoner to the Vengaboys and had to ride it out as best I could. Song two began with air horns blaring and those unmistakable build up lyrics, ""We like to party, we like, we like to party, we like to party, we like, we like to party"". Suddenly a small Nepali man in traditional topi hat who had been sitting half asleep on a sack of flour on the bus aisle came to life and began to bop his head hypnotically from shoulder to shoulder. The song went into brain catchy overdrive.

"The Vengabus is coming
And everybody's jumping
New York to San Francisco
An intercity disco
The wheels of steel are turning
And traffic lights are burning
So if you like to party
Get on and move your body"

I twisted around in my seat to see if Dermot and Ian were sharing my mental distress, but they were both fast asleep, fly catching with open mouths. I wondered did they posses some higher developed mind protection gene than me, which allowed them to go unconscious in these situations. I so wished at that moment I had it. I even felt like giving them both a punch on the shoulder to have someone to share this music torture with. Next up, it was another Venga Boys brain washing favourie "Shalala Lala",

"My heart goes shalala lala, shalala in the morning
Oh oh oh shalala lala, shalala in the sunshine
Shalala lala, shalala lala in the evening
Shalala lala shalala lala just for you."

Other hits endured included "Up&Down" and the artistically composed "Boom, Boom, Boom, Boom!!". I tried to employ some simple breathing meditation techniques to take my mind of it, but the barrage of sound and video was too much to try and ignore. In the end I just gave up and went along with the music. When the final tracked finished in suitable candy flossed pop dramatics, I watched in horror and slow motion disbelief as the bus driver simply raised his hand upwards and pressed play again. I was never so happy to get off a bus in all my life. We arrived in Katmandu by early evening, and checked back into our previous guesthouses.

It was our last night together in Katmandu so we decided to go out for a few beers in the touristy Thamel district. We found a lively Nepali bar with even livelier music and befriended a guy called Ben from New York who had left his job as a high powered lawyer, to travel around Asia for a few years. The live band's front man was a Nepali version of Danny De Vito with a powerful high pitched voice which he used to comical effect. For the band's finale, they were joined on stage by a young sultry Black woman, who began singing down at Ian. We were drinking pint bottles of lager and after a week's high altitude trekking and long bus journey we were soon 'fluttered' to use a diplomatic term for drunk. The live music was followed by a disco downstairs with dance music. All the young Nepali people were dressed in the latest clubbing fashions and many seemed even more intoxicated than us. I felt uncomfortable in such a hazy mind state, after spending weeks up the Himalayan mountains on a clear headed natural high. The techno music got darker and deeper and I felt overly sensitive to the atmosphere and vibes around me. All the young Nepali people in the venue were trying so hard to be Western and cool. I grew up with this insecurity and knew how it had made me feel an embarrassed stranger to much of my own culture. I arranged to meet Ian and Dermot the following morning, then made my excuses and left. My guesthouse was locked up but with the help of a reluctant young Nepali auto rickshaw driver, I managed to climb over the front entrance gate and landed on the far side, uninjured.

Awaking was greeted by an unpleasant hangover and headache focused behind one particular eye socket. The Irish comedian Tommy Tiernan spoke the truth when he proclaimed that from the age of thirty, once manageable hangovers become mininervous breakdowns. I walked with frayed nerves to buy three Langtang badges to mark the completion of our trek together.

When I returned to the guesthouse, Ian and Dermot were sitting around a shaded sun-table wearing dark glasses on. They too, were looking frail around the edges and over breakfast shared stories of late night confusion and alcohol fuelled misadventure on the streets of Katmandu. A standard Irish night out followed by a traditional post match analysis, peppered with sharp humorous jibes, astonished guffaws of 'My God, no way!" and wry statements such as "yous are some boys".

Dermot kindly agreed to take a carrier bag of books home to Ireland for me and I walked Ian and Dermot out to their taxi, after presenting us all with Langtang badges to sew on to our trekking coats like medals of honour. I had to see them off twice, as in a piece of vintage Asian commotion, they got into an imposter's taxi cab just as the real taxi they had ordered arrived. As their taxi cab weaved through the milling streetscape and disappeared down a side street I felt an initial sense of relief. Later that evening though, this changed to melancholy as I began missing their company and familiar chat.

The following day I came down with another more powerful bout of giardia which left me weak and in minor recovery for a week. It was Friday the first of June 2007, and I still had over two months of travel adventure left to unfold. During this time I rang home and shared with my parents the stories about meeting up with Dermot and Ian. It was good to hear their voices on the other end of the phone. They had news of unusually sunny weather in Donegal, Mary Coughlan topping the local polls in the Irish General Election and my sister Donna and boyfriend Brian back home for the Rory Gallagher music festival in Ballyshannon.

With daily medication and meditation, I steadily recovered from my latest bout of giardia, but I seemed to lose any motivation to travel onwards or even visit tourist sites around Katmandu. Our guesthouse was in a way like being on a luxury cruise liner with 3 floors of rooms, a cook and central outdoor dining area for meals, a library, video room, meditation room and rooftop yoga terrace. After so much constant, relentless travel and interaction with people it was like residing in a a sort of cocoon which shielded me from the hectic outside world. A part of me became anxious and I pondered whether I was slipping into a sort of sedentary rut. Then one evening I thought of a story I was once told concerning a party of Native Americans who were assisting an expedition of explorers find a passage across the Rockie Mountains to become the first European white men to reach the Pacific Ocean by land. The Explorers were eager to press on and reach their goal as quickly as possible and were dismayed when one day their Native American guides suddenly stopped in their tracks and started to set up camp. When asked by an irate expedition leader why they were suddenly stopping without reason, they received the reply, "we are waiting here for our spirits to catch up with us."

INNER LANDSCAPES OF THE HEART AND MIND

One evening while staying at the HBMC I literally bumped into a young woman on the stairs coming down from the video room. She asked me straight out, "are you the guy from Ireland that everyone has been telling me about" in an Australian accent to which I replied, "well as long as its all good then I might well be the guy. I'm from the northwest of Ireland, a place called Donegal. "No kidding, my father is from Glencolmcille!", she replied. This was much too nice a chance encounter to pass off and we sat outside, drinking tea and chatting together for hours that first evening. Her name was Rose Gillespie and she was also backpacking around India and trekking in Nepal. Her father, James Gillespie had emigrated to Australia in the 1950's and met and married an Australian woman. Rose was of medium height with wild curly dark hair, large attractive hazel green eyes and body curves that a sculpture would have been proud to recreate. Rose had been back to visit Glencolmcille a few times with family and had some great stories about times spent with her uncle Francie who is affectionately known in the area as one of the 'three wise men'.

Rose also had plenty of fascinating travel tales to share. As well as travelling extensively in West Africa she had worked for five years in a remote Aboriginal community in the far North of Australia, a place called Arnhem land. While there, she taught spoken English to the villagers so that they would be better able to deal with the Australian Government, state officials and communicate with the outside world. Rose had great spirit and spoke elegantly and passionately about the struggle for Aboriginal rights in her home country. She spoke of the terrible Government policies of the past such as the physical removal of Aboriginal children from their parents for 're-education' and the creation of welfare dependency among native communities. This she explained, had destroyed the very fabric of their culture which was to be self sufficient from hunting and gathering in the Bush, (the great expanse of Australian wilderness).

She told me how she had invited her uncle Francie down to visit her in Arnhem land and amazingly he had accepted, though pushing eighty years of age at the time. He was accompanied by a younger cousin Eamonn, also from Glencolmcille and together they took a plane to Australia and on to an airport outside Cairns in the Northern Territory. They stayed at the Aboriginal community in Arnhemland for the best part of a week. Rose smiled broadly, as she conveyed how her uncle who had lived in Donegal all his life, took so easily to his adventure in the remote wilds of Australia. Word had spread through the community to Rose long before they arrived that two white men wearing heavy rain coats had been seen walking through the airport in 100% heat and humidity. One of the highlights of Francie's trip had been helping the villagers drag in a catch of fish from nets cast from the shore. Rose described wonderfully how they had interacted naturally with the people through everyday tasks. Perhaps people who are close to the land and sea and who live in communities like Arnhemland and Glencolmcille share much, without even knowing.

Rose went on to say that unlike Glencolmcille, huge fresh water crocodiles lurk beneath the waves. A bathe in the sea is to be treated with the same caution as a bird does when taking a bath. Crocodiles or 'crocs' are so fast and cunning that all you would hear and see is rows of jagged teeth snapping tight around you, before being dragged away for lunch. Rose informed me that she was coming to the end of her travels in Asia and was returning to Australia in just over a week's time. We hung out together for several special days and enjoyed each other's company in more ways than one. It was a special time after spending so long on the road backpacking by myself. One of the great wonders you discover about travelling is how easy it is to meet and make new friends in the most unexpected of places and situations. You are who you are in the present moment. The only baggage you need to carry is your clothes and belongings.

I used the remainder of my time at the HBMC to write down in a log some of what I had experienced in the last few months and emailed my final travelogues off to the Donegal Democrat who were now serialising my travels. I decided not to continue with the newspaper travelogues beyond my trip to Gokyo Ri and the Himalayas, as my journey was entering a much more personal stage and I was uncertain at the time about sharing it with the general public back home. I had half visions of outraged locals waiting at the bridge in Ballyshannon with burning torches for my return. I imagined someone pointing at the Dublin to Donegal expressway and shouting "that's him on the bus boys, quick now, heat up that barrel of tar Mickey and get that sack of goose feathers I left against the wall". In fairness. this was my mind in complete fantasy mode as Donegal, Ireland and the Western World were all changing rapidly since the late sixties. TV had opened up people's eyes as well as closing down part of their minds. The all powerful spiritual and social authority of the Catholic Church in Ireland had been rocked by one scandal after another since the 1980's and it was now in a definite decline. Many were now reverting back to or seeking a more personally empowered, enquiring spirituality based on intuition, enquiry and trial and error within the existing framework of Church ceremonies such as funerals, weddings and christenings. At the same time Eastern practices such as yoga, homeopathy, meditation and Reiki were being introduced to the West and becoming available to anyone with an enquiring mind and a seeker of inner peace.

During my final week at the HBMC I met with a friendly middle-aged couple while having our evening meals together in the courtyard. Chris was originally from England while Jaal was from France. Chris was a tall well built man who wore glasses and his hair in a long greying ponytail. Jail was petite and delicate in stature, with bright inquisitive kind eyes. They had both met under quite extraordinary circumstances, in an ashram in India a few years back and were literally brought together by a holy man teaching at the centre. They were now both living in Australia and had plans to set up an alternative centre there for meditation and healing. They informed me that they were travelling through Asia, seeking teachings and guidance and were about to travel up to Solu Khumbu, where I had recently been. They seemed to be going through a turbulent time in their personal relationship, which can happen when two people are travelling in such close and constant proximity to one another. We spoke for hours together in an easy flow of conversation. They were clearly genuine seekers of a life lived in spirit and I listened with interest to all they had to say.

It was the end of June and the monsoon season was fast approaching. The weather began following a distinct daily pattern. Each day began bright and clear and by afternoon a hot, sultry sun blazed in the sky. Every evening, cloud would build up and by nightfall thunderstorms lit up the sky. Rain would often suddenly fall at the most unexpected of moments in sheets that quickly turned the narrow streets and alleyways of Katmandu into temporary shallow waterways. The downpours seemed to bring people together in excited conversation wherever they happened to be stranded, similar to a rare snow fall back home.

I could sense my journey was taking on a new form. I had experienced some of India and fulfilled a dream to see and trek through the Himalayas. I still had almost two months left to travel but no pre-planned destinations. I thought of visiting Tibet but after the stories I had heard of the widespread repression and penal laws imposed by China, I did not wish to give money to support the Chinese tourist authorities. Then I thought of Ladakh, also known as Little Tibet and part of Jammu state in the far northwest of India. I knew in some way, that it was time to explore and experience new uncharted internal landscapes of the heart and mind and that Ladakh was one place on that journey.

Over dinner one evening Jaal and Chris informed me of their plans to visit the Lawudu hermitage above Namche Bazaar where I had wished to visit and stay a while. I knew they were travelling on a budget and so offered Chris my heavy trekking coat. When he collected it from my room later that evening, he handed me a card with an address for 'Ananda Mai Ma's guesthouse and ashram in Haridwar. "You might like to check this place out Keith. You can visit Haridwar on your way to Ladakh. Ananda Mai Ma was a very special and spiritual woman and revered as a holy mother. You can still sense her presence there and there is a museum opposite the guesthouse which will make it more clear what I am talking about", he said. I thanked Chris kindly for the card. Although I had my reservations, I did not share them with him. I still had a self created picture in my mind of ashrams being places where wealthy Westerners hung out for years at a time, as a devotee to some holy Indian guru or other. My intuition told me to let go of my pre-conceived assumptions and experience the place for myself.

Before leaving Katmandu I bought a few gifts to take home and posted on CD's for Rose as I promised to. When I asked to settle up for my accommodation I was at first shocked to realise that I had spent twenty six days at the HBMC guesthouse. For this I paid less than one hundred euros. It was then time to part with my snake staff or 'latee surpa' which I gave to one of the kind young porters by the name of Ram, who had been teaching me some basic Nepali. He looked at it with almost theatrical reverence and said he would store it away safely until I returned to Nepal.

It was at first tough to get back into travelling mode after such a sheltered stress-free life at the HBMC. After a short stop in Pokhara, I took a bus back down to the southern lowlands of Nepal known as the 'Terai Plains'. The landscape began now to resemble Northern India and the people were predominantly Hindu again. After about seven hours of steady driving our bus stopped in a busy non-descript town for a short break and to change down to a small mini-bus. We travelled on until midnight when our bus broke down and we chugged slowly into a dark roadside diner. Everyone got out to stretch their legs and our driver disappeared under the bus with a torchlight. Soon, the news went around that we would be delayed for at least an hour. As people waited around or went looking for a snack, I decided on taking a short stroll along the dark deserted road ahead. Opposite the roadside diner stretched a huge field of near ripened maize. The chirping of crickets filled the balmy night. With no electrical light source, the natural world put on a splendid show of its own. A troupe of fire-flies seemed to dance under the spotlight of a milky bright full moon, while lightning flashes pulsed hypnotically on the distant southern horizon, too far off for thunder to be heard.

Back at the bus I got chatting with a Nepali soldier who was returning home from duty to visit his young family. He told me he had served overseas as a UN peacekeeper in Haiti. The light went from his eyes as he described Haiti, "it was not a nice place, very dangerous for people living there, there is no forest, no jungle left, all gone." As if then wishing to lighten the conversation, he quickly produced a brand new mobile phone from his pocket and proceeded to show me a music video of his favourite Hindi pop band, smiling at me in advance, to acknowledge how good it sounded and looked. I didn't ask him to write down the name of the artist for me but it sure was a marked improvement on the Vengaboys.

The bus re-started with a few merciful lively chugs and we took of with a jolt into the dark Nepali night once more. I woke a few hours later to see through sleep filled eyes a digger up ahead with a bright spotlight fixed to the front cab, clearing a mud landslide from our way. Dawn was breaking the next time I woke. I marvelled at how I had slept at all with the constant rattling, shaking and loud engine revs of the bus.

As I continued on my journey to the Indian border with West Nepal, I was torn between travelling on to Rishikesh or Haridwar to visit the Ashram that Chris talked about and had given me a card for. Rishikesh was a town made famous by the Beatles who spent three months there in 1967 staying at the ashram of a famous Indian Yogi by the name of Mahirishi Mahesh. They practiced transcendental meditation under the guidance of the Mahirishi and composed over forty songs while in India. In many ways The Beatles popularised Indian spirituality through much of their music and songs on 'The White Album'. It was a time of huge change in the West, a time of musical, sexual, cultural, social and political expression and liberation. Nothing would ever be the same again. Inner spiritual methods and disciplines from karate to meditation were moving westward as outer modernity such as profit driven business, economic development and pop culture were moving eastwards.

It wasn't until I crossed the border the next morning that I decided on taking a bus directly to Haridwar with a calling card to visit a guesthouse of a revered Indian 'holy mother' or saint who I knew nothing about. On the way to Haridwar, I had great fun at a large bus terminal where we stopped off to change buses. I got talking to the young bus station controller who persuaded me to make a few announcements in English over the intercom. It was comical to see the surprised reactions of people hearing a man in an Irish accent pronouncing Indian destinations and announcing the latest bus timetable. A stern looking Indian official then stormed up to the desk and put a prompt stop to our fun.

It was night when I arrived in Haridwar and I just about managed to find a cheap hotel room quiet enough to sleep in. Stifling heat woke me the next morning and after a short walk up the street to find breakfast, I retreated to the relative cool of my hotel room to read and snooze. By mid-evening, it was cool enough to venture out and explore the town. I found out from the hotel receptionist that Amanda Mai Ma's guesthouse was five miles out of town so I decided to stay an extra night in the hotel. The streets were heaving with people. Built on the banks of the upper River Ganges, Haridwar is one of the most sacred places in all of India for many Hindu pilgrims who travel here from across the sub-continent. The Ganges or Ganga is itself considered sacred and personified as a voluptuous Hindu goddess. I had spent an hour sitting in meditation before leaving my hotel and felt very calm and deeply content as I walked through the streets.

I found myself being swept gently along by a crowd until the narrow streets opened up to a bridge with concrete stepped ghats on either side of the Ganges and ancient looking stone ornate temples for people to deposit their clothes and footwear. The sun was setting the late evening sky on fire with hues of orange, yellow and purples as people gathered in their thousands on either side of the fast flowing dark blue Ganges. Young vendors went through the crowds selling small leaf boats enclosing a small night-light candle and flower petals. As the light faded I sat down amidst the throngs of pilgrims and listened as a song-like chant rose from the crowds as part of evening puja. Indian Puja is modelled on the idea of making an offering to a Hindu God and receiving their blessing. People began lighting their candles and floating their tiny boat offering unto the Ganges. I followed suit. Soon the river was full of hundreds of tiny flickering lights which floated on their fragile leaf vessels for a few moments before being churned up in the fast flowing currents. I thought back to the bodies of dead people I had watched being cremated on the banks of the Ganges in Varinasi and how our individual light has such a short time to shine in the vast scale of time, before we too disappear once again.

The following evening I decided to visit the Mansa Devi Temple perched high on a wooded hill overlooking Haridwar. Due to the sticky pre-monsoon heat it wasn't long before my shirt was stuck to my back with perspiration. Sitting on a wall beside steps were a troop of monkeys, ever vigilant for the chance to snatch some food or jewellery from an unsuspecting pilgrim or tourist. One young monkey played contently with a large silver bracelet, no doubt the proceeds of some earlier snatch and grab heist. I continued on the steep hike until I was rewarded with a panoramic view of Haridwar stretched out below. In Hindi Haridwar means 'God's Gateway or Door' and now I could see how it got its name. The river Ganga passes down a narrow gorge between two prominent steep sided hills before flowing through Haridwar.

I entered the temple as a veteran Indian traveller with a pre-prepared small bundle of ten and twenty rupee notes in my short pocket to pay the sandal man, flower sellers, temple priests etc. I was starting to become more than a little sceptical and cynical of temple visits and the strange looking exotic Hindu Gods and Goddesses that were on display. The heat and humidity was also starting to make me irritated and restless. The streets were so thronged with pilgrims coming and going, that it was an effort to get back to my hotel room. Street vendors seemed extra loud and pushy, beggars more persistent, the sun ever hotter.

It was time to get away from Haridwar, put aside any prejudgements and visit the guesthouse address on the card which Chris had handed me back in Katmandu. The crowds thinned as the auto-rickshaw driver took me across a bridge to the outskirts of Haridwar. The roads became dirt tracks with huge pot holes full of pre-monsoon rain water. A short time later, we drove through bright iron gates and stopped in front of a gleaming white two storey building. It was Anandamayi Ma's International Guesthouse. As I shuffled through the front door with my backpack and extra travel luggage I felt immediately at home and at peace. My bad mood had simply vanished. I was ushered upstairs to a beautiful plush clean room and was requested to attend morning puja at 7.30am the next morning. Soon after getting settled in, I fell into a deep sleep.

Directly next to the guesthouse was a mausoleum built in memory of the Indian holy woman, Anandamayi Ma, who had passed away in 1982. Born in 1896 in modern day Bangladesh, she was regarded as a living saint and her name means 'Joy Permeated Mother'. Although she was married by arrangement at the age of thirteen, which was the custom of that time, her husband Bholanath quickly came to realise her unique divinity and theirs' was a celibate marriage. In later years her husband became one of her devotees. I came to know all this from a book I borrowed while staying at the guesthouse.

More pre-monsoon rains had fallen overnight and the trees outside the guesthouse had flowered in bright yellow and pink blossoms which looked like a colour splashed painting by Monet. I decided to pay a visit to Anandamayi Ma's final resting place and attend the morning service as requested to. The mausoleum was a stately building of white marble-like stone, with a visually stunning stepped cone shaped steeple. Inside, local

worshippers and visitors sat cross-legged on a spotless marble
floor around an interior enclosure cordoned of with a metal railing. A huge mound of fresh flowers covered Anandamayi Ma's
white marble tomb, around which a group of elderly sari clad
women all in white clothing, sang hymns and chanted ancient
Hindu prayers. As the puja went on I began feeling a strange
sensation in my heart area. Anandamayi Ma had died back in
1982 and yet I could feel some unexplainable presence of her
through the ceremony. Just as I was about to leave the grounds
after morning puja a silver haired woman in a white sari caught
up with me and placed a lotus flower in my hand. I thanked her
with a smile, looked at the delicate lotus flower in my hand and
burst into tears.

What happened to me over the next few days I do not fully
understand, but I am sure that there are many so called psychological experts out there that wouldn't be shy in offering
a clinical or case study explanation to help put my mystery to
rest. I returned that evening with red tear softened eyes to the
crowded and chaotic streets of Haridwar. Many Indian people
simply looked into my eyes and gave me a re-assuring, knowing
smile. There was no stress or confusion this time. I stopped for
a moment by a shop window to watch and listen to a beautiful
Indian princess singing like a Hindu nightingale on the TV. I
followed the mass of pilgrims to the banks of the Ganges. This
time I was going in too. Depositing my clothes at a small temple
I walked forward in a pair of black football shorts. I waded out
with a family and holding a safety rope plunged down into the
cold fast flowing waters of the Ganges which tumbled down
from the Himalayas. The water felt indescribably invigorating
in comparison to the sticky humid air. As I ducked down a submerged blurry forest of legs, arms and bodies appeared around
me in the dulled water. Someone reached out a hand and steadied me as I re-surfaced with elation. My eyes met smiles and
nodding heads from young and old around me. Something had
been cleansed no matter what the water quality.

The next few days spent back at the Anandamayi Ma's international guesthouse were quite extraordinary. Each morning

I attended a puja in her honour and each morning my heart burst open in tears either during the hour long ceremony, or a short time afterwards. I felt a little uneasy about this at first, as men are not encouraged to cry in my own culture. The ego part of my mind was starting to come up with some predictable thoughts such as, "you should never have come here in the first place, you have really gone too far this time with all this Indian mysticism baloney. What would people say if they could see you now, crying like a big soft baby?" This was fear, shame and doubt all giving itself an inner voice. I laughed them away, when I came to the conclusion that if anything, I was actually experiencing an 'emotional fix-up' as opposed to an 'emotional break-down'. I could physically feel a tender sensation in the centre of my chest and sensed my mind move down from my head into my heart area.

Each evening I would lie in bed and read a little more about Anandamayi Ma's life. She looked radiantly beautiful in old black and white photos as a young woman. Even as an old woman, she radiated a natural beauty with eyes and face that reflected an inner state of bliss. She seemed the embodiment of her name, 'Joy Permeated Mother'. Throughout her adult life she travelled across India helping to open teaching hospitals and ashrams, healing and caring for the sick and dying while sometimes performing miracles. One such miracle involved the feeding of a huge crowd of pilgrims with a limited amount of food which was verified by scores of people present. This story of course sounded so similar to that involving Jesus and the loaves and fishes. The more I read about Anandamayi Ma's life the more I came to relate to Jesus as a divine being who was born in the Holy Land over two thousand years ago. No longer did I consider the miracles and powers associated with him as fanciful stories put in the bible to impress non-believers and faithful Christians alike. It was strange to think I was finally accepting and making peace with my own Christian faith in an ashram, in Northern India.

What really impressed though, as I read Anandamayi Ma's teachings, was that for her, every religion and spiritual path was right from it's own standpoint. She once stated "how can one impose limitations on the Infinite by declaring, 'This is the only path!" For Anandamayi Ma, the reason there were so many different religions and sects in the world was because there are so many different peoples of diverse cultures and world views. After all, the spokes on a bicycle wheel all lead to the axle at the centre.

There was a small museum across the road from the guest-house, dedicated to the memory of Anandamayi Ma. It looked a little run down and didn't seem to receive many visitors. Displayed all along the walls were a series of glass cabinets containing gifts that she had received in her lifetime. I went from the first one to the next and so forth with increasing amazement. All the leading churches were represented. A Jewish church community in New York. A Muslim association from the Middle East. A Sufi society from the Netherlands. Anandamayi Ma had obviously touched the lives of so many people from around the world. She advocated spiritual equality for women and taught through meditation, songs, jokes and practical instructions on life. She never gave lectures but instead simply answered questions.

Sadhus, scholars, philosophers, politicians, ambassadors, rajas, doctors, writers, lawyers and businessmen from across India and the World came to listen in awe at the spontaneous answers given to their questions. She had a message for everyone and excluded no one. Wrong doers, labourers, farmers and the mentally unbalanced were all treated with equal dignity and without judgement.

The day before I left the guesthouse I met a lovely French couple from Paris called Laurent and Juliette over breakfast. They had travelled to India together many times and every time were drawn back to Anandamayi Ma's final resting place. I shared with them my plans to continue on my journey soon. Upon hearing this they both insisted that I meet with an old *Swami* or Holy Man who was a lifelong devotee of Anandamayi Ma. He was a French doctor who had had travelled to India and met 'Ma' in 1951 at the age of thirty-six. He decided to stay as her disciple and never returned to France again. He now went by the name Vijayananda. We went to see him one evening after puja and found him sitting on a wooden chair with his feet barely touching the ground. He was now almost ninety-five years old and although his body was frail and shrunk with age his eyes sparkled and shone from a wise radiant face. Long white whispy hair flowed to his shoulders and a flowing beard gave him the appearance of a great old wizard. We waited in turn while an Indian family knelt down before him, touching his feet one by one while he raised his hand and nodded, slowly giving each a silent blessing. It was then our turn. Juliette introduced me in French and then in English before explaining that I was travelling through Nepal and India and on my way to Ladakh. I handed him a small bag of fruit I had brought him as a gift and he gestured for us all to sit down. We sat at his feet like children and it felt respectful to be looking up at him as we talked. "Where are you from?", he asked me in a clear French accent.

When I replied Ireland his eyes lit up.

"Ah, Ireland, you know when I was in London after the war I heard many Irish songs, you know the song about Tipperary?"

I guessed the song he was referring to and started into, 'It's a long way to Tipperary'. Amazingly the old French Swami knew the words also and we sang softly together in the grounds of a temple in Northern India,

> "It's a long way to Tipperary
> It's a long way to go
> It's a long way to Tipperary
> To the sweetest girl I know
> Goodbye Picadilly, hello Leicester Square
> It's a long way to Tipperary
> But my heart lies there."

Vijayananda smiled warmly and patted the back of my hand. I then piped up, "Do you know Molly Malone by any chance?" After a slow positive nod from Vijayananda we sang the first verse of it together as well. We were now both smiling brightly with the random merriment of it all. Laurent and Julliette listened in good humour, although they seemed a little taken back by our instant familiarity. After a few moments he then asked me, "so you have been to Nepal?" I explained that I had done a meditation course in Kopan monastery and trekked up through the Himalayas. He then waved a hand over his shoulder as if the Himalayas were right behind us and said, "you know after I met Anandamayi Ma, she sent me on retreat to a cave up in the Himalayas to meditate. Eight years I spent up there. It is quite extraordinary you know, to spend that much time by one's self". He paused and stooped a little closer before joking, "You know, after a while, no need for mobile phones. Like Eskimos hunters out for weeks alone on the ice, I could hear any messages that were sent to me…quite extraordinary."

I nodded and smiled back. This time I knew perfectly well what Vijayananda meant from receiving Ian's long distance transmission while up in the Khumbu.

The skies began to darken overhead and an ominous rumble of thunder echoed off in the distance. Before leaving, I decided to ask Vijayananda for some advice. "Dear Swami", I addressed him, "How do you advise maintaining a grounded spiritual life back in the West, where the pace of life seems to be becoming ever more hectic and the focus seems to be towards having the biggest car, the dream home or apartment, the latest I-phone and the perfect social life?"

He paused for a moment and then looking back towards me intently said, "you know, the people in the West are very fortunate now. They do not have the constant daily struggle that many in the East still have, such as finding the next meal or money for basic survival. These things you speak off are merely distractions. You must create a quiet inspiring space in your house or flat when you return home. Then you can develop a daily practice". He then reached down a little closer again and emphasised his concluding words with an outstretched finger, "All you need then is the spiritual will."

That night back at the guesthouse I watched an awesome electrical thunderstorm from my bedroom window. It seemed that every few moments, the dark night itself was split in two by a flash of intense lightning. Sleep proved difficult in the stifling humidity and my mind was restless for a reason I could not understand. I bought lotus flowers the next morning to leave at Anandamayi Ma's temple and thanked her for helping me open my heart to glimpse its self-healing potential. It would have been nice to have meet her in person. Although she had died in 1982 at the age of eighty-six, it felt like her divine spirit wasn't very far away from this place.

The pre-monsoon heat was beginning to rise steadily with daytime temperatures rising to between 35 and 40 degrees Celsius. I felt empathy for the local people who were lucky if they had small fans, while air conditioning was only a TV induced dream, available to none but rich Indians and wealthy tourists. I had since come up with three additional reasons for travelling on to Ladakh. These were to visit an ecological organisation, escape the relentless heat of the India plains and experience a land similar in culture and landscape to Tibet. Ladakh was over a week's travelling away by bus and experience had taught me to take my time and make a proper journey of it.

From Haridwar I travelled to the city of Dehra Dun. It took me just a day to figure out why there were so few other Western backpackers there. I entertained myself by teaching three young Indian boys at a tea shop how to greet someone in traditional Donegal fashion. I demonstrated the wink and quick head tilt to the left followed by the words, "how's it going there hey?" They were quick learners and eager students. I had great fun watching them approach passer bys' on the street, who reacted with either bemused bewilderment or a confused smile. A tea shop corner in Dehra Dun was transformed into a college for Donegal country greetings. if only for a few light hearted minutes.

From Dehra Dun I bought a bus ticket to Shimla, situated in the foothills of the Himalayas. The bus made its way along bustling rural roads and countryside alive with people working, relaxing or going somewhere. By midday we had reached the city of Chandigarh which borders the states of Punjab and Haryana. It was a strange experience travelling into the city limits, as if someone was playing a practical joke on a huge scale. As India's first planned city, the roads were laid out in grids of wide tree-lined boulevards. Here and there small groups of Indian people had stopped to eat and rest under the shade of trees but even this re-assuring spontaneous behaviour did nothing to diminish the overall feeling of immaculate urban, logical planning. Like the American tourist who longs for the nostalgic 'Old Irish' experience, this was not the India I had come to love and draw from. The city of Chandigarh was a revelation of her emerging economic power and modernising transition to come.

In Chandigarh I switched buses directly for Shimla. The sweat ran in beads down my back as I hauled over my luggage but I didn't mind anymore. We were heading north and to much cooler climes. For hour upon hour our turban wearing Sikh bus driver revved and coaxed our bus up steep hair pin bends. Passengers began sliding open windows to let the fresh sweet air blow through the bus. We were now in the mountainous Indian state of Himachal Pradesh and the landscape changed to thickly forest clad hillsides of pine and oak, with deep rocky ravines. We arrived in Shimla in the middle of a monsoon deluge and I managed to find a room at the YMCA youth hostel. Shimla had an unmistakable old world colonial feel to it. In 1864 Shimla was declared the summer capital of the British Raj and a railway was built to take the entire administration and their families up to the cooler hill station and out of the hot plains far below. Nowadays Shimla has become a popular destination for wealthy Indians, who love to soak up the old world nostalgia, wear wooly tank tops and marvel at the gothic architecture of their former colonial masters.

I felt a distinct chill in the air upon waking the next morning. Outside, a thick mist cloaked Shimla in a grey gloom. It felt like I had left one weather extreme for another. Over breakfast, I watched the YMCA manageress with increasing agitation as she chastised and berated every staff member within ear shot. She had a scowling face that would curdle milk and when she stormed out of the dining room area, she left a cloud of unease in her wake. One of the male staff saw me looking puzzled and returned my glance with a shrug of the shoulders. I felt like fermenting a breakfast staff mutiny but who can truly judge these matters over tea and toast.

I decided to push on through Himachal Pradesh and continue on my journey to Ladakh. My next stop off was a holy lake called Rewalsar, which interested me because of its sacred significance, not only to Hindus and Buddhists but also Sikhs. After an overnight stay in a damp and dingy hotel room in Mandi, I made my way to the lake on board a bus propelled by a young driver who swung around blind hair pin bends with a kamikaze style abandon. My legs were literally shaking upon reaching Rewalsar. In an attempt to eat more healthily and keep down my daily living expenses, I had bought a plastic bag full of fresh fruit and vegetables and a small knife to slice and eat it with. I spotted what appeared to be a nice quiet place to sit and take lunch, just a few hundred metres away on the far side of the lake. The small lake was the size of a large city park-pond, only surrounded on three sides by a total of three Buddhist gompas and three Hindu temples. Rewalsar lake was also surrounded on three sides by steep lush green hills dotted with tall pines that echoed during various times of the day, with the chanting of Buddhist monks, the singing of Sikh holy men and Hindu temple music blaring from loud speakers. I wondered to myself did they ever think of jamming and performing together as the "Rewalsar Trinity Jam Band."

Just as I was setting out my raw vegetable salad to eat on a wall I was distracted by a group of young Indian men who came over to practice their ten standard questions in the English language. They only got as far as question five when one of the group pointed behind me, barely concealing an amused grin, "I think good sir there is a cow and it is eating your lunch." Sure enough a wandering holy cow had jumped up on the verge and was munching contently on my cucumbers and tomatoes. I let a shout which came out as an Irish cattle farmers, "houy houy", but this cow wasn't for taking orders or any ancient cattle herding commands and diligently finished the last cucumber. Grabbing the remainder of my lunch bag, I made my way to a concrete plinth at the edge of the lake. No sooner had I taken a small hand of sweet ripe bananas out of my backpack than a large temple monkey arrived on the scene out of nowhere, then sat down a few yards away pretending to groom himself. At first he just appeared to be seeking company but in the split second it took me to leave down my carrier bag he made a lightning grab and snatch. It happened that quickly I hadn't a chance. To add insult to injury he sat down less than twenty feet away and throwing me a universal thief's look that says, "don't look at me mate, I did nothing", proceeded to carefully peel each banana as a human would do, then one by one, scoffed the lot. Mesmerised by the cheek of this lesser cousin, I tried to console myself by remembering there were still two mandarins and a juicy mango left in the bag. As I rummaged them out I looked up to see three old wrinkly beggar women standing over me, gesturing with outstretched hands to their mouth. Handing out the last of my lunch with bemused bewilderment, I set off back the way I came in a hungry search for some Indian restaurant to eat in relative peace. It was to be my first and last outdoor picnic in Asia.

It was early evening by the time I found a place to stay the night. Low clouds began racing in from the south, dimming the soft sunshine. My guide book said that it was from a cave in the hills above Rewalsar that the famous Indian yogi teacher Padmasambhava went into retreat before leaving for Tibet. He is held in the same regard by Tibetans as Irish people regard St Patrick who helped introduce the Christian faith to Ireland in the 5th Century. Padmasambhava introduced Tantric Buddhism to the Himalayan kingdoms of Tibet and Bhutan in the 8th Century at a time when the people of there lands were ravaged by wars and perpetual violence between feuding warlords and tribes. Tibetan folk culture is full of fantastical stories of how like St Patrick, Padmasambhava travelled through the country with his followers, outwitting powerful druid-like shamans, while doing battle with demons and monsters who feared this new radical Buddhist religion, with its ideas of universal love and pacifying moral codes.

St Patrick was also associated with a sacred lake called Lough Derg, located in a hauntingly wild and remote mountain valley in South Donegal. He retreated to a cave on one of the islands to fast and pray and had a vision of the hell realms, hence the pilgrimage site became known as St Patrick's Purgatory. In Medieval times, Christian pilgrims of all social classes travelled from across Europe and beyond to pray and fast on Station Island in Lough Derg. Many times, I had walked the hills around Lough Derg and imagined what it was like for pilgrims to visit the area in the medieval period when huge oak and pine forests cloaked its shorelines, sheltering wolves, wild boar and deer. The only comfort would have been the famous customary hospitality of the Irish guesthouses.

As I travelled from Lake Rewalsar on the back of an auto rickshaw up to see ancient cave, I had a strange feeling of time and distance dissolving. The houses and countryside felt strangely familiar as if I was travelling through some southern upland area back in Ireland's recent past. Many of the houses were white washed with hip-shaped slate roofs and wooden doors. An elderly farmer carrying a sack of grain over his shoulder saluted us as we passed him. The landscape was a contrast of small lush plateaus and sharply defined creeks, lined with lakes and rough pasture. Sheltered rocky ridges stretched across the skyline crowned with tall pine groves. A light mist then descended like a silvery grey shroud over everything only adding to the sense that I was entering a mythical landscape. The rickshaw driver left me off at a small carpark in front of a large hill peppered with huge rocky outcrops, boulders, paths, prayer flags and haphazardly built stone houses for the resident Buddhist nuns who take care of the holy site. Two young nuns with heads shaved, brushed past me talking energetically. Each carried two pales of water. After a while I found the sacred cave but the entrance was covered with a metal gate which was locked. I sat down on a nearby boulder and decided to take in the atmosphere of the place even if the cave was off-limits to visitors.

A few minutes later the same two nuns appeared with a key to clean the cave. They disappeared for a few moments before one nun reappeared and gestured me with a kind smile and broken English to follow her. A series of worn winding steps, neatly cut out of the rock, led down into a snug but damp cave about fourteen foot by twelve foot in size with an eight foot cave ceiling. As the nuns lit incense and replaced used candles, I marvelled at my luck in getting to see this famous cave where Padmasambhava prepared himself for the journey of his life to Tibet.

A line of altars took up one wall, with beautiful golden statues representing both the Buddha and Padmashambava, each encased in glass. What drew my eyes to one particular corner was, that a smaller statue case was decorated with lumps of a semi precious stone called Lapis Lazuli. It gave off an intense blue hue which seemed to radiate out into the dimly lit cave. Thanking the two nuns for letting me visit this special place, I re-surfaced as the mist was beginning to clear. Again I felt close to tears, and decided to take a walk up into a woodland further up the hill. Finding two straight pine trees growing side by side I took out a roll of prayer flags and tied them like a clothes line, making a few silent prayers for the health and well being of my family back home.

From a high vantage point on the hill I looked down at Rewalsar lake which now appeared the size of a puddle far below me. I then looked north in the direction of the Himalayas and the lands beyond them. I felt an air of anticipation and excitement to think that all going well, I would be in Ladakh in less than a week. Legend has it that Padmasambhava had mastered the laws of physics through deep yoga and meditation practices and flew directly across the Himalayas to Tibet. Saint Patrick on the other hand most probably took the boat across to Ireland. I would be travelling by bus.

After an overnight stay on the shores of Rewalsar I returned down to Mandi to collect my bags and move on. Someone or something had got sick outside my door overnight, and had been simply left there to stew in the heat. What a great sign it was to move on. The rain came down in torrents as I managed to board a bus up the Khulu Valley with my destination, the town of Manali. The bus journey up the Khulu Valley was spectacular even in low mist and heavy rain. It resembled a mountain pass in Donegal called Barnes Mór or 'The Big Gap', but on a scale a hundred times greater. A monster glacier the size of a small country must have at one time carved out this immense valley. After an overnight stay in Manali, I bought a ticket for a mini-bus which was scheduled to leave for Ladakh at 2am the following morning.

LADAKH; A LAND BATHED IN LIGHT

Still half asleep, I boarded a twelve seater mini-bus as the driver skilfully loaded luggage and shop goods unto the roof before strapping them down. We had a nineteen hour journey ahead of us across the Himalayas, over some of the highest road passes in the World. On board, were a collection of tourists and Ladakhis. I sat next to a placid elderly Ladakhi man in a skull cap and long smig beard, who smiled and nodded whenever we made eye contact.

I dozed off for the first few hours but then, as the first light of day broke through the last hour of dark, an immense green mountain loomed up ahead. Our bus swayed and shook along rough-surface roads that 'zig zagged' endlessly down into an immense glacial valley. We stopped in a damp and desolate looking hamlet to have our passports checked and to take tea and an early breakfast snack. There was a powerful sense that nature was still totally master out here, as we huddled together for warmth in a ramshackle tea house. As I was in conversation with a cordial Belgian guy, a middle aged Israeli man rudely butted in and switched the subject to the 'World' as he saw it ."You must see", he began, "that all the greatest composers, scientists and mathematicians have all been Jewish, think of Leonard Bernstein, Albert Einstein. And the best classical musicians... all Jews. Think of all the most successful business men and banking institutions all around the world, all Jews." He wasn't finished yet, "now think of most of the great film directors such as Woody Allen and Steven Spielberg, all Jews, not to mention who runs Hollywood." It was like listening to an inverse speech on behalf of a new master race but everyone was too tired to reply, never mind react.

For the next few hours, we drove west along the side of this immense river valley cloaked in mist and rain, while loud energetic Hindi music blasted at us through the mini-bus stereo provided the soundtrack for our adventure. Our Indian driver sped onwards and upwards along rough, tar patched, loose gravel-surface roads with unstable steep mountain slopes on one side and sheer drops on the other. We passed through the truly frontier town of Keylong around midday and from there, the road wound its way up into the high Himalayas. We were driving along the new Trans-Himalayan Manali-Leh highway, built in the 1980's by the Indian army to transport convoys of infantry trucks, artillery and fuel tankers during its war with Pakistan. Almost five hundred kilometres in length, the road is impassable in winter because of heavy snowfalls from late autumn to late spring. Any lingering mist and cloud disappeared and the mountains became more rugged, dusty and desolate in appearance. Along the way, squads of road-workers with wild hair, sunburnt faces and scarf covered heads toiled with shovels and spades to repair sections of the road as burly tar-lorry drivers sat in their cabs.

We stopped for lunch next to a metal bridge which spanned a wide shallow river. A simple shack served up pastry snacks and rice meals, but there was no sign of any private toilets. A growing cramp below my stomach told its own pressing message. We were now at high altitude and in a mountainous dessert, with not a bush or tree around for a hundred miles or more. Under duress, I spied a small hill and ravine leading behind the shack. Upon reaching it I was frustrated to discover I was still within sight of my fellow travellers, so continued walking backwards until I found a private spot to do my urgent business. As I walked out of the ravine I discovered with growing dismay that I had chosen the same spot as every curry eating, liquor guzzling, vest wearing truck driver from here to Delhi. My sandals and feet were liberally covered with the stuff and flies were beginning to gather. From the corner of my eye I could see that our bus driver was getting ready to move on. With delayed panic and suspended disgust I ran as fast as my legs could carry me down me to the edge of the river and with fistfuls of silt and fine grit, scrubbed my sandals and feet for all I was worth. The river water was ice cold and I could feel my hands going numb as our driver began honking the bus horn from up on the bridge. With survival like effort and haste, I completed the task thoroughly and jumped back on board our mini-bus with jaded relief.

The bus continued up along an epic corkscrew route. The landscape was now an ever changing sandy coloured canvass of bright sunlight and dark cloud shadows, as sheep wool clouds sailed lazily across the azure blue sky. The air became so thin that altitude induced giddiness or nausea was a certainty. For our Israeli traveller with the new master race theory, it was the latter, and he looked two stone lighter by the time we reached our destination.

We were literally driving over the roof of the Earth and it sure felt like it. Huge convoys of Indian army trucks and fuel tankers passed us noisily, spluttering clouds of thick dark exhaust fumes into the once pristine air. Our bus driver worked hard to keep his own line on the road. Many of the army drivers were Sikhs with turbaned heads and handlebar moustaches made from pliable steel wire. They looked as tough as they were.

As evening lengthened we drove across an immense wide dusty plain flanked on its eastern side by striking lime green, high valley pastures. On one slope beneath a conical peak capped with snow, I spotted a distant Khampa nomadic settlement with tents, sheep flocks and horses, barely visible yet striking against the vast sweeping grassland. Suddenly I got a flashback feeling to when I was a young child and first took in the mist covered mountains of Donegal. It was as if time and space stood still for a suspended moment on the bus, while my own spirit connected with something that I could barely begin to fathom. A part of me longed to get off the mini-bus and to ramble over to drink tea and swap stories with the Khampas. I imagined what it would be like to run or ride on horseback across the rolling hills and high open plains. Another part of me though, was quite happy to look out and dream about it from the comfort and security of my back seat.

By late evening we had reached a dusty village settlement with outlying tiny fields of barley and corn. It was hard to imagine a more remote place to live in the world. The bus stopped once again for the Israeli man. It was amazing to think he had anything left in him to evacuate anymore and I began to feel compassion for him. We then travelled down through a deep valley gorge into what seemed like the creation womb of the Himalayas. Huge slabs of mountain were twisted and shaped into the most fantastical folds and ridges, all pastel pinks, yellows, purples and blues. An air of awe inspired silence pervaded the bus. Nature was revealing a geological dream-time for us.

We arrived in Leh shortly after 9pm in the middle of a power outage. Our bus driver had been behind the wheel for close on nineteen hours. Myself and a young Belgian man called Kjert, teamed up to look for accommodation. Despite the darkness, the local guesthouse touts still found us. We managed to shake them off in Leh town centre and after an hour's tiresome searching found a quiet guesthouse and two rooms for the equivalent of three euros per night.

I had fallen asleep before even drawing the curtains and woke at dawn the next morning, with the nearby call of a rooster and my room bathed in bright sunlight. Outside the window, a garden of potatoes stalks reminded me that one of my main reasons for coming to Leh was to visit the Ladakh Ecological Development Centre. While working back in Donegal with Community Creations, a few years previously, I had taken home a video from our resource library entitled 'Ancient Futures'. It was one of those eureka information movies that you sometimes come across which used Ladakh as a modern example to reveal the harmful impact that conventional development and rapid economic growth can have on a traditional society. Before 1975, Ladakh had a strong culture based on community, a pristine environment and sustainable farming practices suitable to the fragile soil and eco-system. With the subsequent opening up and development of the area by India, things changed, not at a natural pace but like a social and environmental tsunami. A Swedish born environmental campaigner and language expert by the name of Helena Norberg Hodge had come to Ladakh with a film crew back in 1975. Over the next twenty years, she returned many times to film and document what happened.

Intensive agriculture destroyed large areas of semi arid land and polluted the rivers and water table. Plastic bags and rubbish clogged up the ancient irrigation systems. Younger people with access to mainstream Western and Indian TV as well as greater contact with tourists became infatuated with the notion that everyone was wealthy and fulfilled in Europe and America. They became insecure and embarrassed by their own traditional way of life and inter-generational contact broke down. New style politics also threatened the cohesive social harmony that existed between the Buddhist majority and Muslim minority who had lived in peace for centuries. As society fragmented, specialisation and competition were introduced, which led to social problems such as unemployment, homelessness and drug abuse for the first time. These mirrored the same problems experienced by the Blackfeet and Northern Cheyenne in Montana.

Change was not all for the worse. Medical health care, living standards and educational opportunities did improve but at what a huge price to the unique cultural, spiritual, psychological, social and environmental health of this special people and land.

I had come to Leh to find out more about the Women's Alliance of Ladakh and the Ladakh Ecology Centre which Helena helped establish. What I hadn't expected is how enchanted I would become by Ladakh itself. Situated on the high Tibetan Plateau, Leh and the fertile Indus valley is surrounded by a ring of high sandy coloured dessert mountains. Each evening I would climb up to the foot of Leh Palace and watch the sunsets which were beautiful beyond words. Although now in ruins, Leh Palace still exuded echoes of past grandeur through its ruined walls. Perched high atop a large rocky escarpment, once the home of the Ladakhi royal family, it still dominates the town's vista.

I spent the next few days exploring Leh and the surrounding countryside. The days were warm but pleasant in near cloudless deep blue skies. On one of the days I joined Kjert and a German lady called Elsey for a day long tour of the Buddhist monasteries in the region. Our first stop off was Stok Palace, another former residence of the Ladakhi royal family. Dating from the 19th century, it was in excellent preservation. A huge telecommunication tower complete with large satellite dishes built right next to it seemed a little out of place. Next stop was the Buddhist monastery of Hemis located at the foot of a spectacularly rugged mountain valley.

Local tradition has it that Jesus, known in Ladakhi as *Isa*, spent time at Hemis and hung out there with yogis and lamas. I was struck after coming upon this information as the Irish word for Jesus is *Íosa*. In fact up until the early 20th Century, there were Buddhist scrolls that claimed to document Isa's time spent in Ladakh and Northern India. These scrolls revealed that Isa was a very outspoken holy man who exposed and criticised the Hindu religion for many of its practices, included the caste system. Many Western explorers and envoys had visited Hemis monastery seeking these scrolls. There is a theory that the scrolls went 'missing' so as to prevent any embarrassment for the Vatican Church, which would then have to revise as to whether or not Jesus spent time in India and the Himalayan region as a young man. When Capuchin missionary priests traversed the whole way from Delhi to Ladakh, to preach about Jesus and his teachings, the local elders faces lit up when they realised they were talking about Isa, who they still revere as a saint. Needless to say the Capuchin missionaries left Ladakh with very few converts as their good news wasn't as fresh as they at first believed.

There was an air of palpable mystery about Hemis which seemed to emanate from the very golden brown rocky outcrops that crowned the monastic citadel. Many of the temples were built tight up against the mountain side. A steep narrow gorge wound its way up one side of Hemis and disappeared into a wilderness of high mountains and secret caves where yogi's and holy men have gone into silent retreat over the last two millennia. The mountains are also home to the semi-mythical snow leopard which is so elusive that only a handful of Ladakhi shepherds have seen it in the wild. I was truly 'monasteried out' after our trip to Hemis. As a result, our visits to Thiksey and Shey monasteries went by in a sort of information overload blur. Tiredness was a constant companion and I began to wonder if the high altitude and dry arid climate were having an adverse affect on my health again.

On our way back to Leh we stopped off at Shey Festival. We had picked up an Israeli gentleman called Adi at Shey monastery and he was happy to join us. We found a tented food area in which to sit and all ordered fried vegetable noodles. Adi told us that his family were now young adults and as he had recently separated from his wife, he had decided to travel the world for a few years. He spoke for everyone when he said, "this place Ladakh is like nowhere I have ever been. I have never been to Tibet but I imagine it must be similar to this. There are times I feel so much peace here even though there are a lot of changes happening."

Our taxi driver had driven back to Leh to collect his family and said he would return later. The festival area was a huge flat sandy field. On one side there were stalls selling everything from kids toys to jewellery while another row of tents sold soft drinks and meals. On the far side of the field was a modern stadium looking unto a performance area. We stood around waiting patiently as night fell and the crowds swelled. The stadium area was a hive of activity with a lot of monks milling around and directing local officials and lamas to their seats. Workers busied themselves erecting a huge screen upon a large scaffold-supported platform. We did not see much by way of traditional Ladakhi dancing or music, but everyone seemed happy to share in the overall excitement. Suddenly a line of large speakers boomed into action and the giant screen came alive with the flicker of images. It was a high quality documentary-style short film about Ladakh and a celebration of Buddhist culture. People in the crowd laughed when they spotted someone they knew or brought their two palms together towards their mouth as if in prayer when they saw a high lama or Rinpoche on the screen. It was all a bit surreal but at least the organisers were promoting and reflecting their own cultural heritage through the popular medium of a big screen video spectacle. Just as the film finished, a large bang went off to the back of the crowd and a few thousand people turned around to watch a huge flare like firework rocket high into the night sky. The fireworks display was amazing and the glow they cast on people faces brought young and old back to a childlike wonder, if only for a magic half hour. With the movie and fireworks display over and the field in darkness, the night sky revealed itself in all its glory. With so little light pollution in this remote Himalayan land, the milky way stretched overhead like a vast, fluorescent, cosmic cloud. Even the light of the crescent moon shone brightly enough for people to pick their way safely back across the festival grounds.

The next few days were spent catching up with family and friends back home via emails and postcards and doing my laundry. My energy levels were very low and sleep was restless and frequently disturbed. Each evening I watched from my bedroom as the guesthouse owner's mother, a stooped elderly lady in a colourful head scarf, came out to weed and water her garden of vegetables. She seemed in a constant state of agitation and frequently barked orders at the guesthouse staff in an unfamiliar language. They seemed to silently humour her by holding a watering can or following her around with an empty bucket for her to fling weeds into.

Whether walking around the quiet suburbs of Leh or sitting indoors near a window, the light was all-pervading. It seemed to wash over and through everything and sometimes it made the mountains, the trees, the houses and even people appear somewhat dreamlike.

After a few days resting, it felt like my energy was returning and I set off looking for the Ladakh Ecological Centre. I found it at the top of a hill overlooking much of Leh. A small striking gompa or Buddhist temple perched atop a steep rocky ridge caught my eye as I turned to push open the front gate. I entered a small tree shaded compound with a vegetable and herb garden growing in the central area. The late morning sun was once again all pervading and seemed to blast light into everywhere, save the most resilient shaded spots. Surrounding the courtyard on the far side, were a collection of small buildings such as a gift shop selling locally produced hand crafts and clothes, an organic kitchen, resource centre and small office.

By midday visitors began arriving for the daily screening of an environmental documentary. Today it was the documentary, 'Ancient Futures', which in many ways had brought me here in the first place. After the movie I got talking to some of the Western volunteers who were working on various projects over the summer months. One of the volunteer was an engaging French student called Francois. He was wearing a traditional style Ladakhi male tunic that is worn from the neck down to the heels. As we spoke the phone rang and one of the staff answered it. I was about to leave, when one of the staff informed me that Helena Norberg Hodge had arrived at Leh airport and was on her way.

She arrived a short time later and instantly lit up the room, such was her radiant yet gentle presence. Although now in her late 50's with long fair hair she still possessed a fresh youthful appearance, the kind only possible by the cultivation of inner beauty. We sat and talked for over an hour about various environmental topics. I shared with her my thoughts on how the Celtic Tiger and intensive agricultural methods had proceeded ahead with little or no regard for the natural environment in Ireland and how community life, even in rural areas was continuing to fragment.

She listened thoughtfully but urged me to remain optimistic, "over the next few years Keith, as climate change and peak oil become such pressing issues, Governments will simply no longer be ale to ignore these problems. They will be forced to change. Opportunities will arise for new ways to organise our economies and societies on a much more humane, sustainable and localised level". She then added, " everything that you do to help bring community together through the different projects you are involved in will ultimately make a positive difference and give people an opportunity to experience real community co-operation."

Before I left, Helena asked me to consider returning to Ladakh at a future date to help manage a project. It was an inspirational chance encounter and I got her to sign my copy of 'Ancient Futures' before leaving. As I closed the gates of the compound behind me I glanced up again at the monastery and decided there and then to pay a visit the next day.

I had set my alarm clock for 5.30am and made my way through the near deserted streets of Leh and up past the ruins of Leh Palace, where a winding foot path led up the mountain side. The views on the way up were spectacular. The air was so clear and still in the dawn light that it felt possible to reach out to the distant sand coloured peaks, some still crowned in last winter's snows. The tiny monastery was still looming high above me when I began to make out its shape in closer detail. It was built in thee split levels. The oldest tower section looked unused while the lower levels were painted bright white and a deep terracotta red. My breath became laboured from the thin air and steep ascent and I stopped again before reaching the summit.

A smiling and unassuming, bespectacled Lama greeted me at the top. I was glad I had remembered to take a small gift with me of an apple and some biscuits. He gestured me to join him into a small dimly lit temple gompa where he was about to perform morning puja. I sat down on the opposite side of the doorway, on what seemed to be an old red leather lorry seat. It was very comfortable to sit cross-legged on it. In front of me was a beautifully altar adorned with shelves of elaborate ornaments and trinkets and miniature gold statues of various Buddhas in meditation pose. After lighting some incense the Lama sat down and without any further ceremony began chanting puja in deep throaty tones. The monotonous primal sounds of the Lama's chanting sent me into a deeply relaxed meditative state. I then watched with detached interest as a little mouse came scuttling into sight from underneath the altar. Upon finding a morsel of food on the floor, it pattered back undercover, without fear or haste.

I remained in deep meditation as the Lama continued chanting. After a time it seemed like a skylight opened in the roof of the gompa above me and a grainy scene began to appear in my mind. I saw the inside of a large furnished tent and a family moving around inside it. The flap of the tent door opened and tethered to ropes were a number of ponies and horses. I saw the face of a young woman who appeared tearful and very sad. I then saw a young boy being led hand in hand by two tall familiar men up to the entrance of a huge imposing looking monastery. The chanting voice of the Lama brought me back as a stream of tears trickled down my face. With a few quick sniffles I composed myself and through blurry eyes, looked up at the roof of the gompa but saw nothing now but decorative plaster on the ceiling.

When the puja was over I wanted to share my strange experience with the Lama but when I approached him, it felt completely unnecessary and futile to mention it. Instead the Lama beckoned me to follow him into a larger temple. Two large wooden doors opened into a dimly lit two storey temple and staring back at me was a huge statue of Maitreya, the future Buddha. In Buddhist cosmology, it is believed that Maitreya's coming will signify the end of the middle age in which humans currently reside, into a third age of higher consciousness. After saying my farewells to the Lama I walked back down the footpath to Leh in a state of mixed emotions. It was the 23rd of July, the date of my birthday.

A few evenings previously, I had bumped into a young women from Finland called Ritva who was also travelling by herself. We agreed to meet for lunch and I chose a restaurant which had outdoor tables spread beneath a grove of apricot trees in summer blossom. It was lovely to share a birthday meal with someone and I insisted she have a dessert. Ritva was a music teacher back in Finland and was travelling in India and Ladakh over her summer holidays. She told me of her plans to go an eight day guided trek in Ladakh and I shared some of my trekking experiences in Nepal. We exchanged emails which is customary when two travellers meet, although each person knows deep down that they will probably not stay in contact or meet again.

That evening back at my guesthouse, I thought back upon my experience while attending morning puja with the Lama on the hill-top gompa. In a most inexplicably, illogical way, what I had seen in my mind's eye seemed to sit quite easily with me. It explained to me why I felt so comfortable with many aspects of the Buddhist religion and so much at home in the Himalayan region. At the same time I understood the importance of not getting carried away with what I had experienced or of thinking too much about past lives. Besides, I had enough on my plate to be dealing with this life as best I could, and learning to be more centred in myself and grounded in this world.

The next few days seemed to slip by at an easy going pace in Leh, until I looked at my Indian visa one morning and with a sudden shock, realised I had to just one week on my Indian visa remaining. It was time to make a new definitive plan and immediately. "Should I fly to New Delhi and get a flight back home?", I asked myself. This option didn't sit so easily with me especially in light of emails from friends and family who painted a picture of an exceptionally wet Irish summer. My second option was to return to Sri Lanka and Nilambe Meditation Centre to seek a deeper understanding of what this journey I was embarked upon was all about. Of course, the thought of lounging on a tropical beach for a few days and enjoying some hot sunshine admittedly also crossed my mind. This gave me one week to travel from Ladakh to the southern tip of India. The very thought gave me goose pimples of new adventure and challenges to come. I managed to book a flight for two days time from Leh airport to New Delhi which then left me four days on my India visa to find the cheapest way possible to get to Sri Lanka.

That night upon returning to my guesthouse, I felt a horrible cold feeling rising in my body. Sleep became next to impossible as I tried in vain to get warm, shivering in a sleeping bag under a pile of heavy blankets. To make matters worse I began having to make a series of rapid visits to the toilet again. As I tossed and turned restlessly in the bed, I could hear the noise of sirens blaring off in the distance which added to my feverish discomfort. By early next morning I was feeling even weaker and had to let my guesthouse owners know. A pretty young Muslim woman appeared from upstairs a short time later, with a set of car keys and brought me down to Leh Hospital in her new car. She would have made a great wife I thought to myself, as she marched me up to the reception desk and demanded that I get to see a doctor. First, I had to pay seven rupees as a standard hospital fee which worked out at about fifteen cents. Within three minutes, I was sitting next to a Ladakhi doctor. This was not my experience of hospitals and I was a bit shocked at the fast pace that medical attention was being offered to me. A doctor asked me how I felt and then quickly took my blood pressure. With one sideway glance he confirmed how I felt, "you have very low blood pressure and need to be admitted to a ward." He scribbled out some words on a form and handed it to a nurse. My surrogate Muslim wife lifted me by the arm and marched me up and around a few corridors and into a ward.

The ward doctor, a tall fresh faced man in his early forties wanted to admit me overnight, but when I explained I had a flight to catch the next morning he insisted I stay until early evening as I needed two glucose drips. Within minutes a squad of awkwardly smiling trainee doctors were busy finding a vein to insert a glucose drip needle in my arm. The beautiful young Muslim woman stood by my bed until I was comfortable and then said she would send someone from the guesthouse to collect me later. While I was lying down and hooked up to the drip, a German woman who had collapsed while on a trek was wheeled into the ward with an anxious Ladakhi trek leader by her side. It turned out that she too had become run down and ill from the dry harsh climate and altitude. The Ladakhi doctor began cracking jokes with her as he hooked her up to a drip. He was the most relaxed and happy-go-lucky doctor I had ever met. From their conversations, I gleamed that the German woman worked as an E.U. official in Brussels. The doctor explained how he had returned from abroad to live and work back home in his native Ladakh and had happily taken a big wage cut from his overseas earnings. The lady guffawed in disbelief as he went on to explain how as a doctor, he was only required to work six hours a day at the hospital and was currently rostered to work from 10am until 4pm. He beamed a large smile as he shared how much he was looking forward to returning home and spending the evening with his family.

By the end of my second glucose drip infusion, I felt like the cartoon character Popeye after gulping down a tin of raw spinach. Sure enough a man from the guesthouse came to collect me. My entire hospital visit had lasted five hours and cost me the equivalent of fifteen cents. On the way back, we passed by the Tibetan quarter where plumes of black smoke drifted high into the sky over Leh. The driver informed me that the Tibetan Market had burnt down overnight and teams of fire crews from all over Ladakh had tried in vain to put the blaze out. I felt sad for these refugees who have already endured oppression and exile from their homeland

A LAST DASH BACK TO SRI LANKA

A small white taxi arrived at 6am the next morning to bring me to the airport. On the way we lifted a bubbly Ladakhi woman who was going to work at the main terminal. She told me that one of her relatives was killed in the September 11th attacks on the World Trade Centre and that she wished some day to visit the memorial which bears his name. Check-in took a matter of minutes. I still felt a bit shaky and weak, but realised that it was best for me to leave the high altitude of Leh even though New Delhi meant a new challenge in the way of humidity and heat. Hours later, I landed into one of the biggest metropolis in the world, home to almost ten million people. As a rural loving person, I was more than a little daunted. Taking a few deep breaths I left the cocoon-like atmosphere of the airport and made my way by bus and auto-rickshaw to the tourist district of Pahar Ganj.

The main bazaar area was pure pandemonium. Weighed down with travel luggage, I was like a sitting duck for hustlers, street vendors, guesthouse touts, beggars and street-kids. I somehow managed to slip away from the throngs and found myself in a labyrinth of narrow streets flanked by towering tenements and guesthouses. The humidity was super-high. I passed a barber shop to see the barber stretched out snoring on the chair and an assistant sprawled fast asleep with head on hands over the cash register.

A visit to a Kashmiri travel agency later in the afternoon offered me two options to get to Trivandrum in the far south of India by Monday. Option one was book a plane seat for 22,000 rupees while my second option was book a passenger class train ticket for 2,400 rupees. My dwindling budget sealed the train ticket deal option. The only catch was the plane took several hours while the train took several days.

I arrived at the station platform the next morning to embark. Heavy monsoon rain clouds and stifling heat intensified through the morning. My mind began fretting about the marathon three day train journey that was ahead of me and I conjured up images of sleepless nights and chaotic overcrowded carriages. Bang on 11.30am, the Kerala Express pulled into the station. It was so long, it was impossible to see from end to the other. I grabbed my bags and boarded apprehensively.

My first surprise was the door to my train carriage slid open smoothly while the second surprise was to feel a cool blast of air greet and refresh me. The carriage was air conditioned with fixed comfortable bunk-bed style sleeping berths. Feeling greatly relieved, I settled in for the long haul. A short time later, I was engaged in conversation with an Indian college lecturer by the name of Mr Jayaraman about the core cultural and philosophical values of India. He talked about his belief in re-incarnation which is a core religous belief to the majority of Hindus.

"We Hindus believe that as humans we have experienced many lifetimes on this Earth and that our essential spirit or higher self experiences a constant cycle of death and re-birth until one has attained perfection. This gives us our spiritual guidance as the laws of karma remind us that how we live in this lifetime, will determine the circumstances of our re-birth and next life." We talked for ages about the War on Terrorism and India's likely emergence as a super-power during the 21st Century. Enthused by my interest, he continued, "India's values are much different than that of China or the United States. Our national motto is, 'Unity in Diversity', and so we do not wish to pressure the world to accept our values or beliefs as we have many. India is rapidly changing and modernising, however, AS she must do, but we will choose our own terms as to how this is achieved."

Mr Jayaranan also talked fondly about his sons who were both qualified doctors. "One of my sons is a doctor in the United States and I have been over to visit him. My other son is working as a doctor in Bulgaria and I hope to go there and see him later this year." He continued, "they hope to return to Kerala soon and set up a specialist clinic together, which I would very much like to support. This would be a good thing to do."

Our conversations were interrupted by a sudden burst of activity as train staff began handing out lunch packets of curry and rice for thirty-five rupees. On a train full of thousands of passengers this was a military style operation.

On the morning of the second day travelling by train, the landscape changed to large fertile plains bursting with luxuriant green growth triggered by the monsoons. The main highlights of each day were receiving lunch and dinner packets of rice and curry with the option of chicken or vegetarian. People spent the time reading, chatting, gazing out the window or dozing in their bunks. My army friend in the bottom bunk had gathered up a few willing volunteers to share a bottle of bourbon but by 10pm it was lights out on the train and the party was over.

By early next morning our train was climbing up over the Western Ghats mountain range which divides Tamil Nadu and Kerala. The train snaked and creaked its way slowly through thick jungle which added greatly to an atmosphere of adventure before descending down into the tropical wetlands of Kerala. Station by station our carriage began emptying of now familiar faces until at 3pm our train pulled into the final stop of Trivandrum, also known as Thiruvananthapuram which I had three whole days on a train to memorise for life. Before disembarking, three smiling toilet cleaner men dressed in light brown shirts and trousers who seemed joined at the hip, thrust a comments book in front of me. Being in no hurry to go anywhere in particular, I took a few minutes to write a glowing report flavoured with some flowery prose for these three men who worked on behalf of the travellers on our train carriage since we departed in New Delhi, almost seventy-two hours ago. Upon handing back the book, they were full of thanks and nodded their head from side to side in genuine appreciation.

After finding a cheap tourist guesthouse not far from the train station, I set about finding a travel agents office to book the next flight possible out of India. I managed to get a flight for one hundred euros to Colombo, Sri Lanka but there was one major hitch, it meant overstaying my India visa by one day. Now one of my many faults which can land me into trouble is an overly complacent attitude, a sort of "ah sure it will be alright, I will just say I'm from Donegal in Ireland and sure we'll have an oul' chat about it over a cup of tea and say no more." Sometimes it works, sometimes it doesn't.

I spent the rest of the evening wandering about Thiruvananthapuram, soaking in the atmosphere of the place. It had a lush green feel to it despite being home to almost one million people. As well as being the administrative capital of Kerala since the days of British rule it also has 3,000 years of history. It is believed that in 1036 BC the ships of King Solomon sailed into the city port which at that time had an established international trade in spices, sandalwood and ivory.

The next morning I took an auto-rickshaw ride to the Indian Passport Office. After a few hours queueing, I was brought into the office of a passport official. A stout sour looking fellow with large jowl cheeks flicked through my passport with indifference, until he came to my Indian visa stamp. When he registered the date, his whole face flinched back in a mixture of excitement and dramatic astonishment. The silence was deafening as I waited with nervous anticipation for him to speak. Inter-locking his fingers over his belly and reclining back on his seat, he delivered his verdict.

"You are in serious trouble if you overstay your visa. If you want my advice you must get a flight out of India today by any means possible."

This was not what I wanted to hear and a sudden heavy discomfort came over me. Mr Passport man maintained a stony expression as I juggled the situation in my head. There was no quarter to be given here, so I thanked him for his time and got an auto-rickshaw back to the travel agents office where I bought my ticket. I should have known by now, that India runs on an archaic set of stringent rules. Some may be broken with a 'donation' of rupees while others are treated as taboo to even consider bending. In a country of one billion self interested human beings, the line has to be drawn somewhere I suppose.

A young lady at the travel agent office I next went to, offered me a cup of chai tea but more importantly a glimmer of hope to avoid coming up against the Indian authorities. Although they couldn't offer me a flight out that day, she wrote down an address for the Superintendent of Police. I instinctively knew that things were about to get much more complicated but I needed a sheet of official looking paper to have any chance of boarding my flight leaving India tomorrow. The auto-rickshaw driver dropped me outside the front pillars of the Police Headquarters, but refused to go any further. After some searching I was escorted to the foreign office where a young unassuming Indian officer produced the biggest book I had ever seen in my life, at least two foot by two foot square. He proceeded to read out aloud to me that foreign nationals other than Pakistanis are allowed to overstay their visa by three or four days at maximum. I made a wild guess that a prison stay and hefty ransom was on the cards if a foreigner overstayed past 'maximum'. I felt a little more relieved but my tribulations were far from over. My hotel manager was in a genuine fluster and wanted me to vacate my hotel room immediately. A heated shouting match ensued. Minutes later I was holding on to the back of the managers motorbike as we sped back to Police Headquarters to consult the man with the giant book again. The manager was clearly frightened of the police, while I felt like a fugitive who's time was running out. The hotel manager waited until he got his official looking sheet of paper and stamp. I figured I'd ask for one too, but was told that airport immigration would not require a police form.

The rain came down in sheets the next morning as I headed to the airport in the back of an auto-rickshaw. It's canvass side flaps were rolled down to keep out most of the large puddles we skimmed through. Only one last customs check separated me from getting on my flight. My heart was pounding as I waited in line at an immigration booth. The senior Indian official took one look at my passport and pointed a hand up at some invisible exit in the roof. "You are refused permission to leave, you must leave the cue please sir." Within seconds two suited officials with walky talkies were by my side. I swallowed my nerves and explained my story as clearly and calmly as I could while adding a wee white lie that I was to pick up essential medicines in Sri

Lanka which were waiting for me at the main post office in Colombo. It was actually a bottle of medicinal shampoo for itchy
scalp which I had asked my parents to send by poste restante for
my collection. I sat like a fugitive outside the immigration police
office for what seemed like a lifetime. It is amazing how other
airport passengers seemed to look at me as they walked by and
sensed I was in trouble with the law. The strange thing was that
nobody seemed surprised to see me there. Most seemed either
curious, indifferent or indignant.

As the clock continued ticking, I began conjuring up images
of sharing a dungeon-like cell with fifty other hapless prisoners
and breaking boulders forever in an oven hot quarry. My day-
mare was interrupted by an immigration official who managed
a half smile and told me I was free to board my flight. I walked
through the custom gates like a man released from prison and a
routine flight to Sri Lanka felt like a laid on luxury sky cruise.

It was good to be back in Sri Lanka and I felt instantly more
relaxed, especially now that I was more familiar with the culture and people. Five months had passed since I left to travel
through India but one thing was for sure, I would never be the
same again. My journey had changed me in ways I was barely
able to comprehend. This was why I was returning to Sri Lanka
and the Nilambe Meditation Centre - to try and get a deeper
understanding and grounding within myself before I returned
home to Ireland.

I felt my homeland was slowly turning into a 21st Century
economy. Media commentators now referred to "Ireland Inc.",
with values pinned optimistically to the mast head of happiness
achieved through individual wealth creation and realising one's
life through conspicious consumption. I had always felt like an
anxious outsider to this materialistic centred philosophy, but
until turning thirty, had lacked the confidence to choose the
path less travelled, to paraphrase the American poet Robert
Frost.

Instead of going directly to Nilambe, I caught a train back
down to Unawatuna for a few days easy living by the beach.

Each morning and evening I would make the two mile trek through jungle paths, down to a secret sea-cove. There I spent the evenings contently by myself, swimming, paddling and diving for shells in the warm clear water. Sometimes I would spy some local fishermen paddling back into the cove on a traditional katamarang boat and we would wave in friendly acknowledgement to each other. Other times, I would seek out pieces of coral or brightly coloured shell from the sea floor and marvel at its colour and intricate design. One evening while floating on my back and gazing up at the bright blue sky, I had a spontaneous feeling of pure joy brought about by nothing in particular, apart from the enjoyment of the moment and the recognition of how fortunate and blessed I was to be here.

After a few more days spent at Unawatuna though, I knew it was time to move on. I had enough time to travel back up to the Central Highlands and do a self guided meditation retreat at Nilambe. Stepping off the train at Kandy, the chief town in the Cenral Highlands I felt right back at home again. It was also good to stay once again with Eva at the Pink House. Something felt strange, however, and the guest rooms were silent and devoid of backpackers. The following evening I caught up with Eva over tea. I enquired about Jim Gilchrist and Eva in her humorous teasing manner said, "Jim is back in Malaysia sorting some muddle out with his ex-wife or ex-girlfriend, its difficult to keep track with him". I had to remind myself again that Jim was seventy-eight years of age. I then asked her about the Pink House and she frowned and rested her face on an upturned hand.

"We are having no luck Keith these past few months. A guest and friend of the family dropped dead in one of the rooms and his family tried to blame us even though they knew he was sick. We also had a number of accidental fires and when we tried to fix the roof, the neighbouring guesthouse complained. Ayayee, what to do? We had both Catholic and Buddhist priests here to say mass but still there is no luck. Now the tourists have stopped coming."

I was sad to hear all this bad news from Eva, especially as I consider the Pink House to be one of the most special guesthouses in the world. I could scarcely believe that the neighbouring guesthouse owner had complained to the authorities, considering that he was building a crazy looking four-storey high extension, which will tower over Eva's backyard.

On my final day in Kandy, I brought back some cake and presents for Eva's grandsons Keeran and Anuk. I also had some pit-stop repair work done on my sandals. After six months of walking and several thousand kilometres on the road, they were beginning to leak water through the soles. The grey spikey haired shoe repair man ushered me to sit cross legged next to him as he began the essential sandle repair work. He first took out a strip of worn Semperit car tyre from his work bag. He then held it up against the worn sandal sole and taking a pair of large scissors in hand, carefully cut out a patch of tyre. A small brush and jar of sticky glue then appeared from his bag and he applied the tyre patch unto my sandal as you would a bike tube puncture. He then use his palms as a vice to squeeze tight the patch. At this stage the operation was only half complete and I watched on mesmerised. Mr 'shoe repair man' then produced a pen sized needle and strong thread from his bag of tricks and proceeded to sow the patch edges unto the sandal sole with tried and tested skill. Crowds of local shoppers and office workers rushed by us on the pavement and yet I was totally immersed in the repair job operation. With the sewing completed, he then placed my sandal on a shoe anvil and tacked small stumpy nails into each corner of the patch. Hobnail sandals were definitely a new innovation in footwear, I thought to myself. Throwing the sandal at my foot, he then beckoned me with a universal hand signal to go for a quick test drive down the street and back. It took a bit of getting used and left me a fraction lopsided but I had developed a fond attachment to these journey worn sandals. He asked for one hundred and fifty rupees or the equivalent of a euro. When I gave him two one hundred rupee notes, he kissed them, put them up to his forehead in praise, before placing the notes in his shirt top pocket. We parted without a word exchanged, but with a mutualy understood nod and smile.

Kandy was in busy preparation mode for one of the most famous street festivals and parades in all of Asia called the Perahera. This spectacle involves thousands of local people dressed in tradition Kandyan costume and almost fifty decorated elephants. I decided if possible to return from Nilambe for the festival which would take place at the next full moon which was just over two weeks away.

On the last night of my stay in the Pink House, I retired to my room at 10pm which is usual in Sri Lanka. My pre-sleep dozing was soon rudely interrupted by the sound of workmen using power drills and hammers. The din seemed to be coming from the guesthouse next door. I quickly got dressed and went out to the front porch where Keeran and Anuk were sitting bleary eyed in their pyjamas along with their Dad. I asked them did this happen regularly and they nodded yes. I returned to my room, put on my good shirt and trousers and slinging my camera over my shoulder stormed out the porch entrance and up the street with Anuk and Keeran close behind. Just inside the front gates I was greeted by the guesthouse owner who was trying to force a smile the way disingenuous people do.

"Ah you are looking for a room sir", he presumed.

"No I am looking for the manager", I replied.

"Yes, how can I help you?", was his now fretful affirmation.

"I am doing a piece for an international travel book and am currently reviewing guesthouses in Kandy. I have a very early start tomorrow morning and yet you have workmen keeping everyone on the street awake. I was wondering how you think I should write about that in my report?", I said with Oscar acting ambitions.

His face dropped and I thought I could hear Anuk and Keeran giggling somewhere nearby, under cover.

"This...this is not a problem", he replied in a strained voice, "the workmen were only working late because they were behind you see. Please be assured that they are now finished."

I accepted his explanation with a nod but no reply and swung round briskly on my heel and back down to the Pink House where Anuk and Keeran were jumping up and down and telling their father what I said to the guesthouse owner. That night at least, we all slept a little more peacefully.

The next day I set off for Nilambe, a journey of over two hours by bus, followed by an auto-rickshaw ride up into the mountains. From a small hamlet called Nilambe Junction I stepped off the bus with my luggage and shared an auto-rickshaw up to Nilambe with a middle aged American woman. On the rocky and bumpy journey she poured out her story to me from which I gathered that she came from a wealthy family in the United States. After visiting Sri Lanka quite a few years ago, she had visited Nilambe Meditation Centre and was so taken by the place, she decided to live in Sri Lanka permanently. This decision had caused consternation and friction between her and her siblings. Her mother had been recently diagnosed with Alzheimer's disease and her sisters had emailed her with an ultimatum. If she did not return to live in the United States by then, they intended to exclude her from her mother's will. After months of mental turmoil and agonising over what to do, she had decided to send an e-mail from the city of Kandy to her family stating she no longer wanted any share of the will, which seemed to involve quite a considerable sum of money. I simply listened and found the good sense to realise that there was nothing much else I could do, but lend a compassionate ear.

Upon checking in I was shown a sparse but clean room. There was no need to hook up a mosquito net as the high altitude and cool night air was mercifully unfavourable for them. I collapsed into bed shortly after 8pm and slept twelve hours straight through. After breakfast the next morning and communal work I attended my first meditation session. The meditation building was a simple plastered structure with windows and a stone bench, two foot high running up both sides of the hall and decked with cushions for those meditating to sit upon. Running up the centre of the hall was a spacious fibrous floor-mat area.

The hall itself was surrounded by tropical trees in luxuriant growth and alive with the calls of birds, chipmunks and insects. At the top of the hall was a simple shrine with a white statue of the Buddha, vases filled with fresh flowers, and a large photograph of Nilambe's first meditation instructor, Godwin Samararatne, who died a few years back.

I was relieved to find it wasn't as difficult to sit in meditative stillness for an hour an a half at a time, as a I had envisaged it would be. When the discomfort got too much, it was a terrific relief to be allowed to get up and stretch aching limbs while doing some mindful walking meditation instead. It is difficult to describe to someone who hasn't tried it, how physically and mentally tough it is to sit cross-legged and still, in complete silence for over an hour. It was dark outside when we finished our final meditation session of my first full day at Nilambe. The moon, although only in its new first quarter was shining brightly in the quiet night sky, while fireflies blazed an ever changing constellation overhead.

I shared Nilambe with a handful of kitchen and office staff and about fifteen other retreatants made up of Sri Lankans and Westerners and of course Opul, the meditation centre instructor. Most of our day was spent in complete silence, except for thirty minutes in the late afternoon over a tea-break. As well as doing over six hours meditation per day, everyone volunteered an hour's time each morning to help prepare food, clean bathrooms, gather crops and sweep the surrounding paths and grounds.

There was no electricity at Nilambe and most of the food, except for rice, was sourced locally or grown in fruit trees which grew throughout the centre's grounds.

I began to develop an annoying cough, whch made me physically weaker and quite self conscious, especially when sitting in during a meditation session. I began to miss meditation sessions and felt a little down about the whole thing. Upon calling into the office one morning, Mr Putigala informed me that a young woman staying at the centre was going to Kandy and would get me some cough medicine, if I left some money with him. Mr Putigala had a very abrupt manner but also a magnetic likeability. He was a Sinhalese man in his late sixties and wore a pair of jam jar glasses with thick black rims around a shaved head.

He was volunteering at the centre as a general administrator and yet speed walked wherever he went, while the rest of us were encouraged to walk slowly and mindfully. That evening I collected my cough mixture from Mr Putigala and by the next morning, began to feel much better.

I now had just over a week left at Nilambe. With my health steadily improving, I made a personal committment to attend as many meditation practices as possible. My first challenge was to start getting up for our 4.30am pre-dawn meditation practices which went on until 6am. I set both my clock and watch alarm for the first morning. It was weird getting up and washing my face and teeth by head-torch light. Looking up into the early morning heavens, the stars seemed to wink back at me, with a friendly extra bright sparkle as if saying, "hey Keith, fancy seeing you up and about at this hour...you sure its not just for a pee!"

Grabbing a few round cushions to sit in half lotus position I got into straight backed meditation posture and began the struggle not to drop off to sleep. This went on for half an hour or more until suddenly, the whole world seemed to very gradually wake up to a new day. The darkness turned first to hazy grey and then to faint light, as the candles on the Buddha altar grew steadily dimmer. First the insects started up in a chirping concert followed by the birds, with their own dawn chorus. Next up were some monkeys and chipmunks, with some personal improvised solo numbers. I thought to myself how magical it must be to wake with the dawn every morning, but conceded that it would take me a few years to aspire to such a challenge. Rather than enjoy a cup of early morning tea, I calculated that it was eighty minutes until breakfast was served so I hastened back to my bed. Just as I was settling into dreamy slumber I heard a quick succession of knuckle taps on my window. It was Mr Putigala and I was caught. "Up! Up! Up! Its time for Up", he exclaimed and then added " Mr Opul wishes to see you this morning at 9.45p.m." He was turned on his heels and off speed-walking back up towards the main centre before I even managed a drowsy reply.

After a tasty breakfast, I resumed my ego-busting toilet cleaning duties as part of our work hour. It wasn't too difficult as the toilets and bathrooms had been cleaned mindfully and with care for many years before I arrived. I managed a quick wash before walking across the centre to to meet Opul, whose house was located about twenty yards from the main meditation hall. Opul was meditation instructor at Nilambe since Godwin Samararatne had passed away in 2000. A tall man in his late thirties, Opul exuded a spiritual presence and energy difficult to put in words. Opul had been a student of Godwin and was his natural successor.

As I approached Opul's house, I spied him sitting beneath a canopy of hanging vines, mindfully reading a book which he closed and left down slowly as I approached. He wore a bright white Sri Lankan style lungi and white shirt and his face and eyes radiated kindness, calm and light. He gestured me to sit across from him. Some of the hanging vines had flowered star shaped orange and yellow blossoms which gave an otherworldly background to our conversations. Opul had a distinct way of talking. Every word was spoken in a careful and measured fashion in a raised tone, a little bit like the way some Swedish or Norwegian people speak English. He also spoke in his native Sinhalese like this.

"How.. was.. your.. journey?", he began by asking. I replied that it had been a good journey but that I felt compelled to return to Sri Lanka and gain some deeper insights before returning to Ireland. "How is your practice here"?, he then asked. I answered that my mind would often race with thoughts especially when I felt my legs getting stiff and painful from meditating for lengthy periods. Opul remained silent for a few moments and then continued with measured speech.

"Mind is essentially conflict. When meditating it is enough to simply observe what conflict arises. Without conflict there would be no mind!" I understood this on some level and we both broke into spontaneous, quiet laughter.

He added, "the mind is clever and will attempt to trick you. If there are no thoughts or conflict arising, then the mind is asleep! By learning to recognise and observe when conflict arises in our minds, we can begin to create some space and inner wisdom around such thoughts that arise. We should not attempt to resist what arises in our minds, but simply recognise it with love and compassion for ourselves. We must say to ourselves, "dear mind, this is conflict arising and I don't wish to react and follow it. This is all we need to do."

I found this shared insight very helpful. I liked the idea of actually talking to my own mind, when recognising it is in a troublesome mood, just not out loud to avoid attracting the attention of men in long white coats! I then asked Opul about meditation techniques he recommended. Again he paused for a while before answering.

"It is good to find 'the middle way'. We must wish love to our own bodies before meditation begins and feel good at the beginning". Opul continued, "always try and avoid extremes of either forcing yourself or being too easy on yourself. The middle way teaches us this. It is not really possible for some people to sit in meditation for one and a half hours and still practice mindfulness. It is better to be skilful and not to meditate with expectation of good results."

We then sat together for a few moments in silence. Sunlight illuminated the back of the hanging garden through a countless pin prick size spaces in the hanging vine foliage. Opul then invited me to sit awhile but said he had to return to other matters. With a surge of heart felt respect I said "thank you", and with a gaze of loving kindness Opul replied, "you.. are.. very.. welcome."

I felt light bulbs going off in my head about my meditation practice as I returned to my room. I was glad to understand how skillfully addressing my own mind and body during meditation, held the key to deepening my practice. Over the remaining few days I managed to rise at 4am every morning, to the point where the stars became used to my early morning manouvres and stopped teasing. I also began to take up yoga in the afternoons, to keep my body stretched and supple for over six hours in meditation posture every day. There were four of us in the class, including a pretty Candian girl called Svea, who teased me in a light hearted way, as I found some of the yoga positions very difficult to maintain.

With each passing meditation session, I felt it easier to remain in a meditative state for longer periods, where little or no thoughts entered my mind, in what is known as clear-light awareness. When I felt my mind clouded with thoughts like, "what am I to do for work and money when I return to Ireland?" or "I wonder what we are having for lunch today", I would think of Opul's advice and say to myself, "dear mind, I invite you to think whatever thoughts you wish and know that I will be friendly and non-judgemental host to whatever arises."

More and more when I did this and sat spaciously waiting for thoughts to arise, none did. On one occasion when I felt my inside legs aching from sitting I asked "dear body, can we just do another five minutes, and then I will move position." When the bong to end the one and a half hour session sounded, I sat perfectly contented for a further twenty minutes. Somehow, any previous discomfort had vanished. I came to value Opul's advice and to respect him as a master meditatation instructor.

On my final day at Nilambe, a feeling of deep inner contentment came over me while in meditation posture. At first my mind felt fear at this new emerging deeper peace, but I remained calm and centred. As I tilted my gaze slightly through an open window across from me, and at the green sheeny leaves of a tropical tree bathed in bright sunlight, I felt a profound sense of well being. There was also something else though, held within this blissful peace. An insight began dawning that everything and everybody from the mightiest elephant to a tiny worm and including human beings and trees and water are all connected. In the way that there would be no life on earth without the moon and sun, and no sun without a galaxy and so on and so forth. That ultimately there is only 'one-ness' in divine light and therefore we are all on a journey back to its source. For a few brief moments I think I experienced this one-ness and made a heart felt wish that I would remember this special experience as the last breath of life leaves my body.

It helped that I remained in silence with other people on retreat for the remainder of the day as to talk about or explain this experience seemed beyond words. I was able to ground myself by remembering the words of an ancient Chinese sage called Lao Tzu, "Those who know do not say, those who say do not know." I had simply skimmed the surface.

That evening I hiked up a forest path above Nilambe to an outcrop of large boulders where a solitary tree grows. I unwrapped some prayer flags from my pocket and carefully tied the two cord ends of the coloured cloth flags across two outstretched branches. I looked north in the direction of the Himalayas where I had bought them and made a wish that the teachings of the East continue to find new roots and expression in the West and help create a new global awareness and respect for this precious planet.

I had mixed feeling about leaving Nilambe the following morning. One part of me felt it was time to be moving on, while another part of me felt that I was leaving a special sanctuary of peace and mindful living. I could now see this as mind conflict in motion. Besides I could always return and would continue this life-time journey back home in Ireland where it all began. After paying for my food and lodgings, I ordered an auto-rickshaw which Mister Pitigala announced I would be sharing. The auto-rickshaw arrived in the front courtyard like the sound of a Honda 50 motorbike and I loaded my backpack in the backseat. As we prepared to depart the extra passenger arrived. It was the Canadian girl Svea. With a beaming smile she introduced herself with, "Hi I'm Svea, I'm the girl that got you your medicine!"

As our auto-rickshaw drove out of the courtyard and Svea and I made a connection, a part of me realised that my journey was drawing to a wonderful conclusion and that all the people, places and situations I encountered from North America to Asia; all the laughs, tears, joys, struggles, setbacks and insights I experienced, all flashed brightly somewhere in my mind, stored in some mysterious hard drive for future reference. As sunlight danced through the tree-lined driveway, casting intri-

cate mosaics of bright and shadow upon the road ahead, a short
verse came to me;

> Passing through, passing through
> Sometimes joyful, sometimes blue
> Happy though to have met all you
> While passing through.

About the Author

Keith Corcoran is a 35 year old writer, community worker and tour guide based in County Donegal, in the scenic North West of Ireland. He is the co-founder of the SpunOut National Youth Organisation (www.spunout.ie) a multi-award winning national youth agency, which reaches over half a million young people per year.

Keith holds qualifications in Journalism, Cultural Studies and Irish History and writes regularly for newspapers on health, social and environmental issues. Keith is currently active in the areas of Irish (Gaelic) language education, Walking Therapy and Cultural Tourism.

He is also in the process of setting up his own website based company called www.journeyinwonder.com to offer unique touring experiences, talks and therapy walks.

For more updates, photos from journey, and info on ordering see
www.journeyinwonder.com